*SEINFELD*

# The Cultural History of Television

Series Editors: Bob Batchelor, M. Keith Booker, and Kathleen M. Turner

*SEINFELD*

*A Cultural History*

**Paul Arras**

ROWMAN & LITTLEFIELD
Lanham • Boulder • New York • London

Published by Rowman & Littlefield
An imprint of The Rowman & Littlefield Publishing Group, Inc.
4501 Forbes Boulevard, Suite 200, Lanham, Maryland 20706
www.rowman.com

6 Tinworth Street, London SE11 5AL

British Library Cataloguing in Publication Information Available

**Library of Congress Cataloging-in-Publication Data**

Names: Arras, Paul, 1981– author.
Title: Seinfeld : a cultural history / Paul Arras.
Description: Lanham : Rowman & Littlefield, [2020] | Series: The cultural history of television |
    Includes bibliographical references and index. | Summary: "This book traces the history of
    Seinfeld's path onto NBC's schedule and rise up the Nielsen ratings, offering a fresh look at
    the episodes themselves. It pays close attention to the writers and writing of the show, careful-
    ly analyzing individual episodes to articulate exactly what was so groundbreaking and assessing
    its broader cultural impact."—Provided by publisher.
Identifiers: LCCN 2019056194 (print) | LCCN 2019056195 (ebook) | ISBN 9781538126875
    (cloth) | ISBN 9781538126882 (epub)
Subjects: LCSH: Seinfeld (Television program)
Classification: LCC PN1992.77.S4285 A88 2020 (print) | LCC PN1992.77.S4285 (ebook) | DDC
    791.45/72—dc23
LC record available at https://lccn.loc.gov/2019056194
LC ebook record available at https://lccn.loc.gov/2019056195

For Mom and Dad

# CONTENTS

# ACKNOWLEDGMENTS

This book doesn't turn into a coffee table. It doesn't have any built-in legs to prop it up. However, there have been many *people* who have helped prop up the project. Foremost, Taylor Arras read the manuscript, rewatched *Seinfeld* with me, and supported me in so many ways. Our boys, Henry (age four) and Matthew (two), also supported me in their own ways, even though they won't be allowed to watch *Seinfeld* for another decade.

I first watched *Seinfeld* with my family—my brother, Dan, who shares my sense of humor, and my parents, Jane and Al, to whom this book is dedicated. I'm grateful that Mom and Dad raised me to be kinder than Jerry, happier than George, and more content than Elaine. They also endowed me with the independence and courage to be a little like Kramer.

At its best, television brings people together for a shared experience of both pleasure and meaning. Over the years, I have shared the experience of *Seinfeld* with so many friends who helped me ponder its meanings. Those friends include: John, James, Chris, Short Paul, Pandeezy, Other Paul, Maarten, Nasdaf, Brendan, General Taft, Em, Jo, Galdo, Brady, Peter (my patron) and his team (including the J.A.M. session), Cousin Mark, Cousin Eric, Cousin Brian, Professor ELQ and the Writing Workshop, Dr. Bob, Steve and Janet, the Crazy Club, Patches and Redfield, SHA, Nathan and Friends Boat Dock Installers and Removers, Bob Sacamano, everyone who has ever been on the Real Paul Arras Tour, and many others. Thanks also to everyone who worked on this book at Rowman & Littlefield—a much better publishing house than Pendant Publishing.

Thanks to you, too, reader! I hope that this book helps you appreciate *Seinfeld* in new ways. Come find me on the internet if you want to argue about my episode rankings, but only if you're as nice as Bizarro Jerry and his friends.

# INTRODUCTION

*Seinfeld*'s success came out of nothing. The show barely made it onto NBC's schedule and barely survived its first few seasons. For several years, *Seinfeld* struggled to gain traction, with only about 15–20 million people tuning in each week during its brief first season.

*Only* 20 million? A few decades later, a sitcom would kill to get an audience of that size, but in 1990, television viewers were still grouped around a few channels. Cable networks claimed a small (but growing) fraction of the audience, while the broadcast networks—NBC, CBS, ABC, and even Fox (launched in 1986)—battled over most of the viewers. *Seinfeld* was the last great sitcom of this broadcast age. After *Seinfeld*, the television audience splintered, chasing content onto different channels and different platforms.

By the time its much-hyped finale aired, it seemed everyone was talking about *Seinfeld*. That feeling of a national audience now seems impossible to duplicate. Shows like *Game of Thrones*, *The Bachelor*, and *The Big Bang Theory* can rise to the top of American culture for a period. But those fleeting moments are nothing like *Seinfeld*'s cultural supremacy in the 1990s. In its final season, NBC was paying record-high salaries to the cast and earning record-high deals from advertisers.

There are some important disclaimers about *Seinfeld*'s popularity. At its peak, it was the most popular show on television. However, in an era when the entertainment business was still overwhelmingly dominated by white men, it was predominantly watched by white Americans. African American and Latinx viewers mostly ignored the show. Like any cultural phenomenon, the show had its detractors. With characters who could behave deplorably, *Seinfeld* could be an easy show to hate. *Seinfeld* was not beloved in every corner of America. Still, at its peak, the show was everywhere in American culture in a way that is impossible to imagine in today's fragmented state of television. So even if you didn't watch *Seinfeld*, if you lived in the United States in the nineties, you probably had *some* opinion about the show.

This book traces *Seinfeld*'s rise, peak, and influence in three parts. Part I explores *Seinfeld*'s origin: the backgrounds of the show's co-creators (chapter 1); the state of television when NBC developed *Seinfeld* (chapter 2); the near-death experience of *Seinfeld*'s pilot episode (chapter 3); and the construction of the show's now-legendary cast (chapter 4).

Part II describes the themes found in the show itself: the four main characters (chapter 5); the vibrant collection of supporting characters (chapter 6); the show's New York City setting and related issues of race and religion (chapter 7); and some of the layered cultural issues of the nineties that the show navigated (chapter 8).

Part III is about *Seinfeld*'s legacy: the final episode's failure to live up to its hype (chapter 9); the show's influence on television comedy (chapter 10); the aspects of the show that are now out-of-date or even offensive (chapter 11); and the ways the show's messages continue to resonate (chapter 12).

I was a kid growing up in an Upstate New York suburb when I first watched *Seinfeld*. At its most popular, the show was dubbed a "water-cooler show," based on the idea that viewers would talk about last night's episode around their office watercoolers the next morning. For me, it was a "vending machine show." I remember rehashing episodes with my friends first thing Friday mornings by the time I was in eighth grade.

During the show's final season, I had an SAT prep class on Thursday nights that ended at 9:00 p.m.—right when *Seinfeld* was starting. I would race home to catch as much of the episode as I could, and then I would rewatch the episode in full to catch the opening minutes. This was still the VCR era, so I became an expert in the notoriously difficult task of programming a VCR to record live TV. With no DVRs, no DVDs, and definitely no streaming services, my collection of *Seinfeld* tapes eventually became the envy of my friends. Long before the binge-watching era, I would host viewing parties where we would watch hours of *Seinfeld* late into the night.

*Seinfeld* taught me a lot about the adult world. It taught me about sex (something I wasn't having). It taught me about singledom (something I have left behind). It taught me that crazy relatives, wacky neighbors, and shrinkage were all normal parts of life.

I watched *Seinfeld*'s final few seasons as I went through adolescence. Critical consensus favors the show's middle seasons, but many of my favorite moments come from the wackier concepts in the last years, like Kramer and his New York University intern trying to solve the world's energy problems by rolling a giant ball of oil out a high-rise window.

Was I too young to watch the show? Nah! By the show's final episode, I had figured out that, as much as the four main characters made me laugh, I didn't really want to be like them. Still, I loved hanging out with them, and I never wanted the show to end.

Now, more than 20 years after the show ended, there have been other comedies that I consider even more brilliant, but *Seinfeld* will always be my first favorite show.

Whew! You know, reader, if you would have told me 25 years ago that someday I'd be standing here about to publish a book about *Seinfeld*, I would have said, "You're crazy!" . . . Now let's push this giant ball of oil out the window.

# Part I


# Making Nothing

# I

# JERRY AND LARRY

Springing, as it did, from two remarkably compatible minds, *Seinfeld* was one of television's great collaborations. Fans and critics may continue to debate who the real genius was behind the show, but both Jerry Seinfeld and Larry David should share the credit for *Seinfeld*'s conception and execution.

Early on, Seinfeld had the edge in the public's view. For most of the show's run, Jerry Seinfeld, already famous as a stand-up comic, was the face of the show that bore his name. When David left the show before its final two seasons, many TV critics fretted over the show's potential decline. But most of the show's audience still didn't even know who Larry David was.

David returned to write the show's finale, and, a few years later, created and starred in his own television series on HBO, *Curb Your Enthusiasm*. Linking the comedy of *Seinfeld* to the comedy of *Curb*, fans of David's new show began to argue that he, not Seinfeld, was the real master of *Seinfeld*'s domain.

*Curb* swung the scales so much that Seinfeld's contributions to his own show might be *underrated* at this point. But before we settle the question of who mattered more, let's explore the backgrounds of *Seinfeld*'s two co-creators.

## LITTLE JERRY'S INFLUENCES

In contrast to the shallow, cackling version of himself he would play on television, Jerry Seinfeld was an introvert from childhood. However, quiet, young Seinfeld was not without an inner self-confidence. He believed he was capable of becoming Superman. He just had to figure out how to remove his Clark Kent disguise and reveal his superpowers to the world.

If he was funny as a kid, few noticed him in the shadow of his father, Kalman Seinfeld, the owner of a sign business and the funniest guy in the family. Jerry would ride around with his father in the Kal Signfeld Sign Co. van, watching his dad crack up his serious-faced customers. Whatever Jerry inherited from Kal, it wasn't his father's direct style of humor. Compared to his dad, Seinfeld says, "I've always kind of been a little on the sly."[1]

Never physically imposing, Seinfeld avoided the spotlight in school. Many of his peers didn't perceive his rich thought life, with unspoken comedic observations running through his head. Then one day he made a friend laugh so hard, the kid spat milk and cookies all over—a deeply satisfying reaction for young Seinfeld. He had found his calling.

Seinfeld became addicted to television, both as a fan and as a student of comedy. At one point, his mother tried to get rid of the television set, but that just sent Seinfeld to his neighbor's house. Born April 29, 1954, many of Seinfeld's comedy influences came from earlier years. Besides Superman (a "comic" of a different sort), the Three Stooges, Laurel and Hardy, and Bugs Bunny are referenced throughout *Seinfeld*, often explicitly.

Bill Cosby was another influence on Seinfeld, as he was for any young comic growing up in the 1960s. Cosby is now disgraced—a convicted sex offender with a list of rape allegations that stretches back half a century. But before his crimes came to light, and even before *The Cosby Show* became NBC's flagship sitcom in the 1980s, Cosby was already a huge star. He first parlayed his success as a stand-up comic into a co-starring role (groundbreaking for an African American at that time) in the adventure series, *I Spy*, which ran on NBC from 1965 to 1968. He followed that up with *The Bill Cosby Show* (NBC, 1969–1971), thus solidifying a path Seinfeld and many other colleagues would follow: from stand-up to television to fame and fortune.

Seinfeld cites Robert Klein as his biggest inspiration in the business. That's an unexpected source of influence as Klein rose to fame in the 1970s with his comedic takes on politics while Seinfeld is one of the more apolitical comics of his generation. But it was Klein's straightforward, uncomplicated style, not his substance, that grabbed Seinfeld's attention. Klein could make a joke about a convoluted topic like Watergate seem accessible and even imitable to the young would-be comic.

Later, when he had achieved success, Seinfeld would cite his buddies as his favorite comedians: Jay Leno, David Letterman, and Larry Miller, who appears as the short-tempered, class-conscious title character in the season 6 episode "The Doorman."

## FROM UMBRELLA HAWKER TO NBC PILOT

For college, Seinfeld spent two years at one of the snowiest places on the planet, SUNY Oswego in Upstate New York, before transferring downstate to Queens College. He double-majored in communications and theater, though his acting ability never matched his wit. Once at Queens College, he earned a small role as a reporter in a drama, but to the director's chagrin, he had the whole audience cracking up throughout his scene.[2]

Successful stand-up comics are men and women of steel who, at some point in their lives, were brave enough to climb onto a stage alone to make a room of strangers laugh, fail to accomplish that goal, and then return again and again until they succeeded. Then, and only then, can the stand-up comic begin to earn even a few bucks at their occupation. After graduating from Queens College in 1976, Seinfeld had some lean years, taking odd jobs to supplement his meager comedy club income.

"The Checks" (season 8, episode 7) offers a humorous retrospective on these years. Kramer encourages Jerry to sign piles of 12-cent royalty checks he is receiving from a repeated appearance in the title sequence of a Japanese TV show. The cash is not worth the cramps in the now-successful Jerry's hand, but, perhaps recalling leaner times, he spends hours endorsing them. Later, Jerry grabs an umbrella from a street vendor to demonstrate the twirl and dance he once used to attract customers, referencing one of the odd jobs Seinfeld took after college. In a parody of joke-stealing—the worst possible sin a stand-up can commit—an old friend from the umbrella business, Teddy, accuses Jerry of taking credit for his twirl technique. It starts to pour, and Teddy offers to sell Jerry an umbrella . . . for $200. Jerry, forced to walk umbrella-less to the bank in the deluge, is quickly drenched, ruining the very checks he was about to cash.

Seinfeld's first breakthrough on television came during the New York–based comic's brief period in Los Angeles.[3] In 1980, he landed a recurring role in *Benson*, a sitcom coming off a modestly successful freshman season. Seinfeld played a joke writer who was bad at writing jokes. The inherently unfunny character was cut after three episodes. As *Benson* aired for a total of seven seasons, it is probably to everyone's benefit that Seinfeld was fired. First, it taught him to insist on full control of his own material. If he was going to be not funny, he would only be not funny with stuff *he* wrote. Second, though he didn't know it then, getting fired freed him up for a true breakthrough that was just around the corner.

Five months after his third and final appearance on *Benson* aired, Seinfeld was back on television. This time, he was delivering his own material. The 27-year-old comic had finally landed an appearance on *The Tonight Show* with Johnny Carson. After the five-minute set featuring the best jokes Seinfeld had in his arsenal, the cameras caught Carson giving the young comic a thumbs-up, a sign of Johnny's sincere approval. In those days, a good appearance on late-night television, especially *The Tonight Show*, was a comic's launchpad. After that, Seinfeld filled his schedule, touring the country and performing 300 days a year, setting a pace he would maintain throughout the decade (figure 1.1).

By 1987, Seinfeld had a strong enough national following to star in his first TV special, *Jerry Seinfeld: Stand-Up Confidential*. Sprinkled throughout the show were sketches reenacting portions of Seinfeld's routine. In short, the special prefigured *Seinfeld*'s original premise.[4]

A year later, NBC reached out for a meeting. Suddenly, Seinfeld had a chance to write, create, and star in his own show. But he had no idea what the show might be about. And he had absolutely no experience writing for television. Fortunately, he was friends with a very funny guy who did.

Figure 1.1.   Jerry Seinfeld. *Photofest*

## WHO IS LARRY DAVID?

Because Larry David became famous for a show in which a character was based on him . . . and more famous for another show in which he played a character named "Larry David" . . . and continued to play characters a lot like himself on television, film, and stage . . . it is difficult to pinpoint the real Larry David.

In the opening exchange of a 2015 *60 Minutes* profile, David and Charlie Rose sound like they are acting out an Abbott and Costello sketch.[5] "Who is Larry David?" asks Rose. David, flagrantly chewing gum throughout the interview, squirms and defers with a wry smile. He starts ranting about how he didn't want to do the interview, but his restrained jubilation gives him away. Eventually, after much back and forth, David confesses, "I'm like everybody else. I'm a jerk." Rose doesn't buy it. He presses further, and the routine continues. Somewhere, David's old friend and colleague, Jerry Seinfeld, is laughing hysterically.

David's oldest friends say the sniveling George Costanza, David's avatar on *Seinfeld*, and the curmudgeon David plays on *Curb Your Enthusiasm*, are just an act for the sake of comedy. They say David is actually a very nice guy.

But David says that very nice guy is the *real* act. He actually *is* a jerk. With his hyper social awareness and his ability to shape-shift depending on the social setting, it is no wonder the success of David's *Curb* aligned with the rise of the millennials, the first digital native generation who understood the malleability of identity in an online world. But David's generation, the baby boomers, didn't need computers to build multifaceted identities as they moved throughout the world. The response to the question, "Who are you?" is an existential question for every generation. *Seinfeld* is one of the great comedic responses to that question for baby boomers.

Who is Larry David? He was born on July 2, 1947, and grew up in an apartment in Sheepshead Bay, Brooklyn, with his father (a clothing salesman), his mother, and his older brother. His cousins lived in the same building so the apartment was busy, as open to unannounced visitors as Jerry's apartment is on *Seinfeld*. Reflecting on his childhood, David claims he participated in nothing and was unaware that his school's prom even existed. He allows that he did perform in one school play when he was 13 years old. It was a late-nineteenth-century farce, *Charlie's Aunt*, and he wore a dress for the part. His mother had high hopes that David would become a mailman. He wouldn't, though David would later explore the career on *Seinfeld* through the character of Newman.[6]

David went to the University of Maryland where he majored in history. In college, he also discovered that others liked his sense of humor, though he did not jump right into comedy. Like Seinfeld, David worked various gigs to make ends meet, some of which, like bra salesman and limo driver, made their way into *Seinfeld*.

More than any other *Seinfeld* writer, including the show's star, David's life was the key source for the show's stories. In the early 1980s, he lived across the hall from a rather strange guy named Kenny Kramer. David once quit a job, had second thoughts, and tried showing up to work like nothing happened. His fiancée died from licking toxic wedding invitation envelopes. OK, I made up the last one. But dozens of other moments from the show came directly from the life of Larry David.

Unlike Seinfeld, David says he did not grow up idolizing comedians. He started to become interested in stand-up comedy around the time his hairline started to recede, as the earliest photos of him performing attest. He first climbed on stage for an open-mike night at a club in Greenwich Village in 1974. David struggled through the 1970s alongside friends and future stars like Richard Lewis and Richard Belzer. They describe his style as a "comic's comic," which David interprets to mean, "I sucked."[7] As much as David wanted to make the audience laugh, he was determined not to compromise himself or his material to keep the crowds happy. And he wouldn't tolerate anything less than their full attention. Once, in a Manhattan comedy club, David walked up to the microphone, surveyed the crowed, said, "Never mind" and bailed on the set.

He met Seinfeld sometime in the 1970s, and it was comedy at first sight. The younger comedian was a few years behind David in experience, but the two quickly became professional allies as well as friends, assisting one another with jokes and routines. Still, their styles remained starkly contrasting; on stage, Seinfeld was ingratiating, while David remained, even then, an unlovable curmudgeon. Other comedians loved watching David perform, both because he was so funny and because he was very likely to spike the microphone to the floor and storm off stage if the show wasn't clicking with the audience.[8]

By the late seventies, David was finding some success. He caught his first break in 1979 when ABC hired him to write and perform in a new comedy show. After losing several members of its original cast, NBC's *Saturday Night Live* appeared to be running out of steam heading into its fifth season. ABC was looking to build on that successful model and maybe even take over the late-night, sketch-comedy throne. They even stole for the title of the show, calling it *Fridays* (figure 1.2). As it turned out, even after *SNL*'s creator, Lorne Michaels, left the show in 1980, *Saturday Night Live* was just fine, thanks in large part to the breakout of 19-year-old Eddie Murphy.

There were no breakouts on *Fridays*—neither David nor his fellow cast member, Michael Richards, managed to grab America's attention—and ABC canceled the sketch show after two seasons. Still, besides a steady paycheck, the role gave David a dash of television experience, both in front of and behind the camera. And besides Richards, David also worked with another brilliant young comedic mind, Larry Charles, whose anarchic voice would be central to *Seinfeld*'s style when David hired him for the show's writing staff in its second season.

*Fridays* ended in 1982. By 1984, David was back in the TV business, writing for *Saturday Night Live*. The experience was miserable. Perhaps the only person more unhappy at *SNL* that year was an underutilized young comedian named Julia Louis-Dreyfus, slogging through her third and final season. In one season writing for *SNL*, David only managed to get one sketch on air. His frustrations peaked one Friday afternoon when David yelled, "I quit!" and stormed off the set. The next Monday, after some encouragement from his neighbor, Kramer, David decided to simply return to work as though his outburst had never happened. While George's attempt to follow this strategy fails in "The Revenge" (season 2, episode 7), it worked for David. He finished out the season on staff, only leaving the show at the end of the year. Apparently, late-night TV bosses are more forgiving than real-estate bosses.

Figure 1.2.    The cast of *Fridays* (ABC, 1980–1982). Shown from left, front row: Mark Blankfield, Melanie Chartoff, Bruce Mahler; center: Larry David, Brandis Kemp, John Roarke, Maryedith Burrell; top: Michael Richards, Darrow Igus. *ABC/Photofest*

## LARRY DAVID AND WOODY ALLEN

Throughout the 1980s, with his stand-up career now more or less steady, David had a few more opportunities to write for television, working with Gilbert Gottfried and Garry Shandling.[9] He also landed two small parts in the Woody Allen films *Radio Days* (1987) and *New York Stories* (1989).[10] Years later, after his success with *Seinfeld* and *Curb*, David would star in Allen's 2009 film, *Whatever Works*. (The movie is one of many Allen films to depict a man's infatuation with a woman much younger than him. This repeated motif has now become downright creepy, to say the least, in light of the public's continued grappling with accusations by Allen's daughter, Dylan Farrow, that her father molested her when she was seven.)

Another New Yorker who grew up in a Jewish family, Allen is an obvious influence on David's neurotic sense of humor, and his films are clear forebears for the comedy of social agony in *Seinfeld*. Jason Alexander has said he initially modeled George after Woody Allen in early episodes of *Seinfeld* until he realized David was the character's true inspiration. But it was Kramer, not George, who landed a part in a "Woody" in "The Alternate Side" (season 3, episode 11). Woody, who did not appear in the episode, even gave Kramer a line: "These pretzels are making me thirsty!"

Both from his known and his alleged actions, Allen's personal reputation is now nearly in shambles, at least in the United States. Still, his creative work is among the most significant of its era, and his influence on both film and comedy is undeniable. Anticipating shows like *Seinfeld*, Allen's movies demonstrated how highbrow existentialist musing could co-exist in a story with laugh-out-loud humor—not simply alongside one another, but intermingled. Even more importantly for *Seinfeld*, Allen's art addressed sex in a matter-of-fact way that was simultaneously true, relatable, and hilarious. It is possible to imagine Jerry Seinfeld and even Larry David finding their styles without Woody Allen's influence. It is harder to imagine *Seinfeld* existing without Allen's films. *Seinfeld* is not as rich a text as the best of Allen's films like *Annie Hall* (1977) or *Crimes and Misdemeanors* (1989), but it *was* a more complex, nuanced show than sitcoms had ever been before. Allen's films laid the groundwork for the American audience in the 1970s and

1980s, preparing them to recognize, grapple with, and appreciate the televised comedy style of *Seinfeld* in the 1990s.

When he starred in *Whatever Works*, David mused on the similarities and differences between him and the director: "Woody's more of a pessimist about the big picture: the hopelessness, meaninglessness of it all, the blackness of eternity. I'm probably more pessimistic about the smaller things: the relationship won't work out, the Yankees will lose, the movie will bomb."[11]

This is how David adapted Allen's style in *Seinfeld*. He and Seinfeld moved from the cosmic-scale musing of Allen's films to the tiny social crises of day-to-day life. In this way, George Costanza is even more pitiful than the archetypal Woody Allen character; he and his friends are more likely to worry about the placement of a button on a shirt than to fret about their utter smallness in the universe.

## JERRY + LARRY

Although his lack of experience concerned NBC, David eventually became *Seinfeld*'s show runner, the industry's name for the person in charge of the show's production, from script to screen, from the writers' room to the set.[12] NBC's decision to let David to run *Seinfeld* was extremely bold. By their own admission, David and Seinfeld knew next to nothing about how a television show was supposed to operate. Even more incredibly, NBC more or less allowed these two novices to operate with minimal network interference. David and Seinfeld pretty much ignored any notes the network sent them. As it turned out, David's inexperience allowed both him and the show to evolve organically. Both David and Seinfeld had the freedom to learn, over the show's early seasons, how to use the language of television to express their own style of comedy.

Depending on how realistic you think his character is on *Curb Your Enthusiasm*, you might expect Larry David to be a difficult guy to work with. The evidence of the seven largely happy seasons he oversaw suggests you'd be wrong. Far from feuding with their cast and crew, David, along with Jerry, had healthy working relationships on *Seinfeld*. Anticipating the improv style of *Curb*, David was always pleased to let the actors explore their characters. If they could come up with a line that got more laughs than the one he had written, he would go with it. Comedy, not Larry David, ruled the set.

On the other hand, Larry David did rule the writers' room. In fact, *Seinfeld* did not have a typical writers' room. Any script started with a pitch. Writers would bring their ideas to the pitch meeting for David and Seinfeld to approve, and then they'd be sent off to write. While traditional television scripts would usually be produced collaboratively, *Seinfeld*'s writers produced their own complete scripts. But once it was done, David and Seinfeld took a final pass, often making substantial changes to the script. A writer like Peter Mehlman, who was on the show for many years, eventually earned the trust to take David's feedback and write the final version on his own, but most writers never earned that status with David. [13]

With network executives, David could be combative. By his own admission, he was always ready for a fight if NBC tried to squelch any of their scripts for issues of form or content. Again, comedy ruled. He went to war for some of his groundbreaking scripts in the early years. He usually won, and the critics and slowly growing audience justified his efforts. Then again, David was realistic about what the network would and would not allow on air, so his scripts came out palatable to NBC, often despite his fears.

Moreover, David respected and enjoyed working with his old friend, the star who had invited him along to NBC, and whose name was the title of the show. To Seinfeld's credit, both NBC executives and his co-stars report that he was one of the easiest network stars to work with, and he deserves much of the credit for the on-set camaraderie among the show's "Big Four." Seinfeld also used his diplomatic temperament to be an intermediary between David and the network.

According to Mehlman, the longtime *Seinfeld* writer, "Larry was much more willing to go to darker places than Jerry." [14] When David departed the show after its seventh season, many critics and fans sensed that the show's crucial edginess departed with him. How you feel about *Seinfeld*'s final two seasons depends on how much you enjoy the goofiness that flourished in place of the darkness that receded when David left and Seinfeld stepped into the role as show runner.

Discussing their partnership, David says, "The show is actually much closer to my life than Jerry's. But Jerry takes our darkest notion and makes it palatable to a mass audience." [15] To put it another way, David is

responsible for the show's ability to feel simultaneously zany and realistic, while Seinfeld deserves the credit for making four fairly obnoxious
human beings likable.


## JERRY OR LARRY?

So, who meant more to the show? To find out, let's play a game. What
would the show look like without Larry David?

For this hypothetical, let's imagine that after season 3, with no great
sitcom replacement for *Cheers* on its schedule, NBC decided to steer
*Seinfeld* in a more mainstream direction by firing the TV novice, David.
Would Seinfeld stay? Perhaps his star power was always David's shield.
Obviously, there's no *Seinfeld* without Seinfeld, so for the sake of this
exercise, let's imagine he does stick around.

Maybe *Seinfeld* still becomes a hit on the strength of its cast, as well
as the characters David created. But there is no way it becomes arguably the greatest show of all time. Gone is David's comedy of whining
about everyday life. Besides writing many classic episodes before and
after season 4, David masterminded the show's season-long arcs, such
as season 4's story about George and Jerry producing a pilot for NBC
and George's season-long engagement in season 7. If the show moves in
a more mainstream direction, as it likely would under David's imaginary
replacement, it's hard to imagine classic episodes like "The Soup Nazi"
or "The Bizarro Jerry" ever getting made. *Seinfeld* would not have become an all-time classic if David was removed after season 3.

I think, in this alternate reality, *Seinfeld* would have lasted through
season 5. I think ratings would have started to slide rather than grow in
seasons 4 and 5. I think Jerry Seinfeld would have grown disinterested
in the show by then and returned to the domain he is truly master of—
the stand-up circuit. In other words, *Seinfeld*'s legacy would be that it
pushed the envelope of the sitcom genre for a little while before bog-
ging down under tension between network and creator.

Now let's flip it around. What if Jerry Seinfeld had left the show
after season 3?

As Seinfeld is the titular star, this scenario is immediately *much* less
plausible than David leaving and the show continuing. Let's say, for
some reason, NBC thinks it still has a show without the Jerry character,

and David stays on to help retool the series. George moves into Jerry's apartment and becomes the central character in the series. Kramer remains his wacky neighbor. The George and Elaine relationship does not make a lot of sense on its own in the absence of Jerry (a fact the show explored from time to time) but, for some reason, Elaine hangs around.

Some of the supporting characters need to be elevated to fill out the show. Newman still has a place as Kramer's buddy, but he's a little less fun as George's nemesis than he was as Jerry's. Here's a fun thought: maybe George's parents get an even bigger role in this version of the show. Also, George's and Elaine's respective workplaces could be more heavily featured.

We need a new title, though. I'm not sure you go *George*. How about . . . oh, I don't know . . . *Curb Your Enthusiasm*?

Realistically, the show would not exist without Seinfeld. His star power made the show possible. But once established, Seinfeld became as crucial to the show's balance as any of the other leads. He was the center of the universe on screen. In retrospect, David has been dubbed the secret genius of the operation, but Seinfeld injected just as much of his own sensibility as David did to the show's comedy.

So, while David's contribution was essential, the show did continue for two very funny seasons without him. Once *Seinfeld* was established, David was arguably the fifth most important person for the show. If Seinfeld, or Louis-Dreyfus, or Alexander, or Richards had said they were done, *Seinfeld* could not be *Seinfeld*.

Among the many lucky breaks that NBC got in the development of *Seinfeld* was Seinfeld's friendship with David, and his insistence that his less-successful friend be a part of the show. The show was also fortunate that *Seinfeld* lasted long enough for Seinfeld and David to figure out what they were doing as TV writers. Even the fact that *Seinfeld* made it to air at all is a television miracle.

# 2

# A GUY WALKS INTO NBC . . .

*Seinfeld* won the Emmy for Outstanding Comedy Series just once, for the show's fourth season (figure 2.1). In *Seinfeld*'s final five seasons the award went to a deserving competitor in *Frasier*, NBC's *Cheers* spin-off.[1]

For that Emmy-winning fourth season, Larry David and Jerry Seinfeld decided to use their experiences developing a TV show with NBC as an overarching story for the entire season. The story kicks off in the opening moments of episode 3, "The Pitch," when two NBC executives approach Jerry at a comedy club. They compliment his set and, after George successfully guesses the spelling of one executive's last name, they invite Jerry to a meeting at NBC. After the executives depart, Jerry turns to George, excited about the opportunity but concerned about the task in front of him.

George scoffs at his nerves, exclaiming, "Look at all the junk that's on TV!" Eventually, George convinces Jerry to let him help try to make more of that junk.

The real story: On November 2, 1988, Seinfeld went to his first meeting with NBC. Joining him for the visit was a guy named George—Seinfeld's agent, George Shapiro, who had been pressing NBC to work with his client. Seinfeld, like his character a few years later, had no ideas for a scripted television show. Nine months later, he and David had written—and NBC had aired—*The Seinfeld Chronicles*. Viewers rated it among the worst pilot episodes in NBC history.

## CHAPTER 2

Figure 2.1.   Michael Richards, Julia Louis-Dreyfus, Jerry Seinfeld, and Jason Alexander at the Primetime Emmy Awards. *Photofest*

*Seinfeld* survived long enough to thrive, thanks to the boldness of David and Seinfeld as well as the few NBC executives who stuck with the show. In addition, the show followed an unconventional path through NBC's development chain. Ultimately, the emergence of *Seinfeld* at NBC owes much to serendipity. The late 1980s was the perfect moment for a revolutionary new sitcom to emerge, and NBC was the perfect network to take such a chance.

## THE 1980s: TV'S SECOND GOLDEN AGE

In 1988, the year Seinfeld walked into the NBC offices, the network happened to have two classic sitcoms at the peak of their popularity: *The Cosby Show*, entering its fifth season, and *Cheers*, going into its seventh season. Including the *Cosby Show* spin-off, *A Different World*, NBC had three of the top four shows on television, all airing on Thursday nights. NBC had depth on its schedule, too, with 17 of the top 30 rated programs in prime-time television. Even in an era dominated by only three broadcast networks, that was an incredible mark of success.

But NBC had started the decade in last place out of the three. That's when the network took a risk and invested in two dramas from MTM Enterprises, the production company Mary Tyler Moore had founded with her husband, Grant Tinker. *Hill Street Blues* (1981–1987) and *St. Elsewhere* (1982–1988) reached a level of quality not seen in scripted television since the first Golden Age of TV in the early 1950s. From their writing to their production style, these shows displayed more cinematic realism than TV had seen in some time; *Hill Street Blues* felt closer to the world of *Taxi Driver* (1976) than *Charlie's Angels* (ABC, 1976–1981).

Barely a top 30 show at its peak, the gritty *Hill Street Blues* never matched the audience size of *Charlie's Angels*, a crime drama built around the sex appeal of its three female stars. However, like *Charlie's Angels*, it did score well among younger adult viewers. Ratings were becoming increasingly specialized, giving advertisers insight into which shows wealthier audiences were watching, and advertisers liked the way *Hill Street Blues* performed in those demographics. This same data set was one of the few things *Seinfeld* had in its favor during its first few seasons.

Other increasingly complex shows followed *Hill Street Blues* throughout the 1980s, including CBS's *Cagney & Lacey* (1982–1988) and ABC's *Moonlighting* (1985–1989). These shows were more serialized than television had ever dared to be before, meaning that storylines continued from episode to episode. Serialization is now commonplace, and almost expected for content on streaming platforms, but it was rare through much of television history. Tracking a story across multiple episodes demands a certain amount of attention from a television viewer.

The risk of losing the audience was balanced by the reward of richer plots and greater depth of characters. Some dramas in the late 1980s and early 1990s, like ABC's much-hyped but short-lived *Twin Peaks* (1990–1991), may have been too dense and demanding for viewers of the time. But by *Seinfeld*'s fourth season in 1992, its audience was ready to follow a season-long storyline about Jerry and George developing a show for NBC. David and his writers rewarded the audience for their attention; every episode in the season connects in some way—major or minor—to another episode.

*Seinfeld* took serialization farther than any sitcom had before, although, as we have seen, it was following the path of MTM Enterprises' dramas. The company's influence is profound—MTM is a kind of illuminati for late-twentieth-century American television. Practically every significant program from the eighties and nineties was created by someone who worked on an MTM show or worked for someone who worked on an MTM show. You can play a version of "six degrees of Kevin Bacon" with MTM's vast web of successful television writers.[2] The great exception to this "six degrees of MTM" rule? *Seinfeld*.

Still, *Seinfeld* owes much to the revolution in quality that MTM sparked. MTM made shows that were more complex and, with their success, networks became bolder with the kinds of shows they were willing to green-light. Ultimately, the failure of *Twin Peaks* dampened the enthusiasm for envelope-pushing dramas on television. Simultaneously, a new wave of sitcoms starring proven stand-up comics rocketed up the TV ratings charts: *Roseanne* (ABC, 1988–1997), *Home Improvement* (ABC, 1991–1999), and *Seinfeld*. Throughout the nineties, networks would lean more on sitcoms than dramas as tent poles for their schedules.

Of course, this was NBC's strategy already. But, as the bigwigs at the Peacock network knew, *Cheers* and *The Cosby Show* wouldn't stay on the air forever. A day of reckoning was coming. It just took NBC a few years to realize that *Seinfeld* might be their savior.

## THE NEXT *COSBY SHOW?*

*The Cosby Show* was *Seinfeld* of the eighties—a sitcom constructed around the most famous stand-up comic of the time that became one of the top-rated shows on television. Before network executives started looking for the next *Seinfeld* in the late nineties, they were looking for the next *Cosby Show* in the late eighties.

ABC found the next *Cosby Show* first, with *Roseanne* ascending to the top of the charts for several years. Created and starring Roseanne Barr, the show's depiction of a working-class, white family was a funny and savvy inversion of the themes in *The Cosby Show*.

For NBC, the search for the next *Cosby Show* was more literal than other networks; *The Cosby Show*, more than *Hill Street Blues* or even *Cheers*, was directly responsible for taking the network from third place to first.

The job of a network scheduling department is hard to explain in the cord-cutting era, but let's start with this reminder—before on-demand streaming and before DVRs, you actually had to *turn on your television set at a specific time to watch a specific show*! This meant that network executives agonized over their schedule—when should a certain show run? One strategy was to build a popular block of programming to keep viewers from changing the channel all night long. NBC's Thursday night was the pinnacle example of this strategy. For eight years, Americans could tune to NBC on Thursday to watch *The Cosby Show* at 8:00 and *Cheers* at 9:00. At 10:00, NBC ran a drama—*Hill Street Blues* for much of the decade, succeeded by *L.A. Law*.

But *The Cosby Show*'s ratings began to sag in its final seasons, and the show ultimately ended in the 1991–1992 season, its eighth. *Cheers* was finished a year later. When Seinfeld walked into his first NBC meeting in 1988, the network executives were not yet desperate to replace their two Thursday night tent poles. But they knew they had to start cultivating a new hit.

Ultimately, it was NBC exec Warren Littlefield who presided over this Thursday night transition. Littlefield had a difficult task. Finding replacements for *The Cosby Show*, *Cheers*, and *L.A. Law* would be like driving a golf ball off a beach into the blowhole of a passing whale . . . three times!

In his efforts to reload Thursday night, Littlefield had his share of whiffs, but ultimately his Thursday night reprogramming was a triumph. The year after *Cheers* ended, *Seinfeld* took the 9:00 p.m. spot in the 1993–1994 season. The next year, *ER* took over for *L.A. Law* at 10:00. And the year after that, *Friends* moved to *The Cosby Show*'s old time slot at 8:00. Of those three ratings superstars, only *Seinfeld* was not an immediate hit. But *Seinfeld* became a hit just in time, bridging the gap for NBC as *ER* and *Friends* arrived.

I know, I know . . . I've yada-yada'd *Seinfeld*'s emergence. We'll cover that in chapter 3. The point is that *Seinfeld* almost single-handedly kept NBC at the top in this moment of transition.

At the same time, it is worth recalling how different *Seinfeld* and *The Cosby Show* are. *Seinfeld* would eventually become the most popular sitcom of its day and take the title of "Best TV Show Named after the Comedian Who Created, Wrote, and Starred in It" from *The Cosby Show* and *Roseanne*. Otherwise, it had little in common with *The Cosby Show*'s sentimental depiction of an upper-middle-class black family.

*The Cosby Show*'s cultural legacy on nineties television was better represented not on NBC's Thursday night, but on ABC's Friday night "TGIF" lineup of family sitcoms, including *Full House* and *Boy Meets World*. These programs skewed a bit more narrowly toward a younger audience than *The Cosby Show*, which enjoyed broad appeal across demographic categories. Aiming at parents stuck at home on a Friday night with kids too young to drive, one of the TGIF stalwarts was *Family Matters*, a family sitcom with a predominantly black cast that featured regular doses of comically delivered lessons about being a parent and/or growing up.

*Seinfeld*, on the other hand, was ambivalent toward families, averse to lessons, and bereft of black characters. The latter characteristic was increasingly embarrassing as the nineties wore on, though, as we shall see, the show was not afraid to acknowledge and own that failure. But the show's cast and writers boasted that *Seinfeld* taught no lessons; "no learning, no hugging" was reportedly the show's motto. And the fraught relationship between the main characters and their aging parents stands in stark contrast to the tight-knit nuclear family in *The Cosby Show*. With the patriarchal, traditionalist humor of Bill Cosby at its core, *The Cosby Show* expressed a modern faith in both the family and the economy as reliable sources of uplift for American life, black or white. *Seinfeld*, on the other hand, manifests a postmodern fear that there is no center to life at all.

Both shows exemplify their eras. *The Cosby Show* was a landmark achievement in its time for normalizing the idea of an upper-middle-class black family, though it has been retrospectively criticized for the way it neglected harsher realities of both class and race in the Reagan era. *Seinfeld* was the first hit sitcom in the nineties about a group of single, professional friends living in a city. Looking back, *Seinfeld* reminds us that Americans were beginning to feel a detachment from their communities even before the emergence of the internet, cell phones, and social media. In its antisocial worldview, *Seinfeld* differs sharply from the other hit sitcom that preceded it on NBC.

## THE NEXT *CHEERS*?

Though it was critically lauded in its first season, *Cheers* was not an immediate hit in the ratings, making it more like *Seinfeld* than NBC's instant winners, such as *The Cosby Show* and *Friends*. In fact, *Cheers* did not become a hit until *The Cosby Show*'s debut season. Just as *Seinfeld* received a huge ratings bump when it moved to Thursday in *Cheers*' final season, a sizable audience finally discovered *Cheers* thanks to *The Cosby Show*.

*Cheers* is a workplace sitcom, only the workplace is a bar, a public space that allows regular customers to be a part of the central cast. Family members, as on *Seinfeld*, are often a burden rather than a source of inspiration and education as they are in *The Cosby Show*. Like *Seinfeld*, the show is often about conversation more than action. On *Seinfeld*, whole scenes revolved around conversations in their favorite coffee shop. On *Cheers*, whole episodes remained in the bar, the barflies glued to their stools, the bartender trapped within the encircling counter. *Cheers* was adult-themed, like *Seinfeld*, with many episodes revolving around sex.

While *Cheers* could be edgy in some of its content and was undeniably an excellent sitcom, it did not advance its genre as much as *Seinfeld*. Unlike *Seinfeld*, it's easy to pin down the premise of *Cheers*: an alcoholic ex-baseball player who owns a bar filled with various amusing characters hires an intelligent, sophisticated woman—his exact opposite—as a waitress. While *Seinfeld* defiantly resisted romantically pairing its male and female stars, "will they/won't they?" was central to *Cheers'* dramatic tension until Shelley Long left the program following its fifth season.

Most distinctively, the ideals of both shows are complete opposites. Emphasized by its theme song, the characters in *Cheers* embrace whomever and whatever comes into the bar. Regular, recurring, and one-off characters of all varieties bring their problems to Cheers, finding a support group who will listen, commiserate, and do their best to help, if at all possible. Whereas on *The Cosby Show* the suburban family is the solution to life's ills, on *Cheers* a lively urban public space is the cornerstone of personal growth and fulfillment.

As much as the characters on *Seinfeld* enjoy hanging out in a public space, they want absolutely nothing to do with the public life going on in their immediate vicinity. They might engage with a passing stranger if there is the opportunity for personal gain or the chance to find a new sexual partner, but most social interactions beyond their core friendships are burdensome. A *Seinfeld-Cheers* crossover would be disastrous, with the *Seinfeld* characters resisting and mocking the attempts the bar's staff and regulars might make to butt into their problems.

So, while *The Cosby Show* and *Cheers* set the bar for commercial success that *Seinfeld* would achieve on NBC's schedule, *Seinfeld* drew minimal influence from its two predecessors. Other than the foundational sources for the senses of humor of its two creators, it is hard to pinpoint obvious television predecessors for *Seinfeld*'s style and substance.

But there is one more NBC show to examine for its relationship to *Seinfeld*. Two of *Seinfeld*'s five most important people worked on one other linchpin of NBC's schedule, a program that has had an ongoing influence on American comedy for more than 40 years. *Seinfeld* does not belong in MTM Productions' influential family tree, but it is a distant cousin of America's greatest sketch comedy show, *Saturday Night Live*.

## SATURDAY NIGHT LIVE **AND** SEINFELD

Larry David's only season writing for *SNL* was Julia Louis-Dreyfus's third and final season performing on its cast. Louis-Dreyfus joined the cast at the age of 21 but found the environment cutthroat, drug-fueled, and sexist; throughout the early eighties, few female performers broke out from their work on the show.[3] While David and Louis-Dreyfus may not have liked their time on the show, that doesn't mean they did not learn anything or that they were not influenced by it.

David, since his earliest years stepping up to the comedy club microphone, has a stubborn belief in his own comedic abilities. That bullheadedness is the kind of temperament needed to succeed in the competitive, fast-paced *SNL* productions. Funny wins at *Saturday Night Live*; that's a commandment Lorne Michaels built into the show's production, and it remained inherent to the show's survival, even if Michaels wasn't in the building when David and Louis-Dreyfus were there. (Michaels left *SNL* in 1980 and returned in 1985.) Funny would win on David's set at *Seinfeld*, too.

David's stubbornness did not help him break through at *Saturday Night Live*, in part because *SNL* also favors collaboration. David not only couldn't find anyone else on the writing staff who shared his comedy sensibilities—he couldn't find anyone else he liked. David remembered this, too, as he became a successful television show runner. He doesn't just work with people who have complementary senses of humor; he works with his friends. He collaborated with a friend to make *Seinfeld* and, given even greater creative control for *Curb Your Enthusiasm*, surrounded himself with friends there.

Louis-Dreyfus took a similar lesson from her time on *SNL*, vowing that she "would not take any jobs that didn't seem as if they would be really fun."[4] That led her to *Seinfeld*, to work with Larry David, one of the few people she felt a connection with from her time at *SNL*.

The content of *SNL* also filtered into *Seinfeld*. *Seinfeld*'s recurring caricature of George Steinbrenner, voiced by David, is more like the kinds of exaggerated celebrity impressions repeated on *SNL* rather than the typical sitcom boss. Kramer's recurring lawyer, Jackie Chiles, was played by actor Phil Morris as essentially an impression of Johnnie Cochran, the celebrity lawyer. Other recurring characters on *Seinfeld* were similarly zany and broad. In another universe, it's not hard to imagine an *SNL* sketch built around Newman, the evil mailman, or Frank and Estelle Costanza, the crazy parents, or Mr. Pitt, the eccentric rich guy.

Both *Seinfeld* and *Saturday Night Live* also lean regularly, though not overwhelmingly, into physical comedy, proving that slapstick, done well, has a place at even the height of American comedy. The pratfalls and gyrating of both Michael Richards and Louis-Dreyfus on *Seinfeld* are on par with the antics of Chevy Chase and Chris Farley on *SNL*.

One final connection between *SNL* and *Seinfeld* steers us back to the strange story of the sitcom's development at NBC. *Seinfeld* was shepherded into existence not by the network's prime-time programming department but by NBC's late-night programming department, the very same department that oversees *Saturday Night Live*. In large part because of its *SNL* pedigree and its development in NBC's late-night division, *Seinfeld* did not look or feel like the prime-time sitcoms of its time. It was different, and ultimately it took someone from the late-night world to appreciate that difference.

## TO THE PILOT

The most powerful of the NBC executives who sat down with Jerry Seinfeld and George Shapiro in November 1988 was Brandon Tartikoff, by then a legend of the industry. Tartikoff took over programming at NBC at the age of 32. President of NBC from 1980 to 1991, Tartikoff gets the credit for the network's turnaround in those years, giving the green light for both the innovative quality of shows like *Hill Street Blues* and the mass-appeal humor of *The Cosby Show* and *Cheers*.

Seinfeld came into that first meeting with nothing, not even an idea for a show about nothing. He had never really thought of himself as a sitcom performer, and he had by then achieved as much success as a stand-up comic as he could have ever hoped. He was performing across the country, 300 dates a year. He had just bought an apartment on Central Park West. "I definitely did not want to be in a sitcom," he recalls.[5]

But history belies Seinfeld's recollection. In fact, he had just auditioned for a lead role on an ABC pilot, *Past Imperfect*. He lost the gig to Howie Mandel, just coming off a star-making role on NBC's *St. Else-*

*where*. The pilot, on which ABC passed, was produced by Castle Rock, a production company co-founded by the actor and filmmaker, Rob Reiner. It's hard to imagine Seinfeld turning any heads with his acting, but Reiner had a good feeling about the comedian.[6]

Back to the first NBC meeting. Tartikoff, in fact, did not have a sitcom in mind for the star comedian. "Would you be interested in a talk show?" Seinfeld recalls the NBC president asking.[7] *The Cosby Show* and *Cheers* weren't the only NBC stalwarts closer to the end than the beginning; another NBC star with a much longer legacy than Bill Cosby or Ted Danson was nearing the end of his career. Johnny Carson would depart his role as host of *The Tonight Show* in 1992, the same year *The Cosby Show* ended. Tartikoff might have been thinking about testing Seinfeld as a potential replacement on the show that had made his career. Seinfeld and his agent, Shapiro, left that meeting with the possibility of a deal for a talk show that would run as a Saturday late-night special, taking *SNL*'s time slot while the sketch comedy show was on a break. Henceforth, Seinfeld's name would come up whenever a late-night talk show hosting job opened up. This seemed like a logical path, both to NBC and to Seinfeld and Shapiro.

Then Larry David got involved.

Sometime after the meeting, the two comedians were hanging out, chatting humorously as usual, when either David or Seinfeld (the story has been told both ways) suggested that their amusing conversation could be the basis of a sitcom. David kept hashing out the idea with Seinfeld and eventually the latter was persuaded. Or maybe, as Seinfeld has recalled, David was his first choice all along. "Whenever Larry and I would chat, it sounded like great dialogue," recalls Seinfeld. "And when I thought of what I wanted the show to sound like, I thought I wanted it to sound like Larry and me talking."[8] Seinfeld's memory should be taken with a grain of salt; as we'll see, he claims that *everyone* who ended up working on the show was his first choice all along.

Early in the process, David and Seinfeld were still thinking the show might be a comedy special, one that demonstrated how a comedian comes up with his material. Eventually, they began to conceive of the show as a sitcom, partly because the characters began to take shape in their drafts, and partly because they could barely come up with enough material for a 30-minute episode. There was no way they could fill a full

90-minute special. David might have quit on the spot if someone told him the show would last nine seasons.

In the fictional version of this story in "The Pitch," a coffee-shop conversation between the two characters leads George to convince Jerry that they should pitch NBC a "show about nothing." For Seinfeld and David, the premise of the show was more about the life of a comedian in New York—two comedians, in fact, as George's character was originally conceived even closer to the real-life David.[9] With the concept crystallizing in Seinfeld's mind, it was time to go back to NBC, this time with David at his side.

NBC was still thinking about some kind of late-night opportunity for Seinfeld, and thus, one of the key figures now involved in the project was Rick Ludwin, the senior vice president who oversaw late-night programming (including *Saturday Night Live* and *The Tonight Show*) as well as NBC's variety shows and specials. Ludwin had first become interested in working with the comic after catching his 1987 TV special, *Jerry Seinfeld: Stand-Up Confidential*. Remember this name—Rick Ludwin is about to play a pivotal role in this story. For now, he was one of many enthusiastic receivers of the duo's pitch.

David and Seinfeld laid out their vision. Seinfeld would not play a doctor or a dad or an antique-store salesman or any other fictionalized role. He'd just play a stand-up comic living in New York. The show would be about his life as a comedian, and the ways that life fed into his act. He'd have a friend he would hang out with and talk to in a diner. And—this was based on David's life—he'd have a zany neighbor who dropped in unannounced from across the hall. It doesn't sound like much, but NBC liked it. Their decision: go find a production company (they did: Rob Reiner's Castle Rock) and make a pilot. Yada, yada, yada . . . *The Seinfeld Chronicles* aired on July 5, 1989. The hard part came next.

# 3

# WHO (ALMOST) KILLED THE PILOT?

So, you have an idea for a TV show and you want to try to sell it to one of the broadcast networks? Thirty years after *The Seinfeld Chronicles*, the television industry is undergoing a complete upheaval, and yet the process for securing a network order for a full season of a show remains similar.

First, you pitch the network your idea for a TV show in the summer. If they like it, they'll ask for a script in the fall. If they don't like it, you can always try another network. You turn in the script, and in January, if they like what they read, they give you a little money to shoot one episode—the pilot. You scramble to cast your show, because other pilots are being cast and filmed around the same time. Then you turn in your pilot to the network.

For creators, the goal of the pilot is to convince the network to order a full season of your show. Network executives will do a few things with your pilot before they make their final decision. First and most importantly, they'll watch it themselves. They believe they are good at their job; they believe they can recognize a show that people might watch, even though, as the great screenwriter William Goldman famously said about Hollywood, nobody knows anything.[1]

Network executives may also show your pilot to test audiences. The public's initial reaction to your pilot is not necessarily more important than the network's opinion, but it can be persuasive. Finally, your pilot will be shown to advertisers, especially if the network is thinking about ordering a full series. Remember: The primary business model for television networks is not, in fact, to create programs for their audience. Television networks make money by creating audiences to sell to their advertisers.

To be sure, this model has become less reliable in the decades since *Seinfeld*, and some content providers have found success with different business models. Subscription cable network HBO and subscription streaming service Netflix do not have advertising. They rely on their subscription fees as their sole source of revenue. Not coincidentally, their programming strategy differs substantially from the traditional development process. While Netflix emphasizes breadth of content and HBO focuses on quality, both providers have found success giving creators more freedom to pursue their own visions. But back in the 1990s, the relative independence that David and Seinfeld enjoyed was unusual.

There are many technological reasons why TV has changed so much since *Seinfeld*'s debut such as the growth of cable television, improvements in recording and on-demand systems, and the rise of the internet. But there are other factors, too. In 1993, the FCC ended restrictions on the amount of programming a network could own. Since then, TV networks have become central players in the production game, edging out independent production companies like MTM Enterprises. If NBC itself, instead of Castle Rock, had created and produced *Seinfeld*, you can imagine they would have a larger incentive in its success—they could get a bigger cut of the syndication revenue if and when other channels bought the rights to air reruns of *Seinfeld*. Streaming rights have become even more valuable than syndication rights, and if you don't have your own library of content, you will not be able to play on the same level with HBO, Netflix, Disney, and other competing platforms. Among the thousands of TV shows created between the end of World War II and 2000, *Seinfeld* is one of the very few to increase in value in this new, very different era of television.

As smart as they think they are, TV executives cannot see the future. In 1988, NBC executives believed that Jerry Seinfeld might be a valuable person with whom to be in business. But the show Seinfeld initially created with Larry David did not look like the kind of sitcom that had succeeded in the past. The fact that *Seinfeld* ever made it onto NBC's schedule is a miracle.

There were a lot of smart minds working at NBC in the late 1980s. Who tried to kill *Seinfeld*? And who deserves the credit for saving one of the most successful—and lucrative—sitcoms in broadcast television history?

## WHAT THEY SAW

The pilot for *The Seinfeld Chronicles* was ready for production in April 1989. The cast and crew gathered to read the script on April 20. They shot the pilot at Ren-Mar Studios in Hollywood, which just so happened to be the same place where *I Love Lucy* and *The Dick Van Dyke Show* were made. Filming wrapped in a week—the typical time frame for a 23-minute TV episode.

Soon after the episode was finished, about two dozen NBC executives gathered to watch it in a screening room in Burbank, California. This room did not exactly represent a cross-section of the country; these were mostly middle-aged white guys, veterans of a successful decade of programming. Included in the group were NBC President Brandon Tartikoff, his deputy and eventual replacement Warren Littlefield, and the head of NBC's late-night programming Rick Ludwin.

Meanwhile, NBC also arranged a test audience for the pilot. Four hundred households across America were invited to watch it. At a pre-arranged time, they could tune in to a cable channel specially designated for testing purposes and see *The Seinfeld Chronicles*. NBC's research department would call these viewers immediately after the show to get their reactions.[2]

The tension at the heart of the episode, titled "Good News, Bad News," is found in Jerry's relationship with Laura, a woman he had met in the past but doesn't know very well. Out of the blue, Laura calls Jerry to let him know she is going to be in New York City. Jerry is interested in Laura, but he and George spend much of the episode wondering whether she is interested in him. They discuss the words and voice inflection of her call. When she calls again and asks to stay in Jerry's apartment, they debate whether this request is a "signal" that Laura is hoping to have sex with Jerry. George goes with Jerry to the airport to meet Laura, where they try but fail to gauge her interest in Jerry by the mannerisms in her greeting.

While later episode plots might elicit a chuckle simply based on their description, let's be honest—that summary probably didn't put you on the floor laughing. As Larry David and Jerry Seinfeld's first crack at a sitcom script, the pilot is rough and far from hilarious. However, *The Seinfeld Chronicles* pulls off a nice trick in building both the sexual and comedic tensions to a simultaneous climax when Jerry and the audience finally discover Laura's intentions.

Once in Jerry's apartment (figure 3.1), Laura seems to be sending signal after signal to Jerry that she is interested in sex. She kicks off her shoes, unbuttons her top blouse button, asks for a glass of wine, and turns down the light. Jerry seems primed to make a move when the phone rings. The call is for Laura, who speaks cheerfully and fairly intimately for a few moments. She hangs up and reveals . . . it was her fiancé.

Interspersed throughout the pilot are four scenes of Jerry performing a stand-up act in a dark comedy club. After the fiancé revelation, the scene cuts right to Jerry on stage. "I have absolutely no idea what women are thinking," Jerry admits to the comedy club audience. Con-

**Figure 3.1.   Jerry's living room and kitchen.** *NBC/Photofest*

fronting the problem of relationship communication, particularly its failures, would become one of *Seinfeld*'s central themes.

The challenge of understanding the opposite sex is a timeless obstacle in storytelling. But nonverbal communication problems transcend gender in this episode, as they will throughout the series. Kramer (called Kessler in *The Seinfeld Chronicles*—Larry David was hoping to avoid any problems from his neighbor and inspiration for the character, Kenny Kramer) bursts into Jerry's apartment at 1:00 a.m. Despite Jerry's annoyed body language and repeated eye-rolling, Kramer makes himself at home with a bowl of cereal on the couch. Jerry could ask him to leave, just as he could ask Laura about her intentions for the visit. He doesn't ask. Speaking up might cause further social awkwardness, something that Jerry and his friends expend so much energy trying to avoid.

Other behaviors that would become familiar throughout *Seinfeld*'s run are present in this pilot, including the intense conversations about seemingly unimportant details of everyday life. The most important scene in the episode has nothing to do with Laura, or sex, or anything important. The pilot opens with a thoughtful conversation between Jerry and George about the placement of a button on a shirt, a discussion that would be reprised in the final moments of the series (see chapter 9).

The episode also goes to great lengths to establish that the audience is watching Jerry's day-to-day life in all its banalities. With no connection to the plot, one of his conversations with George takes place in a laundromat. A few other scenes happen in a coffee shop, where Jerry and George interact with a waitress, Claire. Played by Lee Garlington, Claire is dry but friendly and familiar with the two male characters. She's close enough with the two men that she teases George about slipping him caffeinated coffee.

Even in this first try, David and Seinfeld figured out how to talk about sex without talking about sex, referencing intercourse throughout the script in a manner suitable for FCC-regulated network television. For example, as Jerry prepares for Laura's arrival, he brings an extra mattress into the apartment. George chides him, asking, "Why even give her an option?" The exact option—whether or not to sleep with Jerry—is never spelled out in the dialogue, but we all know what George means. Here, David and Seinfeld showed an early gift for creating humor in these sorts of roundabout and indirect conversations about sex.

So, *The Seinfeld Chronicles*, though rough around the edges, did establish much of what made *Seinfeld* great. The Jerry-George relationship, grounded in and inspired by the Seinfeld-David relationship, was fully formed from the jump. An interest in the nitty-gritty details of social communication had always been a part of the comedy of both co-creators, and thus it is immediately present in the show. As sluggish as the episode feels compared to later episodes, its writing was often quite clever.

Still, there are substantial differences between *The Seinfeld Chronicles* and what *Seinfeld* would become by the end of its first full, twenty-three-episode season almost three years later. Besides the presence of Claire and the absence of Elaine, Kessler was no Kramer. Jerry's neighbor was subdued to the point of being creepy. Fully formed Kramer was full of life and energy, as opposed to the still, sullen character who haunts Jerry's apartment. This Kessler slinks across the hall in the middle of the night, tears up Jerry's magazines, ruins the Mets game Jerry had taped, and, later in the episode, frightens George out of the apartment. In the pilot (and, alas, not for the last time in his career) Michael Richards goes for edginess and darkness at the expense of his more natural, more successful ability to channel manic physicality into a comedy that is, at its heart, joyful. Richards is only partly to blame for the flaws in proto-Kramer. Initially, David and Seinfeld conceived the character as agoraphobic—afraid to leave the building. It is hard to imagine *Seinfeld* with two of its four characters pinned to a single location, Kessler in his apartment and Claire in her diner.

With Kessler so brooding and Claire so sarcastic, the pilot fails to build the momentum so many later episodes would succeed at achieving. For a show that would come to be known as being about people sitting around talking about nothing, there is often quite a lot of action to look at on a typical episode of *Seinfeld*. It is a dynamic show, but *The Seinfeld Chronicles* is often quite still. Half of Kessler's jokes happen as he is sitting on Jerry's couch, not flopping around the set. Surprisingly in retrospect, it is not Richards but Jason Alexander, by then a veteran of live theater, who counterbalances the lack of physicality Seinfeld brought to the set, gesturing wildly at many points during their lengthy conversations.

As sitcom writers, David and Seinfeld still had a few things to learn about adding moments of visual hilarity to humorous dialogue. Eventually, influenced by Seinfeld's deep-rooted love of slapstick, the show would come to rely quite heavily on physical comedy.

*Seinfeld* would also come to be defined by its elaborate, multifaceted, and often intersecting plotlines. The plot of *The Seinfeld Chronicles* is more straightforward than any that would follow. Jerry doesn't know whether or not a female houseguest is interested in sleeping with him. Hilarity ensues? Most of the episode is spent waiting and wondering. The climax of the episode is Laura's arrival and, quickly, the revelation that she is engaged.

Even the colors on *The Seinfeld Chronicles* are neutral, bland, and ponderous. The show's more fully formed seasons would skew toward a palette of primary colors, emphasized even in *Seinfeld's* logo. The future would be much brighter than the pilot suggests, but in the moment, most involved with the show doubted that future would even exist.

## "WEAK"

Some NBC executives and many TV critics DID notice many elements that were different, fresh, and special. One critic loved the blend of stand-up act and sitcom, leading to a "surprising show . . . that takes full advantage of Jerry Seinfeld's skills."[3] Another called the show "innovative . . . the wittiest show we're likely to see on the tube this summer."[4] "NBC is making a mistake if it doesn't pick up *The Seinfeld Chronicles*," warned Ken Tucker of the *Philadelphia Inquirer*. "It's bound to be superior to most of what the network has planned for the fall."[5] Good call, Ken. Of the nine other new comedies NBC debuted that season, eight would be canceled by the end of the next season. Remember *The Nutt House*, the Mel Brooks sitcom about the wacky staff at a run-down old hotel in New York City? Me neither.[6]

The problem for Seinfeld and David, for Castle Rock, and for the show's proponents at NBC was that the test audience wasn't a room full of TV critics. The report came back from the research department even before NBC sent the tape to the critics. At the top of the memo, it read "PILOT PERFORMANCE: Weak."

It is worth noting that NBC executives are not blindly beholden to the testing process. Many shows before and after *Seinfeld* received a series order after a weak pilot test. A few years later, *Friends* scored a "weak" in its testing and went on to its own massive success. But, as one executive recalls, "This was a weak 'weak.'"[7]

Some excerpts from the memo: "As one viewer put it, 'You can't get too excited about going to the laundramat [sic].'" "Viewers were unclear whether Jerry worked as a comedian or if his routines took place outside of the show as commentaries. The movement back and forth was also considered abrupt and somewhat disorienting, especially to elder viewers." "Jerry's 'loser' friend, George, who was not a particularly forceful character, actually appeared somewhat more in charge, and viewers found it annoying that Jerry needed things explained to him." "No segment of the audience was eager to watch the show again." "Lukewarm . . . boring . . . mildly amusing . . . disliked . . . did not identify."[8] Yada, yada, yada.

The screening at Burbank went a little better. It may not have played as well as predecessors like *The Cosby Show* or *Golden Girls* had for executives, but as Tartikoff's then number two, Warren Littlefield, recalls, "People laughed. There was a sense this was something different. The room embraced the humor and the attitude."

But Littlefield was crushed when he read the pilot report. Even worse for him and other remaining proponents at NBC was news of their boss's disapproval. "Too New York, too Jewish," Tartikoff declared.

*Seinfeld* could have died there. Critics like Tucker, quoted above, knew NBC was leaning toward a pass on the show even when they broadcast the pilot to the nation on July 5. Their positive reactions may have helped persuade Littlefield and others at NBC to follow their gut feeling about the show.

Meanwhile, the co-creators were hopeful, but realistic. "If this doesn't work, I think this is it for me in network television," Seinfeld told *USA Today*.[9]

The show's producers at Castle Rock, no novices to the cutthroat business of TV pilots, figured the show was toast. After pitching *The Seinfeld Chronicles* to the fledgling Fox network, which passed, Castle Rock turned its attentions and resources to another new sitcom named after its star—a show with a pilot that had been received much more

WHO (ALMOST) KILLED THE PILOT? 37

favorably. *Ann Jillian* is about a widowed ex-Rockette who moves with her daughter from New York City to a small town in California. NBC canceled it after 13 episodes.

Despite Littlefield's good feeling about the show, NBC was not in a position to gamble. At the beginning of the eighties, mired in third place behind ABC and CBS and performing worse than any network had in a quarter-century, NBC had little to lose in taking some risks with shows like *Hill Street Blues*.[10] As its strategy began to pay dividends and NBC rose in the rankings, the network became more risk-averse. NBC was still at the top of the ratings in 1989, and still in that risk-averse mode. Rather than use its position of safety to try something daring, NBC did what so many big companies do—they decided to stick with their typical process. *Ann Jillian*, with its Rockette in California, looked better than *The Seinfeld Chronicles*, with its comedian in a laundromat.

The critics may have confirmed what Seinfeld and David thought they were doing with the pilot, and what Littlefield sensed when he watched the pilot—*The Seinfeld Chronicles* was different, perhaps niche, but definitely interesting. Sadly, Littlefield didn't have the guts or gusto to get his boss to bet on niche but interesting. Fortunately, one other *Seinfeld* proponent was in a position to place a bet on *Seinfeld*. Rick Ludwin was in the late-night and specials division, not prime time. Technically, sitcoms weren't his domain. But he had a plan.

Ludwin had been involved in the project from the beginning. Like Littlefield, he felt the pilot showed promise in its distinctiveness. Now, he was curious about what this show might become. He wanted to see more episodes and give the audience the opportunity to see a little more, too. The prime-time department was allocating its resources to shows with a better chance of success, like *Down Home*, a comedy about a New York City businesswoman (Judith Ivey) who returns to her Texas hometown to run her father's bait-and-tackle store.[11] The prime-time budget was spent. But Ludwin had a budget, too. Could he spend some of those late-night funds on *The Seinfeld Chronicles*? Basically, Ludwin took a trip to the NBC swap meet.

As the new television season began, it was soon apparent that NBC didn't have a lot of winners among its new shows. *The Nutt House, Ann Jillian*, and other new sitcoms were not long for this world. At a meeting with executives from finance, head of scheduling Preston Beckman (an-

other *Seinfeld* believer), and Littlefield, Ludwin proposed his unortho-
dox idea. What if he cashed in some money from his budget that had
been earmarked for a couple of specials? How many episodes could he
get? The financiers took out their calculators, and I imagine the exchange went something like this:

You're willing to give up two specials?

Well, one is a Bob Hope special, if that helps.

Hmm . . . you can go make four more episodes.

Four? That's it?

Take it or leave it.

He took it, the world lost out on another hour of Bob Hope jokes,
and, henceforth, *Seinfeld* would be overseen by Ludwin's late-night and
specials division rather than the prime-time executives who turned their
backs on the show after the pilot.

Beckman called up Seinfeld with the news.

"In the history of television, has anything ever worked with a four-
episode order?" Seinfeld asked. [12]

Beckman wasn't sure, but Seinfeld took the deal. For the next few
seasons, Seinfeld and David proceeded with the threat of cancellation
constantly hanging over the show. In fact, this state of uncertainty gave
them a sense of liberty, rather than fear. If success was unlikely, then
they may as well do whatever they wanted.

## RETOOLING

With the future still uncertain, the story of *Seinfeld*'s emergence does
not end here. The show had a season order, but it was as short a first
season as any show could get. Its ratings were not very good for this
short season, which NBC ran in the middle of the following summer, a
dead period for television viewing. And the ratings did not improve
much in a slightly longer, but still shortened season 2.

It was never an easy decision to renew *Seinfeld* after those first two seasons. The first season is, relatively speaking, pretty lousy. And the show did not put out a classic episode until the end of season 2. At the very least, *Seinfeld* rewarded its supporters with a few moments that suggested this show was on to something special. Its supporters stuck by it in the hope that, eventually, the audience would grow to love it, too.

How did *Seinfeld* survive from bad pilot to season 1 and season 2? With its ratings still low, how did it last to season 3 and season 4, when the show won its Emmy and entered the top 25 in the ratings?

First, heading into season 1, the television audience had to distinguish the show from *The Marshall Chronicles*, a new sitcom over on ABC.[13] The title was changed to *Seinfeld*. At Seinfeld's insistence, Kessler was renamed Kramer, and David gave up his effort to hide the fact that the character was based on his real-life neighbor. Claire was out. Elaine was in. (We'll cover the addition of Elaine and the casting of Julia Louis-Dreyfus in chapter 4.)

The four-episode order prompted one more addition to the show, a new element with an incalculable yet crucial effect on the series: Jonathan Wolff's *Seinfeld* theme music. *Seinfeld*'s framework poses a unique problem for a television composer. Nowadays, many shows run their opening credits and theme over some sort of visually stylized depiction of the show's theme, mood, and story. Other shows, particularly comedies, barely feature an opening credit sequence at all. The typical sitcom opening credits sequence in 1990, now old-fashioned and clichéd, was built around a montage of the show's characters. *Seinfeld*'s opening and closing credits ran over Jerry performing stand-up. So whatever else the show's theme might be, it had to complement that performance while not conflicting with Jerry's monologue.

Several composers took a crack at the problem, but Seinfeld and David were unhappy with the results. Seinfeld was explaining this problem to his real-life best friend George—the comedian George Wallace—who referred Seinfeld to Wolff. Seinfeld called him on the phone, described what they needed, and then, crucially, left him alone. A television composer by day and a jazz musician by night, Wolff was the perfect person to solve the *Seinfeld* theme puzzle.

Wolff immediately understood that the opening theme song would have to vary every episode, accompanying Jerry's monologue. "I needed to architect it modularly so that it could be shiftable, changeable, like

Lego music," Wolff explains. "It needed to not conflict with his voice. His human voice was really organic. It wasn't a trumpet or a clarinet. It was a human voice. So I chose to build this percolating rhythm, this New York groove."[14]

Using a synthesizer as well as his own mouth, Wolff developed a quirky, funky tune with happy pops and clicks and a slap bass that went up and down as Jerry's jokes built from setup to punch line. Both David and Seinfeld liked what Wolff had come up with. NBC's executives, on the other hand, were not thrilled with the sound, which was so different from the norm. Ultimately, David and Seinfeld won out, and Wolff's music became a classic theme, immediately recognizable as the sound of *Seinfeld*.

At the beginning of the third season, David and Seinfeld suggested that Wolff add background singers, harmonizing scat lyrics over his music. The first episode, "The Note," aired with this updated version before both NBC and Castle Rock discovered the change. The producers immediately axed the singers (for once, the executives were right) and "The Note" was the only episode to air with the altered music.

But as the first season production wrapped up, that conflict over the show's music was two years away. As the four episodes of the first season were completed and ready to air, the show's future still seemed bleak to everyone involved.

## SEASON I HIGHLIGHTS

The first episode, "The Stakeout," which aired on May 31, 1990, was particularly significant for proving *Seinfeld*'s quality to critics and executives alike. If any moment from season 1 could be pointed to as the reason why *Seinfeld* was renewed for a second season, it is the stakeout scene from which this episode gets its name. Critics loved this episode, the first to air during the show's four-episode run in the summer of 1990. According to Seinfeld, Tartikoff—the legendary NBC president who had effectively passed on the show a year before—had this scene queued up in his office to show visitors.

Jerry and George wait excitedly in the elevator lobby, looking for a woman Jerry met at Elaine's friend's birthday party. As they come up with a plan to explain why they are lurking around her workplace, their dialogue is reminiscent of Abbott and Costello, a comedy duo Seinfeld admired. As Seinfeld points out, this exchange "was very important in establishing the way these guys were going to talk . . . and the stupid way they were going to solve problems."[15] Finally, the woman emerges from the elevator. The two clumsily execute their plan, something about meeting their friend Art Corvelay—or maybe Vandelay—an importer/exporter. At one point, apropos of nothing, George blurts out the lie that he is an architect. He always wanted to pretend he was an architect. It's a mess, but it works. Jerry secures a date.

The pacing of this scene, particularly the rapid-fire exchange between the two friends, anticipated the thrilling comedic pace the show would eventually find rather than the slow speed of the rest of the episode and the season.[16] It was definitely faster-paced than the pilot. Jerry and George literally pace back and forth throughout the scene, changing positions on the set several times during their conversation. The chemistry between the two actors is already well-established; Seinfeld isn't the actor Alexander is—he never will be—but even at this early point in his sitcom career he uses his mastery of comedic timing in a way that translates well on television. Alexander's background in live theater helps him weave his dialogue smoothly with Seinfeld in front of the live studio audience.

Further along in the season, episode 3, "Male Unbonding," contains a scene with Jerry and Elaine that is as much about nothing as any other scene throughout the run of the show. The two friends are trying to come up with a plan to do something, anything, to fill their evening. They don't feel like doing anything. Eventually, they agree to go hang out in a coffee shop, but Elaine makes Jerry promise that she does not have to talk. They'll just sit there, enjoying their coffees. The ennui of the scene is so familiar, but the execution is hilarious, most of all for the boldness in putting such a dull exchange on prime-time television.

The next episode, the season finale (if you can get excited about a finale in a four-episode season), "The Stock Tip," contains a line that might have been even more unexpected to see on prime-time television on 1990. George is having a conversation with Jerry at a dry cleaner. (David is, perhaps, thumbing his nose at the people in the pilot's test audience who were so bored with the duo's trip to the laundromat.) George turns away from Jerry for just a moment and then turns back and mutters, "Boy, I have to get to a bathroom!" He realizes, too late, that a woman has stepped between him and Jerry. They both stare awkwardly at each other for a few beats as the audience cackles. *Seinfeld* hadn't yet become known as a show about nothing, but in season 1 it was already a show about some things no one else was talking about.

Season 1 wasn't much, but it earned the show a season 2—a "whopping" 12-episode order, half a typical season. NBC executives continued to believe in the show into its second season, and *Seinfeld* was gaining steam. Literally, in fact, it was speeding up; through season 1, no episode had more than six scenes, but the first episode of season 2, "The Ex-Girlfriend," has nine. Through the second season, the scripts were mainly written by both David and Seinfeld, with the star still finding time to contribute to the writing in these early seasons. These scripts were becoming denser, with snappier dialogue and more jokes. The show itself was building momentum, and NBC liked what it was seeing . . . until the network got the script for "The Chinese Restaurant."

## THE FIRST CLASSIC

"The Chinese Restaurant" (season 2, episode 11) is the episode that gave "the show about nothing" its nickname. It is a bottle episode—a term for episodes in which the main characters are stuck in one location—and the plot unfolds in real time. The stories within the episode are utterly banal. Elaine, Jerry, and George are stopping in for a quick bite before heading off to see *Plan 9 from Outer Space*—"the worst movie ever made," Jerry declares. George needs to use the public phone to call his girlfriend. Jerry recognizes a woman in the restaurant but can't remember how he knows her. Elaine is just very, very hungry.

Confronted with this script, Littlefield was not pleased. "Nothing happens!" he recalls saying. "Am I missing pages?"[17] Even Ludwin was baffled and hesitated to green-light production for an episode that had no plot.[18] David threatened to leave the show if NBC demanded alterations to the script, and Seinfeld stood behind the script as well. To the network's credit, despite their displeasure, they remained hands-off with the still-not-a-hit young sitcom and ran the episode, although they did push it back in the schedule to late spring.

The actors, however, recognized its brilliance from the moment they saw the script. Richards was devastated that Kramer had no part in something he knew was important. (Though it was one of the last to air, "The Chinese Restaurant" was one of the first to be produced that season, and, at that point, the character was still conceived as agoraphobic.) Louis-Dreyfus "adored" the script. Alexander thought the episode "defined the anarchy" that would typify the show. Even now, the episode largely holds up to modern viewers because of its mixture of the relatable (Elaine's desperate hunger) and the absurd (the restaurant manager pronouncing "Costanza" as "Cartwright"). Though it is all set in one small space, the episode doesn't feel static. The writing pops from character to character as George waits for the phone, Jerry stares at the familiar-looking woman, and Elaine moans for food.

Seinfeld, still touring as much as the show's production would allow, now started bragging about his buzzy new show. Swinging through the flyover states, far from the network's coastal headquarters, Seinfeld took NBC to task for being too stuck in old formulas. "I feel the only chance network TV has is to tell some things that are different, to get up to speed," he opined during a stop in Minneapolis. "Some of this crap, what is it, 1971? People are ready for some new TV!"[19]

Critics agreed, recognizing and praising the creative boldness of "The Chinese Restaurant," and promoting the underdog show as "perhaps TV's funniest half-hour."[20] Viewers were starting to catch up, and "The Chinese Restaurant" did surprisingly well for its late-spring air date. Finally, NBC decided to order a 23-episode full third season of the show.[21] Without "The Chinese Restaurant," an episode that even *Seinfeld*'s strongest defenders at NBC thought was a bridge too far from typical TV, *Seinfeld* might have ended after two very short seasons.

Despite its rough edges, watching "The Chinese Restaurant" with an awareness of its place in television history is like gazing at a Van Gogh. It only takes a bit of consideration to see layers beneath the familiar story of helpless waiting. At its finest, *Seinfeld* finds humankind's existential crisis lurking just beneath the surface of everyday problems. The Chinese restaurant's waiting room is purgatory, as the three characters wrestle with flaws of the head (Jerry's memory), heart (George's romance), and gut (Elaine's hunger).

Imperfect and impatient, the trio gives up and leaves the restaurant, moments before the manager calls, "Seinfeld, four?" The characters had left, but the show had arrived.

# 4

# ENSEMBLE ALCHEMY

**W**hile "The Chinese Restaurant" firmly established *Seinfeld*'s interest in examining the everyday, the familiar, and the "nothing," one plot device that would become a signature for the series was still missing. The episode peters out, rather than bringing multiple plotlines together into a climactic scene. Larry David first experimented with this atom-smashing in "The Busboy," the twelfth and final episode to air in season 2. "The Busboy" is less memorable than "The Chinese Restaurant," but it is equally crucial to the early development of the show's style. At the climax of the episode, two characters involved in separate storylines literally run into each other in the hallway and get into a fight. As David recalls, "That left an impression on me, how those two stories really collided like—like freight trains. And I remember thinking how I really liked how that happened."[1]

NBC, however, did not like "The Busboy." In fact, the network's executives were even more displeased with this episode than they were with "The Chinese Restaurant," dumping it in late June—over a month after "The Chinese Restaurant" aired—even though it was completed long before. Their problem this time: the show was called *Seinfeld*, so where was Jerry Seinfeld? For the first time on the show, the episode included scenes without Jerry.

Of course, that only happened because Seinfeld himself co-wrote those scenes. "That showed a generosity of spirit," says Alexander, "that I can't imagine in any other situation." Adds the director, Tom Cherones, "I don't think it ever bothered him if somebody else got the laugh instead of him."[2]

The idea of following the lives of George or Elaine or Kramer beyond Jerry's perspective was seminal. Yes, Jerry is the title character, played by a recognizable star. But, starting with "The Busboy," the show began to discover who its other characters were, independent of Jerry. More importantly, it discovered they could be funny without him, too.

"The Busboy" thus underscores a crucial aspect of the show—perhaps no television show constructed around a single comic persona ultimately relied on that persona less than *Seinfeld*. Remember: Seinfeld was an established comic star when his sitcom debuted, and even while he embedded his comedy within the show's writing, he was willing to spread the wealth of his humor among the four main characters and beyond. Bill Cosby, Roseanne Barr, and Tim Allen were on-screen suns around which the rest of their shows' characters rotated. Only Seinfeld was just one of four main planets, revolving around the show itself, which shined equally on all four characters (figure 4.1).

It is perhaps surprising that Seinfeld was so generous given his background—he was used to standing on stage alone, in complete control of his delivery and his environment. Then again, he was always a student of comedy. He had grown up watching all those classic comedy teams. When the time came for him to share the stage, his ability to mesh with his fellow cast members seemed innate.

It is not that Seinfeld is a good actor—he pretty much always behaves like a guy who is having a good time being funny on television—but he did improve as a sitcom actor. Learning from the talent around him and recognizing the detail that the television audience could pick up through the camera, he got better at using his face and body to punctuate his lines. Belying his reputation for being a control freak, both as a person and as a performer, Seinfeld became increasingly willing to let his character look ridiculous for a laugh.

The traditional production elements of a sitcom also played into Seinfeld's strengths. Like almost every pre-2000 network comedy, *Seinfeld* is a multi-camera sitcom. The single-camera method, used in *Curb Your Enthusiasm*, for example, has since become increasingly popular on television, though the multi-camera style remains. Shows like *Seinfeld* are filmed on a set with several cameras operating at once, some

Figure 4.1.   George (Jason Alexander), Jerry (Jerry Seinfeld), Elaine (Julia Louis-Dreyfus), and Kramer (Michael Richards). *NBC/Photofest*

covering a wide angle of the set and some close up on the main characters in each scene.

During rehearsals, Seinfeld could work out all the details of his performance, both his delivery and his movement, all carefully choreographed in consultation with the director.[3] Seinfeld, always a perfectionist with his own routine, implicitly understood the importance of these details. Also, the multi-camera setup, with the cameras essentially in the front row of the studio audience, feels theatrical—Seinfeld knew how to stand on a brightly lit stage and deliver jokes while facing forward. Performing in front of a live studio audience gave the comic the useful feedback of laughter throughout the filming process. As the history of television has shown, from Milton Berle to Amy Schumer, television can be a natural leap for a stand-up comic. The detail-minded Seinfeld brought a good sense of both timing and delivery to the medium, and thus he had all the potential to be funny on TV.

Of course, it helped that he surrounded himself with such a talented cast, a quartet that would, in time, become regarded as one of the funniest foursomes in television history. As we will see, the paths the other three cast members took to get to *Seinfeld* are as distinct as the abilities they brought to the show.

## JASON ALEXANDER

From the show's first conception, the George Costanza character was always based on Larry David. George would be Jerry's counterpart and confidant, an understanding conversation partner with a similar yet distinct understanding of both himself and the universe. The actor who played George needed to be able to humorously embody a character who, let's be honest, is not lovable at first sight. Also, it wouldn't hurt if George was physically complementary to Jerry, in the tradition of the great comedy duos Seinfeld grew up idolizing. If *Seinfeld* was going to be built around two guys sitting in a coffee shop talking about their lives, the two guys should be a visually interesting pair.

David *could* have played the role, but he claims he was uninterested. He wanted to write for the show and, as co-creator, he was in the best position to be its show runner . . . aside from the whole "lack of experience" thing. It's hard to believe David didn't consider playing himself on the show, but it's easy to understand why he and Seinfeld would have assumed the idea was a nonstarter. Even if David did want the part, NBC would have been taking a huge risk in building the show around two stand-up comics with barely any acting experience. Larry David as George Costanza is an interesting exercise in alternate history but, let's be honest, it turned out better this way. David is hilarious on television, but he can be just as stiff an actor as Seinfeld. Nowadays, any network would pay wheelbarrows of money for a David-Seinfeld sit-com, and I would definitely watch it. But a sitcom starring David and Seinfeld in 1989 would have been dead on arrival. The show needed a person with reliable acting chops to play opposite its stand-up star.

Seinfeld had the perfect person in mind for the role of George. Someone whose balding, round head complemented Seinfeld's full hair and angular face. Someone whose thicker build would contrast nicely with the thin Seinfeld. Someone with a distinct style and energy as a performer. The person happened to be one of Seinfeld's very best friends and a fellow comedian, Larry Miller.

Actually, in 1989, Miller had even fewer TV or movie credits than David. Around the time David and Seinfeld were casting for *The Seinfeld Chronicles*, Miller landed a small part as a Beverly Hills store manager in *Pretty Woman*. Released in 1990, *Pretty Woman* not only catapulted Julia Roberts into super-stardom, it also jump-started Miller's career as a comedic actor. While still primarily doing stand-up, Miller landed many supporting roles in Hollywood throughout the 1990s and 2000s.

Another actor landed his biggest movie role to date in *Pretty Woman*: Jason Alexander. In the film, Alexander plays a villainous lawyer who attacks Julia Roberts's character. Meanwhile, NBC was casting a wide net to fill the cast for *The Seinfeld Chronicles*. Alexander sent in an audition tape, which earned him an invitation to Los Angeles for a second audition.

Alexander, based in New York, headed out to Los Angeles, saw Seinfeld's friend, Larry Miller, also waiting to audition, and immediately thought his trip had been a complete waste of time. "Oh, I get it now," Alexander recalls thinking when he spotted Miller. "They flew me out here to keep him from negotiating too high a salary."[4]

Hollywood casting what-ifs are notoriously murky, but according to Alexander, NBC also brought in Nathan Lane, Danny DeVito, David Alan Grier, and Brad Hall—almost a year before Hall's wife, Julia Louis-Dreyfus, joined the show.[5] While Alexander says he has heard that some of those more established actors were offered the role ahead of him, both Seinfeld and David insist they loved Alexander even before that second audition, from the moment they pressed play on his audition tape.[6] Alexander was shocked when he got the part.

It would be a pivotal year for Alexander, though not for the reasons he might have expected at the time. In February 1989, he began a run as the star of the Broadway musical *Jerome Robbins' Broadway*. Toward the end of April, he flew out to Los Angeles to film *The Seinfeld Chronicles*. On June 4, Alexander won the Tony Award for Best Leading Actor in a Musical. Surely, he partied all night and saw the sunrise at Liza's. About two months later, *Pretty Woman* started filming. Little did he know that his most famous work of the year would be in the barely noticed pilot NBC had dumped in early July.

Throughout the eighties, Alexander was much more active on Broadway than on television or film, and the stage has always been the place where Alexander feels most at home. He remembers seeing *Fiddler on the Roof* when he was four years old. Aside from an aborted attempt at a career in magic, for most of Alexander's life "the theater was everything. . . . It was all I ever wanted to do."[7]

As the Tony proved, Alexander is a multifaceted talent, a song-and-dance man who landed one of the funniest supporting roles in television history. He didn't get to sing much on *Seinfeld*, and when he did, he struggled to tamp down his talent. One episode ("The Susie," season 8, episode 15) catches George screening his answering machine, and the audience gets to hear George's message, which is a riff on the theme from *The Greatest American Hero*. It's hard for a good singer to sing poorly, and Alexander had to record the message several times before it sounded bad enough to be funny.

By all accounts, Alexander is nothing like George. He doesn't wear glasses, and, even at the height of the series, he struck people as younger and thinner in person than when he was in character.[8] A Tony winner by age 29 and a sitcom superstar in his 30s, Alexander was justifiably full of self-confidence throughout the run of the show, in contrast to the fatalistic George. Alexander's home life is refreshingly stable; as of this writing, he and his wife, Daena Title, have been married for 37 years and have two kids. In short, the only things the five-foot, five-inch actor has in common with his character are height and lack of hair.

When Alexander first saw the script for his audition, the material reminded him of dialogue from Woody Allen's movies, and so in the audition, *The Seinfeld Chronicles*, and the first several episodes of the series, Alexander channeled an Allen impression into his characterization of George. It was only later that the actor discovered his character was based on David. After receiving a script for an early episode, Alexander was concerned with the realism of George's behavior. He approached David. "This could never happen to anyone," protested Alexander. "And even if it did, no human being would react like this." David responded, "What do you mean? This happened to me once, and this is exactly how I reacted."[9] From then on, Alexander had a clearer understanding of the character, and he started doing "a shameless impression of Larry David."

When the show began, Alexander had the most acting experience in the main cast, and his embodiment of his character, George, anchored the show from the first moments of the pilot. George is an emotionally complex human being, and Alexander conveys that complexity into a character who is as believable as he is ridiculous. By "The Chinese Restaurant," Alexander was exploring the full range of the character's raging self-doubt even within the limits of that episode's plot. Waiting for his girlfriend, Tatiana, to call the restaurant, Alexander's George runs a gamut of emotions. He's typically insecure in his relationship to the unseen Tatiana. He rants at the world when other customers use the pay phone in front of him. He is too wimpy to try bribing the restaurant manager for a table but is disgusted when Elaine fails in her own attempt to get them seats. Alexander dominates the scene in his turn, but plays off the other characters when it is their time to shine.

## MICHAEL RICHARDS

*Seinfeld* was certainly the breakout role for Richards, though he had been working steadily in television and film throughout the eighties and since first working with David when they were both in the cast of *Fridays*. Like Alexander, Richards started on the stage, studying theater in college. He had always been a cutup, though; one high school classmate recalls that Richards couldn't enter a room without tumbling over a desk.[10] Finding the comedy club microphone more accessible than the theater stage in Los Angeles, Richards turned to stand-up as a "last resort" opportunity to perform.[11] Developing his own inimitable persona, Richards's stand-up work eventually led to the gig on *Fridays*.

Richards is intensely thoughtful about all of his characters, both comic and serious. It is easy to suspect, despite his natural gifts, that he would have preferred a career that had led to more opportunities to do the latter. His idol is Peter Sellers, who could be as hysterically profound as he could be profoundly hysterical.[12]

NBC was no stranger to Richards's work. Besides a recurring role on *St. Elsewhere*, Richards appeared on *Cheers*, *Hill Street Blues*, and *Miami Vice*—all NBC shows. In 1987, he landed a recurring role on the sitcom *Marblehead Manor*. He appeared in 11 of the 18 episodes produced, working alongside Phil Morris. Years later, the two would share the screen on *Seinfeld* when Morris played the lawyer Jackie Chiles in several episodes.

Also like Alexander, Richards might have guessed his biggest break of 1989 was something other than *The Seinfeld Chronicles*. He had a major supporting role in "Weird Al" Yankovic's cult film, *UHF*, which was released July 21, less than three weeks after *Seinfeld*'s pilot aired.

Richards played oddballs in most of these roles, some of them kooky, some of them edgy. He often employed his gangly frame to slapstick success. Prior to *Seinfeld*, his knack for slapstick was best seen in his character of Dick Williams, fitness guru. Richards had first developed the character on *Fridays*, and later performed as Williams on *The Tonight Show*. Williams was simultaneously self-assured and hopelessly clumsy; his humor came from Richards's ability and willingness to bonk, squash, and twist his body as he grappled with various workout implements.

In casting for Kramer, Richards's competition for the role included talented character actors like Tony Shaloub, Steve Vinovich, and Larry Hankin. Before landing his career-defining role on *Monk* in 2002 (a part that ABC originally conceived for Richards), Shaloub eventually ended up as a scene-stealer on *Wings*, the NBC sitcom about a small airport in Nantucket that aired throughout the nineties. Vinovich continues to work steadily on film and TV, but Hankin's lanky figure is perhaps even more recognizable, playing recurring characters in shows from *Friends* to *Breaking Bad*. Hankin also returned to *Seinfeld*, playing the role of . . . Kramer! It happened in season 4, when Jerry and

George make a show for NBC which includes a character based on Jerry's kooky neighbor, just as David had based Kramer on his real-life kooky neighbor, Kenny Kramer. Hankin's characters are often soft-spoken and restrained in their weirdness, characteristics that would have fit with the original conception of Kessler, though not the beloved character Kramer would become.

As with Alexander, David and Seinfeld claim that Richards was their first choice for the role. "When I heard he was available, my mind was made up," says Seinfeld. In Richards, Seinfeld had someone who shared his passion for classic American comedy. But where Seinfeld studied the old masters for their delivery and timing, Richards was drawn to their physicality, even researching exactly how they prepared and executed their best falls.[13] Indeed, a physical feat of his own may have ultimately won him the part. For no apparent reason, in the middle of his audition, Richards flipped into a headstand. The job was his.

As Richards added his ability for violent slapstick to his character on *Seinfeld*, Kramer emerged as a fan favorite. The transition from the shadowy, humorous yet bizarre Kessler to the still-odd, yet far more energetic and animated Kramer occurred over the first few seasons. A key turning point came in season 2's seventh episode, "The Revenge." Kramer encourages Jerry to put cement in the washing machine of a local laundromat (another clothes-cleaning scene!) whose owner, the two mistakenly believe, took $1500 that Jerry accidentally left in his pants pocket. While Jerry distracts the owner, Kramer attempts to lift and pour the cement into the machine. For the scene, Richards insisted on using an actual bag of cement. It does make a difference for the scene, but only because Richards throws all his physical talents into bumbling, thrashing, and falling with the heavy bag.

Richards would go on to win three Emmys for his portrayal of Kramer. Alexander, blocked in the same category by his fellow cast member, did not win any, despite his many nominations.

## CLAIRE OUT, ELAINE IN

In *The Seinfeld Chronicles*, Richards did his Kessler, Alexander did his Woody Allen impression, and Seinfeld did a sitcom version of himself. Lee Garlington did her best to earn a few laughs as Claire, the waitress, though she only had seven lines in her one and only scene. Garlington also apparently did her best to rewrite some of the lines from David's script; this has often been cited as the reason why she was replaced on the show. While the theory is a juicy one, and both Alexander and Seinfeld have confirmed that it happened, the truth is more complex. [14] If David was unhappy with Garlington's behavior, why not simply recast the role of Claire after the pilot, filling the same part with a new actor?

Another theory is that Garlington was replaced by Louis-Dreyfus because the latter was seen as having more sex appeal. This theory may have some merit given the male-dominated production of the show. Again, though, if sex appeal was the only factor, why not just recast the role?

The decision to drop Claire, the waitress, and replace her with Elaine, the ex-girlfriend, seems to be the one major suggestion David and Seinfeld took from NBC after the pilot. NBC suggested that the waitress character was too limited in her potential interactions with the rest of the cast—her role kept her stuck in the diner. Just as Kramer inevitably had to lose his agoraphobia, a successful female character on the show had to be free to get mixed up in whatever adventures befell the gang that week.

Also, there was a difference in class between the waitress character and her middle-class customers. *Seinfeld* could have explored this difference, or the show could have been about a struggling comedian, but neither angle seemed to interest the co-creators.

As a solution, David and Seinfeld came up with the idea of cutting the waitress and adding an ex-girlfriend as a female character for the show. Some have suggested they based the character on Carol Leifer, a mutual friend and fellow comic who had a brief romance with Seinfeld in the 1970s and who would join the writers room in the show's fifth season. [15] However the idea came about, the ex-girlfriend role was the perfect way to blend a female friend into the gang if the audience could suspend their disbelief over the unlikelihood of one of Jerry's former flames becoming a close friend. Little explanation is given for Elaine's ability to remain friends with Jerry, while so many other women come and go in his life. But Louis-Dreyfus's chemistry with the rest of the cast banished any questions about why Elaine kept hanging around her old flame's apartment.

## JULIA LOUIS-DREYFUS

Having gone through the ringer during her time at the hyper-masculine, drug-fueled, tumultuous *Saturday Night Live* of the early eighties, Louis-Dreyfus was well-suited and eager to take advantage of the collaborative spirit she found with her fellow cast members on *Seinfeld*. Joining *SNL* at the age of 21, Louis-Dreyfus was the youngest female cast member in the show's history to that point. She was invited to join the show along with two other members of the Practical Theater Company, her Chicago improv team: David Kroeger and her then-boyfriend and future husband, Brad Hall.

The three arrived at *SNL* in Eddie Murphy's third season. Murphy, still a few months younger than Louis-Dreyfus, was the standout personality of the show and a rapidly rising star about to embark on a successful transition to the big screen. While he was on the show, he was the center of its universe. When he departed the show a season and a half after Louis-Dreyfus arrived, he left a vacuum that many observers suspected the show could never fill. Dick Ebersol, producing the show at the time, attempted to solve the problem by bringing in a bunch of stars to make up for the loss of one: Billy Crystal, Martin Short, and Christopher Guest were among the many new cast members added to *SNL* in Louis-Dreyfus's final season. Needless to say, it was easy to feel overlooked on the backbench of *SNL*'s performers.

No one at *SNL* was looking to do her any favors, but Louis-Dreyfus admits her own cockeyed optimism didn't help her in the high-stakes game of late-night comedy. At her very first table read, she, Hall, and Kroeger were invited to present their best material. "Here we were coming in as these stupid-ass new kids who had not a clue doing our goofy Chicago sketch comedy in front of a bunch of kiss-off, more experienced, bitter people," recalls Louis-Dreyfus. They didn't get a single chuckle.[16]

"It was this very chauvinistic situation back then," she says. "Very few women, lots of sexism, issues of sexual harassment and some really big-time drugs. Of course, I was so oblivious." Things only got worse when Hall was fired after their second season on the show. Her consolation prize: a funny, yet somewhat morose loner joined the writing staff—Larry David. Louis-Dreyfus stuck it out for her third and final season before Lorne Michaels returned and overhauled the entire show. David and Louis-Dreyfus went their separate ways.

She caught a few post-*SNL* breaks. Woody Allen cast Louis-Dreyfus in her first film, *Hannah and Her Sisters* (1986). Her subsequent credits included *National Lampoon's Christmas Vacation* (1989), which was out in theaters around the time David called her about the Elaine role.

A couple of years earlier, Louis-Dreyfus had landed a role on another NBC sitcom, *Day by Day*, where she played the kid-hating, next-door neighbor to a couple who opens a daycare center. A mid-season replacement in 1988, *Day by Day* ran for 33 episodes before NBC cut the show. Meanwhile, Louis-Dreyfus landed an exciting development deal with Warner Bros.—an opportunity to create and star in her own show. Luckily for *Seinfeld*, that script never got off the ground, and Louis-Dreyfus soured on the project. [17]

Meanwhile, after *The Seinfeld Chronicles*, David and Seinfeld had decided to cut the Claire character and introduce Elaine, Jerry's ex-girlfriend-turned-friend. As with George and Kramer, the show ran through a long list of potential actors for the part, including Rosie O'Donnell, Patricia Heaton, and Megan Mullally. David deserves credit for bringing in Louis-Dreyfus, his old friend from *SNL*. In Seinfeld's memory, as usual, he knew Louis-Dreyfus was right for the part from her first audition. She met the show's two creators at the studio and clicked with Seinfeld.

"I sat with Julia and read a few pages of dialogue," remembers Jerry, "and I could tell immediately that she knew how to play this game. The ball comes up to her, it's up, and she's firing it right back to you with the kind of energy I was looking for." [18]

But was this the opportunity Louis-Dreyfus was looking for? Another likely short-lived NBC sitcom? A half-hearted, four-episode order on the heels of a dismally rated pilot? A fourth-wheel role behind three dynamic male characters? It seemed, perhaps, a step back from the potential she had sensed in the Warner Bros. deal, a step away from the decent film roles she had been landing, and a step into the dead-end role she had in *Day by Day*.

On the other hand, she had a feeling. Just as Rick Ludwin, Warren Littlefield, and maybe even Brandon Tartikoff had had a feeling—there was something different about *Seinfeld*. And that something different might turn into something special. "It was not written like standard sitcom fare," Louis-Dreyfus remembers. "The rhythm was entirely different. The jokes were subtler, and they had a different tone."[19]

But before she could take the role, NBC had to offer it to her, and once again, Tartikoff was in the way. The NBC chief, recalling her from a pilot for a *Family Ties* spin-off that was never picked up, felt she was too short and "not hot."[20] Fortunately, other NBC executives were paying attention to her comedic talent.

The perpetually unsatisfied character of Elaine was thus rooted in Louis-Dreyfus's own struggle to emerge from the male-dominated television business, from her early misery on *SNL* to the chauvinism of the casting process. But Elaine did not arrive fully formed.

The trouble was David and Seinfeld didn't know how to write for a female character. No wonder Claire only had one scene in the pilot! In the third episode of season 1, "Male Unbonding," Elaine does not appear until two-thirds of the way through the episode. True to form, Louis-Dreyfus did the best she could in the scenes she had, and eventually she got more to do as David, Seinfeld, and the other writers began packing scripts with three, and even four storylines—twice as many as the traditional sitcom formula.

In a way, David and Seinfeld's inexperience ultimately may have allowed the Elaine character to emerge (figure 4.2). NBC wanted them to include a "girl," but they didn't know how to write typical sitcom material for a typical female supporting character. So, they wrote what they thought was funny, and, eventually, doled out the humor to the cast in equal portions. As the show became a hit, the writers room remained dominated by men. Still, Louis-Dreyfus shaped Elaine into as well-rounded a female character as had ever appeared on a sitcom.

At five feet, three inches, Louis-Dreyfus is undeniably short, and yet her characters have always found a way to exude physical strength even as they struggle through emotional and psychological strain. The actor's physical talents are noticeable from her *SNL* days, and her old improv teammates remember that Louis-Dreyfus's "physicality was on display very early."[21] Even behind the scenes, she would give her larger male counterparts a big shove to playfully express moments of frustration. On *Seinfeld*, Elaine would employ the same kind of shove on her male friends.

Often overshadowed by Richards's antics on *Seinfeld*, Louis-Dreyfus is nearly equal to his physical abilities. Exhibit A for this argument is, of

**Figure 4.2.    Elaine (Julia Louis-Dreyfus) and Jerry (Jerry Seinfeld).** *NBC/Photofest*

course, the season 8 episode "The Little Kicks." Elaine dances at her office party, if you can call it dancing, and hilarity ensues. As George reports to Jerry, "It was more like a full-body dry heave set to music."

Prior to filming the scene, Louis-Dreyfus was concerned that she would look embarrassingly foolish, but not funny. When they started shooting, director Andy Ackerman coached her to try to dance off-beat to the music. When that didn't work, Ackerman decided to have Louis-Dreyfus dance without music playing.[22] The result was magic, delighting both her co-workers at the party and viewers at home.

She will be forever associated with that scene, but Louis-Dreyfus was throwing her body around in hilarious ways long before season 8. While *Seinfeld* is beloved for its memorable lines and elaborate plots, the show's visual comedy is equally superb, thanks especially to Richards and Louis-Dreyfus.

## TEAMWORK AND TENSION

The main cast of *Seinfeld* is a perfect balance of talent, from the physical prowess of Richards and Louis-Dreyfus to the stagecraft of the stand-up, Seinfeld, and the theater whiz, Alexander. The personalities of the cast, too, would prove to be complementary. The goofball, Richards, was ironically the most serious of the four toward his craft. The titular star, Seinfeld, was willing to share the spotlight with his co-stars. Alexander quickly found his inner Larry David, while Louis-Dreyfus knew how to scrap and claw for her fair share.

As far as fans and the media could tell, the four stars appeared to get along well throughout the run of the show. The quartet were not, in fact, close friends off the set. Considering the different life circumstances each of the four had at the time, it is understandable that they weren't best buddies.

As *Seinfeld* become a massive hit, the stars found themselves in front of cameras even when they were not filming the show. Seinfeld's love life became a particular interest to the tabloids, especially when, in 1993, he started dating a 17-year-old high school student, Shoshanna Lonstein.

On the other hand, Alexander and Louis-Dreyfus were both raising young families, a shared circumstance that made the pair a bit closer within the foursome. Both had two kids born during the show's run, though only one of them was pregnant on set. Louis-Dreyfus had to conceal her baby bumps throughout season 3 and for portions of season 8 with a variety of costumes and props.

As for Richards, he went through a separation and divorce in the first few years of the show. He had one child—a daughter, who, as it happens, was born the same year as Lonstein.

With such different off-set lives, it is a wonder the four got along as well as they did, for as long as they did. Ultimately, their relationships did fray in the final years of the show, worn down by a classic source of tension: money.

Seinfeld, as the show's star and co-creator, was always going to make a higher salary than his three co-stars. The show's rise lifted the boats of everyone involved, but the *S.S. Seinfeld* rose far higher than any other. Most lucratively, co-creators Seinfeld and David owned a share of the show's syndication value. (A show's syndication rights are, simply, the rights to rerun previously aired episodes.)

Seinfeld was born and raised without streaming services, DVRs, or even DVDs. Thus, unless they carefully curated their own collection of recorded episodes on VHS tapes, the only way for fans to watch old episodes of Seinfeld was in syndication. Local broadcast affiliates (and not necessarily NBC stations) would bid for the right to exclusively air old Seinfeld episodes for a fixed period of time. For most shows, if they are worth anything in syndication at all, they will be worth the most the first time their rights are put up for sale. In the case of Seinfeld, the show's value in syndication was clearly going up even before the show's final season aired. It soon became obvious that David and Seinfeld would make more money for their permanent and lasting share in Seinfeld's syndication value than they would even with their lucrative NBC deals. And, unless they could negotiate for a piece of the pie, how much would Alexander, Louis-Dreyfus, and Richards make in royalties from those skyrocketing syndication deals?

Nothing.

The three actors had little leverage to use in negotiations with either the show's producers (Castle Rock) or its creators (David and Seinfeld). They could quit, or threaten to quit, but that would end the show and cost them their paychecks. Instead, they tried asking politely. They were rebuffed.

It is unclear whether Seinfeld himself had the muscle to get his co-stars a piece of the long-term royalties. He and David split a 25 percent permanent share of the show's revenues.[23] By the show's final seasons, Castle Rock had been bought by media mogul Ted Turner, who merged Turner Broadcasting with Time Warner, making Seinfeld a small but profitable piece within a large, publicly traded entertainment empire. For Alexander, Louis-Dreyfus, and Richards to get a share of the show's long-term revenues, some or all of the show's shareholders would have had to give up some of their own shares.

Perhaps Seinfeld could have used his clout to make that happen, but he did not. Years later, Alexander laid the blame at his co-star's feet, saying it created a "chasm" and a "rift" in the quartet. "The day will come when you regret this decision," Alexander recalls telling Seinfeld while the show was still on, "only because it's going to put us in a position eventually of seemingly tainting the wonderful impression of what this was for the four of us."[24]

The next move for Alexander, Louis-Dreyfus, and Richards was to band together in salary negotiations heading into the final season of the show. Using their lack of back-end ownership as a talking point, they asked to be paid the same as show's nominal star: $1 million per episode, a huge increase from the $160,000 they were making per episode in the eighth season. Eventually, they would agree to $600,000 an episode for the 22-episode final season, a year when *Seinfeld* was once again the top-rated show on television.[25]

Despite the record-breaking new contracts, the cast's relationships were strained. Alexander, Louis-Dreyfus, and Richards held a lasting resentment from being cut out of the show's royalties, which continued to rise as the DVD era began. So, in 2003, when the three were invited to participate in the special features for the new *Seinfeld* DVD box sets, they flatly declined.

This was the leverage the three actors had long sought in their pursuit of a cut of the show's royalties. Five years after it ended, *Seinfeld* was still a tremendously valuable asset, with profits over $1 billion and still climbing. Alexander, Louis-Dreyfus, and Richards *were* earning residuals—a small amount standard for any Screen Actors Guild member. At the time, Alexander estimated the trio had earned about a quarter million dollars each—less than their per-episode salaries for the final season—compared to the hundreds of millions earned by Seinfeld and David.[26]

Enough was enough. If *Seinfeld*'s owners refused to cut them in for a fair share, why should the three stars help those owners earn more profits? They refused to participate in the DVD production. The feud went public, and plans for the DVD release, perhaps one of the most hotly anticipated TV series to hit the medium, ground to a halt. Happily, a deal was eventually reached, and the three actors received a portion of the DVD revenue in exchange for participating in DVD commentaries and other special features.[27]

Not only did that deal allow the *Seinfeld* DVDs to come into existence, it also helped mend the rift between Seinfeld and his fellow cast members. Since then, each have appeared together in a variety of projects, including Seinfeld's *Comedians in Cars Getting Coffee* and David's *Curb Your Enthusiasm*.

Ultimately, it is best to think of these four stars as workplace buddies. They appreciated one another for what each brought to the show,
and they genuinely enjoyed working with one another. As the show
slowly grew into a hit, the actors had time to form their characters. By
its fourth season, the show was a hit, and the world of the show was fully
formed. To understand that world, we must start with the four characters these performers created.

# Part II

# The World in *Seinfeld*

# 5

# THE FOUR

NBC finally ordered a full, 23-episode season of *Seinfeld* in 1991. Still, it struggled in the ratings, finishing 42nd overall, a mere four spots higher than its second season.[1] Heading into *Seinfeld*'s fourth season, 1992–1993, Warren Littlefield got a long-dreaded call from Ted Danson, the star of *Cheers*—it would be Danson's, and thus *Cheers*', final season.

Littlefield had succeeded his mentor, Tartikoff, as network president in 1990, the summer after *Seinfeld*'s short first season. Now, in the middle of this pivotal 1992–1993 season, Littlefield gambled on *Seinfeld*, moving it from Wednesdays to Thursdays. By the end of the year, *Seinfeld* had cracked the top 25 in the ratings. This was the Emmy-winning "show within a show" season, when Larry David came up with the season-long idea of George and Jerry pitching a show to NBC.

The following year, *Cheers* was gone, but *Seinfeld* still finished number three overall. In its final four seasons, the only show to beat it for the number-one spot was *ER*, NBC's hit hospital drama that held down the 10:00 p.m. slot on Thursdays. In those four years, *Seinfeld* averaged more than 30 million viewers an episode.

From season 4 on, the show could rely on audience familiarity as a source of humor. *Seinfeld*'s season 5 finale, "The Opposite" is a good example of how the show relied on this familiarity. In the opening scene, Elaine notices a woman looking at George in the diner. George scoffs at her suggestion that he go talk to her: "Bald men with no jobs and no money who live with their parents don't approach strange women." Today, however, would be a different story for this unemployed bald man.

George had spent the morning sitting alone, staring at the ocean, mulling over his many failures. Arriving at the diner, he declares to his friends that every decision he has made in his life has been wrong and that everything about him is the opposite of what he would have hoped. The waitress comes to take his order, and an idea suddenly springs into his mind. He should do the opposite of every instinct he has. Instead of tuna on toast, he orders chicken salad on untoasted rye.

A few moments later, his instinct is telling him not to approach the woman sitting at the counter. Jerry points out that this is a perfect opportunity to try out his new modus operandi. George should ignore his intimidation and go right up to her.

Emboldened by his friend, he walks over to the woman. It turns out she, too, has ordered chicken salad on rye! George takes a deep breath and introduces himself. Presumably, his instinct is telling him to lie about his occupation and living arrangement. Instead, he blurts out, "I'm unemployed and I live with my parents!" Inexplicably, the woman is charmed.

Thus begins the greatest run of success and achievement in George Costanza's sad little life. By the end of the episode, he lands a dream job with the New York Yankees and moves out of his parents' house. After five seasons of being a loser, it's delightful to see George run up a string of victories. Instead of simply having the character's luck turn around for an episode, George turns himself around.

Meanwhile, Elaine goes into a spiral, losing her boyfriend, her apartment, and her job. Jerry, watching his friends' lives transform, realizes he is "Even Steven"—things always end up pretty much back to their comfortable status quo. Elaine is horrified that she is becoming George, but Jerry reassures her that everything will eventually even out. Of course, he's right; the laws of the traditional sitcom dictate the show maintain a certain equilibrium. Both characters do settle back into their usual roles in season 6—George schemes and lazes his way through his Yankees job, while Elaine rediscovers her pride with a seemingly glitzy job as a personal assistant that turns out to be miserable.

## THE FOUR MAIN CHARACTERS

Rather than simply summarizing the four characters, I'd like to think about them in their context. Taking a close look at their quirks and flaws, I'm going to suggest how each character embodies something about American culture in the nineties (figure 5.1). "The Opposite" offers a good overview of these embodiments, and the rest of the chapter examines each character in greater depth.

Let's start with Jerry's character in "The Opposite." Throughout the episode, Jerry is fixated on his "Even Steven" theory. Typical of the character, he shows absolutely no concern for Elaine's mounting misery, nor is he too excited about George's string of victories. In the middle of the episode, Jerry's girlfriend breaks up with him, and Jerry brushes it off with no emotional reaction whatsoever, assuring her that he'll just find another girlfriend, as he always does. Jerry does not exhibit any signs of personal growth, and that's just fine with him. This is because Jerry is the show's *embodiment of delayed adulthood*: the lengthening period of post-adolescence increasingly present in American culture in the generations following the baby boomers.

George is similarly stuck in one place. But while Jerry sees this stasis as comforting and liberating, George finds it terrifying. He is painfully aware of his own inadequacies, as "The Opposite" shows from its opening scenes. Worse, George fears he cannot escape or grow out of these personal failings and suspects he just might be doomed to remain a loser forever. What are the biggest sources of George's self-loathing? Put simply, his physical attributes (lack of hair and unimpressive physique) and his economic failures (unemployed and living with his parents) forever limit his access to pleasure. And yet, even when George does manage to get the job and land the girl, his inner desperation remains. George is thus the *embodiment of the crisis of modernity*, the creeping sense that life is meaningless. Even when he lands a great job and a beautiful girlfriend, the daily grind of satisfying his basic desires seems to draw George farther from finding inner satisfaction.

While George is a perfect conversation partner for Jerry, "The Opposite" suggests that George's real counterpart within the show is actually Elaine. Everything George fears he may never have again—sex, a job, the world's respect—Elaine assumes is right around the corner. Her failures in "The Opposite" present a true crisis of identity because,

**Figure 5.1.   Kramer (Michael Richards), George (Jason Alexander), Elaine (Julia Louis-Dreyfus), and Jerry (Jerry Seinfeld).** *NBC/Photofest*

unlike George, she expects daily fulfillment. However, the main reason Elaine is such a funny character is that she is never quite as smart, impressive, or charming as she believes herself to be. Occasionally, she senses the truth about herself, and those moments of realization are quite painful for her self-image. Elaine is the *embodiment of the crisis of the yuppie*. Riding the rising New York City economy to a comfortable career in the publishing industry, Elaine has a sense of entitlement that comes from her self-confidence; she believes she deserves the success in life and love that is coming to her. Yet, when she stumbles in those categories, she is reminded of a nagging sense that, somewhere, somehow, she took a wrong turn. While George fears that nothing will ever go right, Elaine fears that something is not quite right.

Throughout his friends' personal crises, both in "The Opposite" and throughout the series, Kramer coasts blissfully through his own life, pursuing his own schemes and dreams. In "The Opposite," he appears on *Regis and Kathy Lee* to promote the book he has been working on throughout the season—a coffee-table book about coffee tables. Unlike his friends, Kramer is a generally happy person. He is filled with contradictions and idiosyncrasies—quirky, yet lovable; a mooch, yet generous. He is brimming with ideas and energy. He has a familiar strangeness to him. He is a true individual, yet he gets along with everyone. In these ways and many others, Kramer is the *embodiment of New York City*. He is the show's setting come to life.

## JERRY'S DELAYED ADULTHOOD

Like the real Jerry Seinfeld, the character on *Seinfeld* is a professional comic. He is enjoying a successful career in show business, though *Seinfeld*'s Jerry is not quite as successful and definitely not as rich as the real one. Sometimes an episode shows him traveling for gigs, sometimes he is depicted performing at a New York City comedy club. The entire premise of the show—how a comedian comes up with his ideas—was based on Jerry's occupation. However, once the show found its footing, Jerry's job barely mattered. The stand-up scenes that formerly bracketed the action were even scrapped in the final two seasons.

With his occupation gradually sidelined, *who* Jerry is as a person in the world is much more important than what he does for work. The show came to focus on Jerry's inner life, as much as an emotionally repressed, closed-off, immature, thirty-something bachelor can have an inner life. More than that, *Seinfeld* was about how this naturally solitary guy expresses that inner life to his friends, thus allowing him to make it through the day.

Jerry, George, Elaine, and Kramer are not good people. And yet, in a few ways, they are good for one another. They serve as each other's support group, willing to listen to whatever new social debacle has befallen one of their members. In his typical passive-aggressive manner, Jerry often implies that he'd be happier if his friends just left him alone. But, like a grumpy adolescent who just wants to be alone in his room, these are the only three people whose regular company he tolerates. And they tolerate him, despite his self-confidence that often borders on arrogance, and his dry snark that he directs toward even his closest friends. Elaine is often cruelly dismissive of George, but no one makes fun of George more than his best friend, Jerry.

Other than his parents—who, to Jerry's satisfaction, live far away in Florida—Jerry's longest relationship is his friendship with George. *Seinfeld* does not give us a lot of detail about the characters' histories, but a rare flashback in "The Library" (season 3, episode 5) shows us George and Jerry have been friends since at least high school. With that long history comes a unique intimacy that the two friends often take advantage of. They can talk about anything together. This spirit of openness spreads to Elaine and Kramer as well and forms the basis for the comedy of conversation that flows throughout the series. But that free-flowing conversation starts with the two old friends, who are so close they are mistaken for a gay couple in "The Outing" (season 4, episode 17) when a New York University reporter observes them bickering over whether a pear has been washed or whether a new shirt looks nice.

Jerry's actual romances are short-lived, rarely lasting more than an episode. Only Elaine managed to remain on friendly terms with the bachelor. There is little evidence that Jerry gets anything more than sex out of his romantic relationships. He is uninterested in a long-term commitment. Among the many petty reasons he has found to break up with his girlfriends, Jerry ends one relationship because the woman "shushed" him while they were watching TV.

This is the season 7 premiere, "The Engagement," an episode that begins with George and Jerry having a deep conversation about their shallow lives. George has just broken up with his girlfriend because she beat him at chess. George and Jerry agree to change their ways—as George believes, they make a pact—and they head out with more mature attitudes about their romantic lives. Almost immediately, George runs off and gets engaged to his old girlfriend, Susan, thus setting up the season's overarching plot. Jerry tries getting back together with the "Shusher" until a talk with Kramer reminds him of his terror at being trapped in a marriage. He re-ends the relationship when, out at a restaurant, his girlfriend eats her peas one at a time.

Jerry's career leaves him just as unfettered as his love life. As a stand-up comic, he is in charge of his own schedule. He reports to no one, and, as he smugly notes in "The Stranded" (season 3, episode 10), he has never worked a "real job." Jerry does his best to avoid any responsibility to anyone at all. He is detached from the life going on around him in his apartment and neighborhood and often dismissive of the idea of community service. As the heart of the show, Jerry is a dark heart. He is reasonably loyal, though he is never completely happy when he has to go out of his way for a friend. Even his three closest buddies seem to be a burden. He buzzes them up resignedly when they arrive at his apartment building.

Jerry is emotionally and psychologically immature and not a little narcissistic; he may be dimly aware that the world exists beyond his purview, but he barely cares about anything that does not involve him. He is childlike and childish, both in his inner life and his behavior.

His favorite food is cereal; he eats it throughout the day, and boxes are prominently displayed in the kitchen of his apartment. In fact, the real Seinfeld shares this preference. Also like the real Seinfeld, Jerry loves cartoons, particularly Superman. While the legend that Superman can be spotted in some form in every episode of *Seinfeld* is not true, a Superman refrigerator magnet and a Superman figurine are visible in Jerry's apartment for much of the later years of the series. An entire episode is constructed around Jerry's fascination with the Man of Steel: "The Race" (season 6, episode 10). In it, Jerry is delighted to be dating a woman named Lois. Throughout the episode, Jerry makes comic book–like speeches about how his nemesis, Duncan Meyer, is back and reassures Lois that he'll "think of something" to foil Duncan's schemes. The final slow-motion race against his archenemy is set to John Williams's theme from the original Superman film.

In another episode, Jerry gets a Tweety Bird Pez dispenser ("The Pez Dispenser," season 3, episode 14). He takes it to George's girl-friend's piano recital and puts it on his lap when the recital begins, causing Elaine to burst into uncontrollable laughter. Jerry, and the show as a whole, is disdainful of highbrow culture like classical music and opera. As Elaine points out in another episode, "The Opera" (season 4, episode 9) Jerry's knowledge of performance arts comes entirely from cartoons.

*Seinfeld* is nostalgic for childhood, often through the childishness of its titular character. Children do not worry about society, self-image, and every other thing the adults on the show obsess over. Playing with toys and returning to childhood is an escape from these stresses of adulthood. Perhaps Jerry's most childish moment comes in season 9's "The Merv Griffin Show" (episode 6). Jerry's girlfriend has a collection of antique toys but, priceless antiques that they are, she forbids him from playing with them. After a heavy meal of turkey and some sleep-inducing Costanza family home movies, Jerry manages to get his friends into the apartment so they can play while his girlfriend sleeps.

Perhaps the most immature aspect of Jerry's personality is his deep superficiality. While the show is lighthearted in the humor it draws from Jerry's interest in childish pop culture, *Seinfeld* mocks Jerry's superficiality to the point of ridicule. The best way to explain this side of Jerry is that he wishes to avoid pollution on two fronts. First, he does not want the image he presents to the world around him to be polluted. Other than Elaine, George, and Kramer, who know him well enough to mock his superficial eccentricities, Jerry wants everyone else to think he is flawless. Second, Jerry also wants to avoid polluting his personal space.

One of the best examples of Jerry's image-consciousness comes in "The Van Buren Boys" (season 8, episode 14). Jerry has a new girlfriend, Ellen. As far as Jerry can tell, Ellen is beautiful, charming, and perfect in every way. To the audience, Ellen seems flawless; she's friendly, cheery, and attractive by contemporary standards. Therefore Jerry is confused when Ellen's friends thank him profusely for dating her, as though she is a charity case. He's even more perplexed when Kramer and George tell him he's dating a loser. Neither he nor the audience can see anything wrong with Ellen. When George asks him if he is looking at who Ellen really is inside, Jerry, hilariously, insists he is "being as superficial as I possibly can!"

Jerry keeps looking for a problem with Ellen, but he can't find one. Finally, he introduces her to his parents. He's reassured when they tell him they like her, but the more they gush about her, the more troubled he becomes. Finally, their exuberant compliments convince him there really *is* something wrong with her. Jerry's superficiality reaches a new low as he decides to move on from Ellen. Despite all observable evidence, Jerry dismisses her solely based on the comments of other people.

Jerry's romances often come to a ridiculous end, sometimes because of his fear of polluting his personal space and body. In "The Pothole" (season 8, episode 16), his fussiness drives his storyline. In the beginning of the episode, he accidentally knocks his girlfriend's toothbrush into the toilet. Before he can warn her, Jenna, the girlfriend, uses the tainted toothbrush to brush her teeth. Disgusted, Jerry can't kiss her. Without telling Jenna what happened, he buys her a new electric toothbrush and discreetly adds bleach to her mouthwash. Still, Jerry refuses to kiss her. He lies and says he's coming down with a cold.

Later, Elaine warns him that his excessive fussiness is approaching the level of "disorder." Jerry doesn't like the sound of that, not because he wants to be a psychologically healthy person, but because he wants the world to *see* him as psychologically healthy. Avoiding the chance to actually learn a lesson, Jerry's immaturity remains.

Eventually, Jerry tells Jenna about the toothbrush. Angry, she locks him out of his apartment for a moment while she puts something in the toilet, and then she leaves without telling him what it is. He freaks out and starts throwing out every item he owns. Finally, Jenna tells him what it was—his toilet brush. Jerry, noting with relief that he can replace his toilet brush, heads to Jenna's for dinner. They can't eat at his apartment because he threw out all his dishes. Once there, Jerry and Jenna put the toilet incident behind them. Meanwhile, outside, George's own storyline in the episode has led to him jackhammering a pothole to retrieve a dropped set of keys. He hits a pipe which (somehow) causes Jenna's toilet to explode all over her. Jerry takes one look at his soaked girlfriend and bids her, "Have a nice life!"

Jerry's tendencies remain, but he can still occupy the center of the show. He did make a noble effort to make things work with Jenna. Even as his weaknesses endure, his sarcastic attitude toward the tendencies of his world—his own and those of the people around him—establish him as a central authority on *Seinfeld*. He is the judge. And his proclamations about the behavior he observes, rooted in his own lack of growth as a human being, are often bitter and cynical. Still, they are also honest, often refreshingly so. Despite his deep, irredeemable flaws, Jerry is far more stable, happy, and content than his best friend, George.

## GEORGE'S CRISIS OF MODERNITY

George Costanza is virtually peerless in television sitcom history. Other than Larry David's own character in *Curb Your Enthusiasm*, he has no close comparisons. To be sure, there have been plenty of bumbling losers over the years. But as much as the audience laughed at hapless characters like Barney Fife on *The Andy Griffith Show*, Cliff Clavin on *Cheers*, or Homer Simpson, patron saint of all TV losers, these characters are all a little too dumb to be consistently relatable. More than any of these other characters, George's hopes and fears are terrifyingly relatable. We see the idiocy of the world in Homer Simpson. We see the idiocy of ourselves in George Costanza.

George's foibles often make him a sympathetic character, but his flaws just as often lead him into loathsome behavior. George is an admitted coward. When a small kitchen fire breaks out at a kid's birthday party, George pushes both grandparents and little children aside in his rush for the exit ("The Fire," season 5, episode 19). He is also lazy, once hiring a carpenter to build a little hideout under his desk at work where he sleeps the day away ("The Nap," season 8, episode 18).

George lies to an almost pathological degree and seems proud of his ability to spin tales. Lying seems to offer him an opportunity to fabricate personal success. In more than one episode, starting with "The Stakeout," the first episode of the first season, George expresses a desire to pretend he is an architect. Usually, George lies to impress a woman. He spends entire episodes pretending to be a marine biologist ("The Marine Biologist," season 5, episode 14), a "bad boy" ("The Little Kicks," season 8, episode 4), and a tourist from out of town ("The Muffin Tops," season 8, episode 21). Most of these lies reveal George's deep unhappiness and a feeling that he has not lived up to society's expectations of success. His career is one of many things that have not gone as well as he would have hoped.

While Jerry intentionally avoids landing in a position of steady responsibility, George, though his own missteps, cannot hold a job for very long. Early in the series, George works in real estate and then, thanks to Elaine, publishing. After getting fired for sleeping with the office cleaning woman, he's unemployed for a long stretch before landing his job with the Yankees. The dream job lasts three years, from the end of season 5 to the end of season 8. Working at the Yankees, George feels cool for the only time in his life. After that job ends, George stays within the sports industry, at least by his definition, briefly holding a job with a playground equipment company.

For most of the final season, George works for Kruger Industrial Smoothing. This appears to be a different kind of dream job, as the company is such a mess, George feels no pressure to perform. The Kruger job is one of many times when George feels a fleeting sense of joy from a sudden liberation from social expectations. Unfortunately, George's boss, Kruger, is so incompetent that lazy George Costanza actually feels like he has to pick up the slack.

Throughout season 5 and until his experiment doing the opposite of his instincts in the season finale, George is unemployed and living with his parents. This, the ultimate symbol of adult failure in contemporary American culture, underscores George's incompetence within the late capitalist economy. Though George's parents drive him nuts with their eccentricities, Jerry would probably choose homelessness over the indignity of living with his own relatively even-keeled parents. Unlike Jerry, George isn't deliberately avoiding adult responsibilities. He's just terrible at keeping those responsibilities.

Of course, in the grand scheme of human history, George's rock bottom isn't so terrible. He has his health, despite occasional panics of hypochondria and, even more frequently, instances of faking an illness or injury. George never seems to worry about food or shelter. At the end of the twentieth century, life in American society—even for a short, stocky, slow-witted bald man—is not so nasty, brutish, or short. In *Seinfeld*, even a conniving loser like George has all his needs fulfilled so that he can focus on his futile pursuit of satisfying his wants.

While Jerry's mission is to appear as successful as possible while avoiding commitment and responsibility, George's is to find lasting comfort. He seeks worldly satisfaction from material and physical pleasures in the false hope that they may provide him with a lasting feeling of internal comfort. But external pleasure is always temporary, and his brief moments of freedom from social pressure quickly dissipate. Thus, George's insecurities inevitably return.

George's pursuit of pleasure often leads him to hilarious bouts of pure hedonism, though his idea of a bachelor paradise is sitting shirtless on the couch eating "a block of cheese the size of a car battery" ("The Foundation," season 8, episode 1). In another episode, George stumbles upon the realization that he enjoys eating while he has sex ("The Blood," season 9, episode 4). He secretly sneaks a sandwich into the bedroom and later tries to complete the modern hedonist triple-play by bringing a wireless TV under the sheets. The television and the sandwich distract him from his girlfriend, however, and she kicks him out of the bedroom.

While Jerry has the most sexual partners of any of the four main characters, all four of them have an active sex life. George goes through dozens of girlfriends throughout the show, despite the fact that he fears every time he has sex might be his last.

George observes Jerry's sex life with envy, and his occasional sarcastic jibes at Jerry's comedy may also come from a place of jealousy. He is even more jealous of Elaine's success, especially when he misreads her generosity as attempts to show off her relative success. In fact, it is Kramer, not Jerry or Elaine, who lives the kind of life George wishes he had. When Kramer goes to a fantasy camp in "The Visa" (season 4, episode 15), George laughs that people should pay to live Kramer's life. Getting money without working, food without paying, and sex without dating is George's perfect existence. Jerry and Elaine would be too proud to sign up for Kramer's life. George, though, recognizes and desires Kramer's freedom from social conventions. George lacks the inner strength to pursue a life like Kramer's. Ultimately, he is trapped by the social conventions that he and his friends analyze at length in their conversations.

Both George and Jerry can be terribly shallow men. Jerry, however, uses his charm to get away with his shallowness. George knows he shouldn't be so shallow, but he also knows he can't help it. As its title indicates, few episodes delve into the shallowness of the show's characters as much as "The Nose Job" (season 3, episode 9). George's girlfriend in this episode, Audrey, has a huge nose. This is amusingly demonstrated to the audience with several close-up, fish-eye-lens shots of her massive nose. George is consumed with guilt over his own superficiality, but he can't overcome it. After Kramer, typically unrestrained by conventions of etiquette, nonchalantly recommends to Audrey that she get a nose job, George prods Audrey to have the surgery. When the operation is initially botched, George is so disappointed he faints. He can't even look at her, and he takes off his glasses to talk to her. Repulsed by his behavior, Audrey dumps George and then goes on to have the nose job fixed.

Jerry tells George to stop being too concerned with Audrey's looks, but Jerry's own shallowness is emphasized throughout the episode. He describes his current girlfriend as "the most despicable woman" he has ever met, yet he keeps dating her because she is attractive. Ultimately, Kramer ends up with Audrey after her second surgery is a success. Is Kramer less superficial than George or Jerry? Not really, as Kramer was the one who recommended the nose job in the first place.

So all three male characters are superficial, but George's complete lack of self-confidence makes his superficiality even more crippling. In "The Doodle" (season 6, episode 19), George discovers an unflattering drawing of himself in his new girlfriend's purse. Elaine checks with the woman, Paula, and reports back to George: looks aren't important to Paula. Elaine regrets the phrase as it comes out of her mouth, as George is devastated. Elaine and Jerry console George, emphasizing the fact that Paula actually *likes* George. Distraught, George tells them he'd trade her affection for confirmation of his attractiveness; at least then he could hope to find another girlfriend. Soon, with Paula's help, George will find a silver lining.

Skipping his morning shave—what's the point?—he runs into Paula on the street. To his misery, she confirms that his disheveled appearance means nothing to her. He untucks his shirt. She doesn't care. George, she tells him, could wear sweatpants or even drape himself in velvet and she'd still like him. George is suddenly intrigued.

George discovers his girlfriend's attitude has freed him from his superficial anxieties. Instead of worrying about how he looks to her, she gives him permission to be comfortable. Here, we find a key difference in George and Jerry's superficialities. One woman's opinion would never be enough for Jerry to relinquish his own angst over his appearance. Jerry's self-confidence is based on the image he projects to the entire world. George, so limited in his own self-confidence, is grateful for any other person's permission to relax his endless effort to meet the world's expectations.

George's baldness, an oft-discussed physical trait, is more than just a signal of his failure to live up to modern conventions of male beauty; it is a symbol of the hopelessness of his position. Despite the rumor in one episode that a company in China has created a cure for baldness ("The Tape," season 3, episode 8), there is nothing George can do to put hair on his head, just as there is seemingly nothing George can do to change his identity as a loser. He briefly tries a toupee (season 6, episodes 13 and 14), but this is just another form of lying about who he is. Being bald—like being a loser—is a curse, as emphasized in "The Little Jerry" (season 8, episode 11), when Elaine's boyfriend, Kurt, discovers he is going bald. George tells Kurt there is nothing to do but live as though his last year before he goes bald is the last year of his life.

In the same episode, George dates a woman who is serving time in prison. Fearing he will be deprived of the pleasure of their conjugal visits, George sabotages her parole hearing, prompting her to break out of prison. She turns up at George's apartment where she runs into Kurt, there for more advice about life as a bald man. The police arrive and arrest Kurt, mistaking him for George simply because of his baldness. Kurt punches the cop because, as he explains later to Elaine, "I'm not *that* bald!" He is sentenced to jail for the assault. Elaine, realizing he'll be bald by the time he is free, decides to break up with him.

The irony of the episode is that Kurt has lived for years with a shaved head, and only discovers he is going bald when he decides to grow it back. Elaine is ridiculous for rejecting bald Kurt when she had previously approved of his shaved head, but even Kurt seems to acknowledge that there is a difference between being bald and shaving his head.

Perhaps the problem with baldness is more than aesthetic. Perhaps it signifies a character fault. Does baldness cause George to be a loser? Does being a loser cause George to go bald? Or is the baldness merely an external indicator of his internal condition? Kurt is going bald. Therefore, he is becoming a loser like George.

George's pitiable life is memorably summarized in "The Andrea Doria" (season 8, episode 10), when George describes his many misadventures to a tenant association. He makes this presentation because the association was going to give an available apartment to a survivor of a shipwreck. George sets out to prove that he is far more deserving of their sympathy and offers a convincing laundry list of sad tales from seven-plus seasons of the show. They are convinced, but George loses again when a third party bribes the tenant association with $40 to get the apartment.

George's life is a shipwreck in its modern American context. He fails in all of the modern categories of success, from career to good looks. That these categories themselves are superficial is no solace because George himself is just as shallow. George does find scattered moments of joy, but they never last. Still, his only goal seems to be to string together as many happy moments as he can before he dies. Insecure and weak-willed, George pursues whatever opportunities for pleasure he has before him today, for tomorrow is certain to bring misery. Alas, this is how many live in the modern world—detached from all sources of meaning. Since society gives him nothing but sorrow, why should George give anything back to society? The meaning of his life in this modern world is reduced to his daily pursuit of sex, food, and TV.

And what does George get from his three close friends? They do not dissuade his insecurities; if anything, they acknowledge George's failings directly to his face. His friends do not help him solve his problems, though they are a source of reliable companionship. George will never find meaning or happiness, but at least he isn't alone.

## ELAINE'S CRISIS OF THE YUPPIE

Had *Seinfeld* aired most of its episodes in the 1980s, rather than just one, it would surely have been known as the quintessential yuppie sitcom. The word "yuppie" emerged in the early eighties as a pejorative term for a young urban professional. In 1984, Gary Hart was the first yuppie presidential candidate until America's first modern political sex scandal derailed his campaign. President Reagan was far too old to be a yuppie, but his economic deregulation shifted the balance of economic growth to the financial sector. Young professionals followed the money to urban opportunities, not only in high finance but in other white-collar occupations like real estate, where George works when *Seinfeld* began, or publishing, where Elaine spends much of her career on the show.

Elaine is *Seinfeld*'s premiere yuppie because she encapsulates the inherent hypocrisy of the yuppie. While George and Jerry aggressively seek to detach themselves from all social responsibilities, Elaine maintains a facade of liberal awareness. As occasionally referenced on the show, Elaine is pro-choice and anti-fur. Not referenced in the show, but almost definitely true: Elaine supported Gary Hart.

Elaine perhaps best encapsulates the yuppie mind-set in a season 5 episode when she is trying to convince her friends (and herself) that she is a good person. She lists behavior like not throwing things at squirrels and keeping her hair down at movies so people behind her can see. She also says that when she sees "freaks" in the streets of New York, she avoids staring and yet at the same time does not completely look away, thus ensuring "the freaks feel comfortable" ("The Lip Reader," season 5, episode 6). An image of Elaine taking such care with her nonverbal behavior en route to her well-paying job in the New York City publishing industry should appear next to "yuppie" in some dictionary. In Elaine, as in America, the countercultural activism of the sixties has been absorbed into brief expressions of meaningless etiquette in the nineties.

While Elaine ostensibly adheres to liberal concerns about politics and society, she lives her life just as detached from the needs of the rest of the world as her friends. That is not to say that the character of Elaine is utterly irredeemable. On the contrary, Elaine was a great leap forward in feminist characterization on television. As Louis-Dreyfus's television career continued to soar after *Seinfeld* with two other remarkable and remarkably flawed television women—on *The New Adventures of Old Christine* (CBS, 2006–2010) and *Veep* (HBO, 2012–2019)—retrospectives hail her Elaine as a touchstone in the progress of women on TV.

Elaine is sexual without being an object. She has her own fashion style; Louis-Dreyfus clearly had more of a say in what Elaine wore than the men upstairs at NBC, like Brandon Tartikoff, who said she was "too short" and "not hot." Elaine is tough, too. She scares the other men, especially George. In "The Dinner Party" (season 5, episode 13), George is terrified to be late in picking her up, recalling another time when his tardiness infuriated Elaine; she got so mad that she pulled his Panama hat down hard enough for his head to pop out the top.

Elaine has been referred to as "one of the guys" on the show, though the phrase does not do enough justice to her character's strong sense of self. She can handle herself within the male-dominated action of the other three characters, and she generally fits into the male-oriented perspective of the show. This is useful for the flow of the show because it allows her to be a part of all the other characters' conversations, including the subject of sex. A frequent topic of conversation on *Seinfeld*, Elaine always seems perfectly comfortable when she is discussing sex with her male counterparts.

Louis-Dreyfus certainly performs Elaine as a feminine, sexual woman of the period. It's just that the material her character gets was predominantly written by men; only a few women worked on the show's writing staff over its nine seasons. Thus, as has been true throughout the history of American entertainment, the show's storylines and worldviews were inherently male-centric.

Despite (or, perhaps because of?) the fact that Elaine is the sole female in the quartet of friends, she is also the most self-assured, at least ostensibly. In contrast to the dithering George, Elaine knows who she is, what she wants, and how she plans to get it. She runs into trouble when her plans collapse, or the things she wants turn out to be not as good as she expects. George assumes the worst for himself and is usually proved correct. Elaine assumes the best for herself and is regularly disappointed.

This is the source of the character's crisis; Elaine thinks she makes all the right moves and is puzzled by the sense that her life is never quite as good as she expects. The crisis of the yuppie is neither new nor bound to its era; it is a timeless truth. Elaine proves—but never understands—that happiness has nothing to do with intelligence or beauty or wealth.

While Elaine hits a couple of bumps in her career path, she is never as low as George. Though, like George, she is not as smart as she thinks she is, Elaine is pretty sharp and on top of things at work, while George is incompetent and lazy. When Elaine does lose a job, it is usually due to a series of unfortunate events only tangentially related to her character flaws.

After the publishing firm she works for folds, she gets a job as a personal assistant to a wealthy, and rather eccentric, publishing executive, Mr. Pitt. After that, she ends up working as a writer for J. Peterman, creator of a high-end clothing catalog. Both jobs position Elaine in close proximity to great wealth, yet never close enough to truly enjoy prosperity. The irascible Mr. Pitt actually adores Elaine, who, in their first meeting, reminds him of Jackie Kennedy Onassis. He adds her to his will, only to cut her out and dismiss her when he comes to the mistaken conclusion that she and Jerry are trying to murder him. At the J. Peterman catalog, Elaine is responsible for writing descriptions of fancy, if idiosyncratic, clothing; she sells things rich people buy. Elaine briefly ascends to the top of the company when the catalog's founder goes AWOL in Burma, but he eventually returns, putting her back in her former position. Yet again, just as Elaine thinks she is on the verge of greatness, it turns out she is merely spinning her wheels.

Elaine has a high sense of her own abilities, perhaps even higher than the responsibility-avoiding Jerry. When Kramer describes her as "a calculating, coldhearted businesswoman" who is not afraid to stomp "on a few throats," she takes it as both complimentary and correct ("The Comeback," season 8, episode 13).

As a potential girlfriend and mate, she sees herself as sexy and charming; she is baffled when her romantic pursuits fail over and over again. All four characters are often dismayed when they discover someone else doesn't like them, but this realization drives Elaine particularly crazy. For example, in "The Secret Code" (season 7, episode 7), Elaine is incredulous when a man keeps forgetting her name and even stands her up for a date. She pursues him, despite the fact that he is both dull and disinterested in her, simply to affirm her own vision of herself as desirable.

Elaine's on-again, off-again relationship with the handsome yet dim-witted David Puddy, which spans most of the later years of the show, epitomizes her flaws. At the beginning of their relationship he is working as a car mechanic, and his masculinity seems to represent an intriguing contrast to Jerry ("The Fusilli Jerry," season 6, episode 20). Gradually, she finds herself trapped with Puddy, enjoying him as a sexual partner but repulsed by every other attribute.

Elaine starts to see the downside of Puddy's boorishness when she discovers he paints his face red for New Jersey Devils hockey games ("The Face Painter," season 6, episode 22). It's a behavior she finds baffling and would have been a dealbreaker if he hadn't agreed to stop painting his face on her behalf—a sacrifice she finds oddly charming. Of course, he takes advantage of a loophole in their agreement and paints his chest instead. Puddy's caveman masculinity affirms Elaine's belief that she is superior to him, as she believes she is better than all men. But her sexual appetite trumps her desire for long-term romantic satisfaction, which she knows she will never have with Puddy.

Puddy perfectly sums up Elaine's fate. He is handsome, strong, and sexually appealing, yet completely unfulfilling. Overall, Elaine's life is materialistically successful, but emotionally, psychologically, and spiritually unfulfilling. She does not even find fulfillment in her friendships. Like Jerry and George, the quartet serves a useful purpose in helping her get through each day. Their friendship is far more intellectually stimulating than anything Puddy or her other boyfriends seem to offer her. Still, she senses even Jerry, George, and Kramer are not quite the group of friends she would like to have.

In "The Bizarro Jerry" (season 8, episode 3), Elaine has an opportunity to ditch Jerry, George, and Kramer for three guys who are their "bizarro" counterparts, opposite in every way. She is attracted and delighted by the kindness and decency she finds in this bizarro world. Tragically though, her behavior is too far gone to be acceptable in this world. The bizarro friend group rejects her, and she ends up back where she belongs, like it or not, with her three other equally flawed friends. Elaine can never be as great as she thinks she is.

## KRAMER, THE EMBODIMENT OF NEW YORK CITY

At first glance, and in the early days, Kramer was the weirdo of the quartet. While Jerry, George, and Elaine struggle to navigate social conventions, Kramer's own behavior is far removed from the social norm. Eventually, he becomes arguably the kindest of all four characters, though to say Kramer is *good* would be to oversimplify him. His inner life may be simplest of the four—he's a whimsical, merry individualist who lives in the moment. His endless schemes coupled with his exuberant energy lead him into a variety of life experiences, making his true nature somewhat difficult to categorize.

By season 3, Kramer's complexity was fully formed, and the show's writers winked at his many layers in "The Letter" (episode 21). Jerry is dating an artist, who is painting a portrait titled The Kramer; the addition of the article "the" suggests he is either more special than a typical human or some other creature all together. Kramer is depicted from waist up, standing in a buttoned-up, gray suit coat with a shimmery glow that suggests it might be suede. Both the length of the coat and the painting's proportions emphasize Kramer's above-average height. Kramer's arms hang with his hands comfortably folded below his belly button. A bright, sky-blue, patterned rayon shirt pops with the only color of the painting, visible under the coat from mid-chest to collar. Kramer wears such old-fashioned clothing habitually, but this isn't a sign that his entire character is retro. Richards himself curated Kramer's clothing, envisioning that the character never throws anything out and thus has no need to update his wardrobe.[2]

In the portrait, Kramer's face draws the viewer's gaze. He looks directly and quizzically at the viewer, mouth slightly open, eyebrows slightly arched. Shadows emphasize the many angles of his face, particularly around his eyes, though the brown in them betrays a hint of warmth. He is interested but not judgmental, and likewise unconcerned with being judged. He appears more ponderous than either happy or sad, and yet this moment of introspection does not disengage him from the world; on the contrary, the parted lips suggest he is ready to respond and then act.

More than a quarter-century after the episode, the picture remains available for purchase as a poster, coffee mug, and other forms of reproduction. I still have my T-shirt with the painting on it, a birthday gift I received back in high school when the show was still on.

Just as memorable as the painting is the scene in which a husband and wife—two aged, cultured, well-mannered art collectors—consider the painting. Mrs. Armstrong sees a vulnerable, innocent man-child, orphaned out of time in the postmodern world. Mr. Armstrong sees a parasite seeking to gratify his basest urges, a loathsome, offensive brute. Mrs. Armstrong's spirit is lifted. Mr. Armstrong is sickened. They both love it.

It is a contradictory portrait of a contradictory man. Both Armstrongs are correct in their assessment of Kramer's character. He is sometimes an innocent, sometimes a parasite. Richards was always calculating in his development of Kramer. "I work very hard to make this character three-dimensional," he explains.[3] As cartoonish as Kramer can be, Richards keeps him from becoming a cartoon. Often, it is his lovability that makes him realistic; he has a willingness to be decent that his friends completely lack. Sometimes, though, Kramer flashes a dark side—the creepy Kessler still alive. "Kramer is full of facets and contradictions," explains longtime *Seinfeld* writer Larry Charles, who mined more of Kramer's character than any other writer. "He's real and unreal. He's like an adult and a child. He's like neutered yet very sexual. He's very light yet very dark. He can be idiotic and yet very wise."[4]

Kramer is many things. He might even contain *all* things, if we had a lifetime to explore him. He is as multifaceted as the city in which he resides, from which he was spawned. In these and many other ways, Kramer embodies New York City in the nineties. He even towers like a skyscraper over the people around him.

So much of Kramer is a mystery. He hides his first name, Cosmo, until season 6's eleventh episode, "The Switch." He keeps another secret until the tenth episode of the final season, "The Strike," when we learn that Kramer has apparently been on strike from his job at a bagel shop. For the most part, he has no discernible source of income, pursuing one business idea, invention, or get-rich-quick scheme after another. Where did Kramer come from? In "The Betrayal," aka the backwards episode (season 9, episode 8), we learn only that he was living in the apartment across the hall when Jerry moved in. At their first meeting, Jerry neighborly insists on sharing a pizza with Kramer, thus unintentionally giving Kramer the green light to mooch off Jerry from that point forward.

Kramer's zany life constantly spills into Jerry's apartment, at any and all hours, like the city that never sleeps. "Giddyup!" is Kramer's fitting catchphrase. In a city filled with endless possibility, Kramer is adventurous and up for anything. On the other hand, his friends have little interest in joining in Kramer's various plans, and he is rarely the impetus for group adventures. Though he can be persuasive and manipulative, his strangeness keeps him from being a truly effective leader. Though his friends have learned to steer clear of Kramer's zany ideas, the consequences of his adventures often ricochet back on his friends.

This dynamic is perfectly encapsulated in "The Marine Biologist" (season 5, episode 14). Rarely is Kramer as enthusiastic as he is in this episode when he comes up with the idea of taking a big bucket of golf balls out to the beach and hitting them into the ocean. No one shows the faintest interest in the plan, which turns out to be a bust anyway when Kramer can't make contact with the ball. The one golf ball he does hit ends up in the blowhole of a whale that George, pretending he is a marine biologist to impress a woman, must rescue.

Like New York, Kramer can be both hard and friendly. Often, especially in earlier seasons, he smirks at his friend's various miseries, though all of his friends display at least as much schadenfreude as Kramer throughout the series. Kramer, loyal in his own idiosyncratic way, cares about his friends, and he is always ready to lend a hand. Though Elaine thinks of herself as more socially minded, Kramer is more likely to actually go out of his way to perform a good deed—though, true to the show's antisocial outlook, most of his selfless acts rebound back on him. In "The Sponge" (season 7, episode 9), Kramer signs up for an AIDS walk but, ever the individualist, refuses to accept and wear the AIDS ribbon pin offered at registration. A mob of other participants read this as a slight against the cause and beat Kramer up.

Much more than his friends, Kramer is driven by his instincts. He is the "id" of the group, even more interested in the pursuit of sex and food than George or Jerry, and more successful in this pursuit than George precisely because he follows his instincts and ignores the moderating voice of the superego. Furthermore, Kramer often encourages his friends to ignore their own consciences. In the season 2 opener, "The Ex-Girlfriend," Kramer encourages Jerry to ignore his hesitancy and pursue a romance with George's ex-girlfriend. "Why would George want to deprive you of pleasure?" he asks Jerry.

Here, as elsewhere, Kramer is a critic of the social norms entrapping his friends. Kramer so easily dismisses the structures of culture that Jerry is too nonconfrontational and George is too timid to take on. He encourages his friends to give in to their natural urges, to seek pleasure. More than his friends, Kramer is uninhibited. He enjoys sex without guilt. He appreciates a good meal, whether in the diner or in Jerry's kitchen. He is an epicurean in his own way, seeking out and savoring the finer things in life, from a succulent Mackinaw peach to a delicious artisanal soup. He savors all that New York City has to offer.

It is thus alarming when, in an arc that carries from the end of season 3 into the first two episodes of season 4, Kramer abandons New York to pursue a fresh start in Los Angeles ("The Keys," season 3, episode 23; "The Trip," season 4, episodes 1 and 2). "I yearn," he tells George as he explains his impending departure, though George has no idea what his strange friend is talking about. As a further impetus to leave, Kramer and Jerry have a fight, sparked by Kramer's continued interruptions of Jerry's space. This leads to Jerry asking Kramer to return the spare key to his apartment.

After Kramer departs abruptly for the west coast, a contrite Jerry flies with George to Los Angeles to bring their friend home. At the end of the arc, even after floundering as an actor and being mistaken for a serial killer, Kramer decides to remain in LA. To an extent, this is his New York stubbornness. He is not one to be talked into decisions, big or small, nor is he one to admit defeat. So he stays in Hollywood . . . for three more days.

Jerry and George are watching television when Kramer enters the apartment, as he has many times before. Acting like all is as it should be, Kramer offers a quick greeting and then heads straight for Jerry's fridge, where he helps himself to some sandwich toppings. George and Jerry exchange looks, but they don't press Kramer for an explanation. Instead, in perhaps the most touching moment in the entire series, Jerry tosses Kramer his spare set of keys, symbolically reconciling with his quixotic neighbor. Kramer smiles gently and disappears into the hall. He returns and, more comically, lobs his massive key chain at Jerry. It knocks Jerry's drink off the coffee table, breaking the uncharacteristically sentimental mood.

What happened to Kramer's yearning? Ultimately, Kramer returns to his comfort zone. As independent a character as he is, he is lost without his New York social network. Surprisingly, the individualist Kramer is the most helpless of the four characters. He is the most childish for his stubbornness, for his inability to care for himself, and for his unwillingness to play by the conventions of adulthood that Jerry, George, and Elaine so strongly subscribe to.

Pulled into the drama over the spare keys, Elaine comments, "I gotta get some new friends." It's not the last time she contemplates cutting ties with this group but, like Kramer, she is unable to break free. The four friends are all stuck with each other. Kramer cannot survive alone. None of them can face the world alone. They are each other's relief from the world's insanity. They release their stresses and neuroses to each other through sarcasm as well as brutal honesty. Their ability to share nothingness is what gets them through the day, and their ability to laugh at each other's misfortunes is what distracts them from their own desperate yearnings.

# 6

# THE PEOPLE IN THEIR NEIGHBORHOOD

They say New York City is a place where you can find anything in the world. For the creators of *Seinfeld*, the city was a place where they could find any*one* in the world. Whatever character type a script might require, that person could conceivably be found living in New York City. Over nine seasons, *Seinfeld* developed a deep and eclectic stable of supporting characters. For a show that featured such antisocial main characters, the world of *Seinfeld* was surprisingly crowded. And while other comedies used intrusions from people beyond the central cast as a basic plot device, *Seinfeld* developed a remarkably deep bench of recurring characters.

For this, Larry David deserves particular credit. As over-the-top as the show could be, David insisted on a few rules of realism that made *Seinfeld* feel true to life in many of its details. For example, Jerry's father was recast after the character's first appearance. Barney Martin took the part from Phil Bruns, and David insisted on reshooting Bruns's scenes with Martin before the episode went into reruns and syndication.

Another example of David's attention to detail in casting comes in "The Stock Tip," the last of the four-episode first season. Jerry's story involved him taking a girlfriend for an ill-fated weekend getaway to Vermont. Since the show had not shown him breaking up with the woman he began dating in the first episode of the season, David reasoned that the same character, Vanessa, should return as Jerry's girlfriend, played by the same actress, Lynn Clark.

Clark was the first of many actors who performed as the same character in *exactly* two different episodes of *Seinfeld*. Almost fifty different actors would do the same throughout the run of the show.[1] These include characters like girlfriends and boyfriends, neighbors, waitresses, and many others who would logically reappear to characters hanging out in the same neighborhood, week after week. If the characters had to go back to a veterinarian, a doctor's office, or a bakery, why wouldn't they see the same person still working there? *Seinfeld* did all it could to bring back actors for recurring parts—big parts *and* small parts—simply to maintain the show's internal logic.

Most of these two-and-out characters are not memorable, though a few stand out, such as Izzy Mandelbaum (the late, great Lloyd Bridges in one of his final roles), real-life Yankee slugger Danny Tartabull, and the Maestro, Bob Cobb (played by Mark Metcalf, who is so funny I can't believe he was *only* in two episodes).

Jerry sees his parents' neighbor, Evelyn, on two separate visits to Florida, five years apart. Even if a *Seinfeld* viewer didn't remember that it was the same actress, Ann Morgan Guilbert, the vague sense of familiarity to the character adds a sense of realism in the viewer's subconscious. There is something familiar about her.

## RECURRING TYPES

Complications are essential to any sitcom plot, and *Seinfeld*'s recurring characters are often the source of a given episode's complications. These recurring characters can be placed in two broad categories: *burdens* and *objects of desire*. In the first category, we find family burdens and acquaintance burdens. In the second category, we have objects of romantic desire and objects of career desire.

Of course, *all* of the people Jerry and his friends encounter are burdensome. Romantic partners have burdensome quirks that must be negotiated for the main characters to achieve one of their basic desires: sex. Similarly, the characters' various employers also have a number of burdensome quirks that must be negotiated for economic reasons.

Jerry, George, Elaine, and Kramer don't like people very much. However, they need money, and they want sex. Jerry seems fortunate in finding a career that minimizes his human interactions; he gets to be alone on stage and be his own boss. When his manager, Katie, does appear in two episodes of the series, her entire character is built around her being an annoying burden who creates more problems than she is worth. She gets Jerry kicked off a flight ("The Diplomat's Club," season 6, episode 21), and books Jerry a ridiculously long two-hour assembly at his old junior high school that does not go well ("The Abstinence," season 8, episode 9).

Kramer somehow avoids regular employment, and his various get-rich-quick schemes create a sort of complication different from the interpersonal woes of his friends. Though George jealously observes that Kramer finds a way to have sex without dating, Kramer, too, gets caught up in the complications created by objects of romantic desire. Usually, for Kramer, he is his *own* burden. As Jerry's zany neighbor, inherently a burden on both Jerry's fridge and his sex life, Kramer is, in a way, the prototype for all recurring characters throughout the run of the show.

Let's take a closer look at some of the more interesting and amusing examples of these recurring character types.

## OBJECTS OF CAREER DESIRE

Though he denies being interested in playing George on *Seinfeld*, David's career before, during, and after the show suggests that he always wanted to be in front of the cameras, perhaps even more than his buddy, Seinfeld. Thus, he managed to find many ways to sneak into a number of episodes of the show, as a variety of characters, sometimes appearing on screen, sometimes heard as an off-screen voice, and always uncredited.

He appeared or had a line in 38 episodes of the series. That is more appearances than all but six people. Obviously, the four main cast members appeared in the most episodes. Wayne Knight appeared as Newman in 45 episodes. (Don't worry, we'll get to Newman!) And Ruth "Ruthie" Cohen appeared in 101 episodes, more than Knight and David combined, sitting at the cash register in Monk's, behind the characters' preferred booth. She only spoke in a few episodes, most notably "The Gum" (season 7, episode 10), when George accuses her of shortchanging him and, stoic in the face of George's accusations, Ruthie helpfully points out that his car is on fire.

One other ubiquitous uncredited performer also deserves a mention here. Norman Brenner lands just behind David with 29 appearances on *Seinfeld*. The tall, red-haired actor's primary job was working as Michael Richards's stand-in, but he made it into many episodes as a pedestrian or a customer or a co-worker or a salesman . . . Within the world of *Seinfeld*, I like to think he is a guy named Ian who lives in the same neighborhood and has worked a variety of jobs in the area, but he has avoided the misfortune of getting to know Jerry and his gang. Though they have a few brief interactions with him over the years, true to their antisocial nature, Jerry and his friends never cared to strike up a conversation, much less a friendship, with the familiar face.

David, on the other hand, definitely played many different people on the show. He appears as a newsstand owner in "The Gum" to reject a drawn-on $20 bill from George, the same bill he mistakenly thought he gave Ruthie. He is a voice on a subway speaker, a baseball announcer, and even a character overheard in *Checkmate*, one of the many fake movies that exist in the world of the show. My personal favorite David cameo comes in "The Chinese Woman" (season 6, episode 4), when he plays "Man with Cape," or, as the character refers to himself, "Frank Costanza's lawyer."

But David's best-known role on the show came as the voice of George Steinbrenner. Every scene of the Yankees owner was shot from behind, with actor Lee Bear embodying the character in a suit and a white wig, sitting at his desk as George timidly enters the room. Parodying the real Steinbrenner' s erratic reputation, the owner would inevitably launch into some absurd tangent. Bear would flail his arms wildly while David read the part off-camera, creating a disjointedness between the character's words and gestures that only added to the insanity.

While the character is a rare example of the show satirizing a real-life person, Steinbrenner is also prototypical for the other bosses depicted on the show. George even encounters a couple of Steinbrenner doppelgangers—Cuban dictator Fidel Castro and Tyler Chicken CEO Johnny Tyler—who are filmed from behind at the same angle and voiced off-camera to emphasize their resemblance.

Steinbrenner is similar to other *Seinfeld* bosses in several ways. First of all, he is a white man, and older than the main characters. He is a self-assured blowhard with a monarchical management style. And he is a source of discomfort because of his combination of power and eccentricity.

Both George and Elaine worked for a number of bosses who fit this characterization, starting with the very first boss depicted on the series, Mr. Levitan, who George tries to poison in "The Revenge" (season 2, episode 7). George's last job on the series is working for one of the shows particularly bonkers recurring characters, Mr. Kruger, who is a blend of George's laziness and Steinbrenner's childlike whimsy—a perfectly imperfect employer for George.

The fits and starts of Elaine's career eventually lead her to work as a personal assistant for Mr. Pitt, a publishing executive who mainly has Elaine fulfilling his own peculiarities, like finding the perfect pair of socks or removing the salt from every pretzel stick in the bag. It is a perfect job for her character—the pay and prestige suit her ego, but the work is comically demeaning and the position leaves her hopelessly trapped.

She surely misses her old job at Pendant Publishing, where she worked for the relatively even-keeled Mr. Lippman, the most "normal" boss on the show. After Pendant folds, Lippman himself starts acting a bit silly. In one episode, Elaine discovers he has opened Top of the Muffin to You!, a muffin shop that only sells the top portion of the muffin. In another episode, Lippman's son and Lippman himself develop an infatuation with Elaine, and, in separate scenes, both ambush her with an unwanted kiss. The most normal boss depicted on the series thus transforms into another Burdensome Acquaintance.

If there is one boss who exceeds Steinbrenner both as a fan favorite and as an eccentric, it is Elaine's last boss on the series, the clothing catalog publisher J. Peterman, based on a real retail entrepreneur of the same name. Elaine first meets Peterman two episodes after Mr. Pitt fires her. Wandering the streets aimlessly, Elaine bumps into Peterman, who tells her that being lost is the best way to end up somewhere you've never been. This is how Peterman speaks, as though every sentence could potentially work as a romantic description in his high-end catalog.

But while Peterman is ostensibly dapper and put together, he turns out to be just as loony as the other bosses on the show. He fires Elaine on two separate occasions, once when she flunks a drug test after her fondness for poppy-seed muffins results in her testing positive for opium, and once when she confesses that she doesn't like the film *The English Patient*. Both times she manages to get her job back, returning to work on writing blurbs for Peterman products like the Himalayan Walking Shoes, the Gatsby Swing Top (a brassiere worn as a top), and an Urban Sombrero of Elaine's own design. For a period, Elaine herself takes control of the company when Peterman disappears on an excursion of self-discovery deep in the jungles of the country known as Myanmar (though it'll always be Burma to me). Eventually, Peterman returns and demotes Elaine back to her old position (and salary), acknowledging her not for a job done well, but for a job, simply, done, and reasserting his erratic leadership.

Overall, these Objects of Career Desire, who must be tolerated for the characters to maintain their own economic well-being, represent a late-twentieth-century dissatisfaction with the working life. The various professional, white-collar jobs Elaine and George hold throughout the series are barely tolerable for them, but they do their best to appease their superiors so that they can maintain their livelihoods. As George knows all too well, the only thing worse than being stuck in a hard job with a crazy boss is being unemployed.

These maniacal bosses, from Peterman to Steinbrenner, hold king-like power over George's and Elaine's careers, just as a girlfriend holds queen-like power over George's sex life. George schmoozes Steinbrenner much like he or Jerry would oblige the wants and whims of a girlfriend. The characters' pursuit of sex mirrors their self-demeaning pursuit of money.

## OBJECTS OF ROMANTIC DESIRE

By any metric—live audience response, critical acclaim, cultural resonance—one of the most famous moments for a character outside the central quartet belongs to Sidra, Jerry's girlfriend played by Teri Hatcher in "The Implant" (season 4, episode 19). In the episode, Sidra goes to the same gym as the other characters. After she spots Jerry ogling Sidra, Elaine, with a hint of jealously, tells him she thinks his new girlfriend's breasts are implants. Jerry is dismissive but, after Elaine sees her in the club's sauna, he is eventually convinced, and he decides to dump Sidra.

A day or two later Elaine sees Sidra in the sauna again, overhearing her describe Jerry's obsession for cleanliness and love for Superman. They strike up a conversation, and when Elaine rises to shake Sidra's hand, she trips and falls into the bosom in question.

Sheepishly, Elaine admits to Jerry that the breasts might be genuine. Jerry manages to get another date with Sidra. Just as he is about to make his move on the couch, Kramer interrupts him to borrow a bathing suit. Moments later, Elaine arrives, and before Jerry can get his friends out of the apartment, Sidra concludes that Elaine had been sent on an exploratory mission by Jerry. She storms out of the apartment, then returns to Jerry's doorway to deliver her instantly classic zinger: "And by the way, they're real, and they're spectacular."

As Hatcher recalls, the line was not in the script, but, after running a few other versions capping the scene, David came up with it on the spot.[2] Hatcher, mixing spite and sexuality, nailed the delivery, and the studio audience exploded.

Beyond the comedic elements of the moment itself, the line and the scenario capture the inherent struggles and flaws of Jerry's character. His shallowness has already found a new dimension when he dumps Sidra on the mere suspicion that her breasts might be fake. Convinced otherwise, he resumes his singular pursuit—sex with a conventionally beautiful woman. On the cusp of his goal, he is thwarted when Sidra draws a false conclusion from circumstantial evidence. Then again, even if Elaine did not deliberately fall on Sidra at Jerry's request, Jerry did ask his ex-girlfriend for more information about his new girlfriend. Jerry wasn't guilty of the letter of Sidra's accusation, but he was guilty of its spirit.

Sidra's departing words tease Jerry's sexual frustration. She is basically saying, "No sex for you!" It's a feeling both Jerry and George have experienced before on the show and will experience again—the object of desire slipping away just as it is about to be secured.

A staple of sex comedies, this is not a new formula. What is distinct in *Seinfeld* are the elaborate, and generally futile, strategies the characters undertake to bed the object of desire. Besides the authenticity question, "The Implant" also includes a running joke about how both George and Jerry need to be sitting on a certain side of the couch in order to make a move.

While Jerry is pondering issues of truth and fabrication, George tries to manipulate the death of his girlfriend's aunt for his own sexual gratification. At the funeral reception, held in Detroit, he is unable to use his role as consoling boyfriend as a springboard to coitus, and he fails to secure a death certificate to save money on the air fare. Then he gets into a tussle after his girlfriend's brother spots him double-dipping a chip. No sex for George, either. Incidentally, George's girlfriend, Betsy, is played by another rising television star, Megan Mullally, who landed a lead role on *Will & Grace* a few years later.

The roster of actors and actresses who played an Object of Romantic Desire on *Seinfeld* en route to bigger and better things in Hollywood goes far beyond Hatcher and Mullally, a testament to the work of the show's casting department, particularly Marc Hirschfeld, who was with the show throughout its run. Kramer had the fewest partners, but one of his girlfriends was played by Sarah Silverman. Elaine went on several dates with baseball star Keith Hernandez, playing himself, and George almost managed to date an Academy Award–winning actress, Marisa Tomei, playing herself. The long list of actresses who played a girlfriend of Jerry's include future Gilmore Girl Lauren Graham; pre-*Friends* Courtney Cox; Debra Messing, who would later join Mullally on *Will & Grace*; Kristin Davis, future star on *Sex and the City*; pre-*Frasier* Jane Leeves; and pre-breakout Amanda Peet.

Half the future main cast of *Breaking Bad* was on *Seinfeld*. Bob Odenkirk played Elaine's boyfriend in one episode, and Anna Gunn played Jerry's girlfriend in another. But one of the most retrospectively famous guest stars on *Seinfeld* was the "one who knocks," Walter White himself, Bryan Cranston. On *Seinfeld*, Cranston plays Dr. Tim Whatley, a dentist and a friend of Jerry's. He is also infatuated with Elaine, briefly dating her, which makes him a perfect transition into our next category.

## BURDENSOME ACQUAINTANCES

Whatley first appears in "The Mom and Pop Store" (season 6, episode 8). Thanks to Cranston's scene-stealing panache, Whatley would appear in four more episodes, thus transcending the gang's long list of acquaintances who typically remained minor characters on the show: people like The Drake, Alec Berg, and Joe Mayo. There is also another entirely different category of acquaintances—associates of Kramer, who often represent the seedier side of New York City life: Grossbard, Shlomo, Slippery Pete, and, of course, the unseen yet oft-mentioned Bob Sacamano. The Whatleys of the *Seinfeld* world are from a more respectable tier of society, though, as Whatley proves, this type of person can be just as sleazy.

Cranston was 38 years old when he was first cast as Whatley. With dozens of roles under his belt, Cranston was long overdue for a breakout.[3] Like other recurring characters on the show, Whatley was seemingly created to fill a role for one story. Only through his multiple appearances does his character evolve into a full-blown Burdensome Acquaintance. In "The Mom and Pop Store," he is throwing a Thanksgiving party because his apartment overlooks the route for the Macy's Thanksgiving Day parade. Jerry is perturbed, because even though Whatley called him to get the addresses to invite his three friends, Jerry is the only one not to receive an invitation. The dentist's apartment serves as the perfect intersection for the episode's various plotlines to collide at the climax. Elaine has helped her employer, Mr. Pitt, win a spot holding a rope for the Woody Woodpecker balloon by correctly guessing the name of a big band song, but to collect the tickets—as well as a dangerously sharp trophy—she has to sacrifice her hearing by sitting through an hour of live band music in a small room. And George is investigating whether the bite marks on the pencil he found in his newly purchased car, a 1989 LeBaron that the dealer *claims* was previously owned by Jon Voight, match the bite marks on Kramer, left there by the actor, Jon Voight, who bit Kramer's arm when Kramer approached the star to ask about the LeBaron. The Academy Award–winning Voight appears in the episode just for the scene where he bites Kramer's arm, making Cranston only the second-most famous guest star in the episode. Anyway, Jerry is stuck wearing cowboy boots after Kramer takes all his other shoes to the mom and pop store down the street. Kramer is trying to keep them in business, but inadvertently gets them busted for bad electrical wiring, leading them to close the shop, disappearing with all of Jerry's sneakers. Stuck in the cowboy boots, Jerry slips on some ice and injures his mouth before the big party at Whatley's.

Needless to say, it's an episode packed with more intrigue and plot twists than an entire season of *Breaking Bad*.

At Whatley's party, Elaine is hoping to connect with the host, but with her ears still ringing, she can't hear Whatley when he asks her on a date. Jerry, uncertain of whether Whatley invited him to the party, tries to hide from the host while searching for a dentist to examine his injured mouth at the beginning of the long holiday weekend. George, with Kramer in tow, is also looking for a dentist to compare the bite marks on the pencil with the bite marks on Kramer's arm. Eventually, he finds a dentist who knows the Voight who owned the LeBaron. Sadly, it is John Voight, a periodontist with whom he went to medical school. Jerry, getting his mouth examined, tips his head back, knocking Elaine's trophy out the window, which pops the Woody Woodpecker balloon. Whatley outs Jerry as an uninvited guest and a troublemaker, to which Jerry responds with the Woody Woodpecker laugh.

In the same episode, Whatley pulls off the rare double play for a *Seinfeld* supporting character. He is a Burdensome Acquaintance for Jerry, and he is an Object of Romantic Desire for Elaine. Jerry, in his typical socially anxious way, frets over whether he was invited to the party and is embarrassed when he shows up and discovers he was not. Here, as in later episodes, Whatley uses Jerry, whom he clearly does not like, to get closer to Elaine, whom he is interested in.

Hinted at here, but only elaborated in a later episode featuring Cranston as Whatley, is Jerry's disdain for dentists. In "The Yada Yada" (season 8, episode 19), Whatley has converted to Judaism, and Jerry is upset as he begins to suspect the dentist's only motivation is so that he can make jokes about the religion. Whatley brushes off the accusation, but further infuriates Jerry when he keeps making Catholic jokes because he used to be Catholic.

Jerry eventually goes to Catholic confession just to tattle on Whatley. "The Yada Yada" deals as much with Jerry's Jewish identity as any episode. Jerry, as he tells the priest, is not offended by Whatley's behavior because he is Jewish but rather because he is a comedian. He holds his profession in much higher esteem than his family's faith.

At the end of the episode, Jerry confesses to his girlfriend that he is an "anti-dentite." He is happy to discover his girlfriend shares his disgust of dentists, but his pleasure is punctured when she lumps in "blacks and Jews" as equally detestable groups.

As much as Jerry grows to dislike Whatley, at least he can do his best to avoid him. His parents, on the other hand, are part of his life, whether he likes it or not. The best he can do is try to fulfill his responsibilities as a loving, loyal son even while keeping them out of his life as much as possible. As he and George learn throughout the show, this is easier said than done.

## BURDENSOME FAMILY MEMBERS

Before we get to their parents, we should mention Jerry's Uncle Leo. Jerry is burdened by his familial ties to his uncle, but Uncle Leo also lives near enough that Jerry risks bumping into him on the street, yet another neighbor Jerry would rather avoid. Uncle Leo's catchphrase— an exuberant "Hello!"—is a loaded phrase for Jerry; the simple greeting means a trap has suddenly closed, sticking Jerry in an unwanted conversation for an unknown period of time. Blowing off his uncle, as Jerry is caught doing several times, leads to an even worse fate—a stern phone call from his mother.

George's parents, Frank and Estelle, live out in Queens, meaning that while he does not face a regular risk of bumping into them around his Manhattan neighborhood, they are a regular part of his life and a consistent source of problems. Jerry is more pleased with his situation; his parents, Morty and Helen, live in a retirement community in Florida. They visit New York occasionally, and he visits Florida just as often, but they cannot possibly be as present in Jerry's life as George's parents are in his.

These situations briefly reverse in season 7's "The Shower Head" (episode 15). Jerry's parents end up living in New York temporarily while preparing to move to a new community in Florida, Del Boca Vista. Eventually, the zigs and zags of the episode lead them to move into Jerry's apartment, completely eviscerating the buffer, as Jerry refers to it, that has kept his parents a comfortable distance away.

George, meanwhile, manages to manipulate his parents into deciding to move to Florida, giving them a Del Boca Vista pamphlet. When the Seinfelds hear that the Costanzas are moving into the same neighborhood, they refuse to leave New York; as Morty says, he and Helen need their own buffer from the Costanzas. "We can't stand them," Morty declares.

Jerry is crushed that his own buffer has evaporated, but George resentfully proclaims that it is his turn to enjoy a buffer. Of course, George's dreams come crashing down; his parents are afraid to move too far from their son. That frees up the Seinfelds to move back to Florida. The status quo is restored.

George sees one more opportunity to enjoy a buffer from his parents in "The Money" (season 8, episode 12). Ever the miser, George starts to contemplate how much his parents will leave him when they die. He pesters them for details on the family's health history, hoping that they might kick the bucket sooner rather than later. His inquiries backfire when his parents recognize their own mortality and decide to start spending their money. Taking money advice from Kramer, they realize they can't spend it fast enough in New York—this doesn't make sense, but Frank and Kramer aren't the brightest bulbs—and they can blow through their savings far faster in Florida.

George is torn between his love of money and his dislike of his parents. Ultimately, he tells his parents he wants them to stay . . . at which point they inform him they are moving to Florida and were only humoring him by asking for his opinion. That's okay with George, who immediately starts basking in his buffer zone. The arrangement is short-lived, however. In Florida, Frank spots a man sleeping in the back of a Cadillac; he doesn't know it's Jerry, and the car is a gift Jerry gave his father in the previous season, which he has bought back after his parents sold it. In his tireless efforts to be generous to his parents and prove to them that he is economically secure, Jerry has maxed out his credit card and can't afford a hotel. Deciding that there are too many bums in Florida, Frank announces that they are moving back to New York. (Again, the plot makes no sense.)

"The Money" isn't the first time George wishes his father were dead. In "The Raincoats" (season 5, episode 18), George sees another opportunity to profit off his parents. He pretends his father is dead in order to make a quick buck selling Frank's old clothes to a vintage clothing store.

George's relationship with his parents hinges on the fact that he is bound to them by blood. He feels a responsibility to them, and as crazy as they are, he can't shake his connection. He might love them on some deeper level, but he certainly doesn't like them.

Jerry is kinder to his parents, but ultimately his relationship with them is also purely based on blood. Typical of his character, he goes through the motions that he believes a good son is expected to go through. He will let his parents stay with him when they are in New York. He won't ask them to give him space while they are in town, no matter how much they cramp his style. He'll do all the things that make his parents declare him to be such a good son, but he'll do them more out of responsibility than genuine love.

On *Seinfeld*, family relationships are nowhere near as intimate as the relationships between friends. Families are more a responsibility than a blessing. Families are more likely to create problems than to help solve problems. This is an inversion of the values traditionally seen in an American sitcom. The classic domestic comedy portrays the family as the cornerstone of life and the pursuit of happiness. *Seinfeld* emphasizes the threat family responsibility poses to personal liberty.

Both Elaine's father, Alton, and Kramer's mother, Babs, appear in one episode apiece, aside from a brief appearance by Babs in the series finale. Kramer is estranged from his mother, but the two reconcile in "The Switch" (season 6, episode 11) long enough for George to discover Kramer's long-hidden first name, Cosmo.

In "The Jacket" (season 2, episode 3), Alton Benes comes into town for dinner with Elaine, Jerry, and George. Elaine's father was played by famous tough-guy character actor Lawrence Tierney, who was just as difficult to deal with on set as his character was for Jerry and George. The pair find themselves entertaining the curmudgeon while they wait for Elaine, who is running very late, doing a favor for Kramer. Alton spends the time reminiscing to Jerry and George about his experience in the Korean War and ranting about how the United States should have overthrown Castro long ago. Jerry and George meekly sip their orders of cranberry juice with two limes and a club soda with no ice. Alton drinks scotch on the rocks.

Like the other representatives of his generation depicted on *Seinfeld*, Alton is portrayed as comically out of touch with the modern world. This was an early episode in the run of the show, but *Seinfeld* had already found comedy in the characters' grappling with the generational gap between them and their aging parents, a factor of life for baby boomers in the nineties.

For four characters obsessed with pursuing their own fleeting pleasures, the past that their parents represent is of no interest. Indeed, the characters are often ambivalent to all things in the past. In "The Frogger" (season 9, episode 18), Jerry and George allow themselves a bit of nostalgia and return to an old favorite pizza place. Mario's rude service reminds them of why they stopped coming to the restaurant. He is going out of business, and it's easy to see why.

Two other objects from the past are destroyed in the episode. One is the Frogger arcade machine that George tries to rescue from the restaurant because he still holds the high score. The other is a piece of wedding cake preserved from the wedding of Edward VIII to Wallis Simpson in 1937. Elaine finds it in Peterman's office and, not knowing its romantic history, eats it all up. George and Peterman's shared desire to preserve the past is played as foolish, and, judging by *Seinfeld*'s treatment of the past, so are all such efforts. (As we will see in chapter 7, the show treats religion similarly—religious faith is a relic of the past and, often, an object of ridicule.)

The past, like the character's parents, is a reminder of both time and mortality. From annoying neighbors to difficult relatives to the specter of death itself, *Seinfeld*'s four characters hate anything that adds a burden to their day-to-day, episode-to-episode pursuit of pleasure.

## THE BURDEN'S REVENGE?

But even as *Seinfeld* was more anti-community than perhaps any show to precede it, few shows were as communal in their central dynamic. The four friends, who serve as both a support group and a family for one another, share every aspect of their lives with one another. The "hands-in" cheer that the four characters do in the final episode of the series is quintessential for the characters, not merely because this is a show about friends as family but also because it is a show about them going out from the safety of their weekly huddle, interacting with all sorts of oddballs, and returning to their foursome for support, guidance, or simply a listening ear.

As *Seinfeld* approached its own ending, and as David and Seinfeld contemplated the show's mortality, it made sense that they would develop a story that allowed all those oddballs to return, and flip nine seasons of selfishness back on top of the characters.

This brings us, finally, to Newman (Wayne Knight), the epitome of the intrusive neighbor. In the finale, it is Newman who warns Jerry that his comeuppance is nigh. In one of the final scenes of the series, New-man's is the loudest voice in the mob, cackling at their fate.

Jerry singles out Newman as his nemesis throughout the series, but as we've seen, just about everyone he and his friends meet is a potential nuisance to Jerry. Newman is singular only in the sense that he is the ultimate embodiment of that nuisance. Worse, while Jerry faces the potential of bumping into a Burdensome Acquaintance every time he leaves the sanctity of his building, Newman is the barbarian inside the gates. When Jerry greets Newman's appearance with his exasperated, repulsed, "Hello Newman," all of the disgust he feels about dealing with human beings in general are channeled into the figure at his door-way.

Fittingly, Newman is a mailman, a symbol of the American neigh-borhood and thus traditionally an honorable profession. But in *Seinfeld*, the neighborhood is a dangerous place, filled as it is with burdensome neighbors. The mailman's job is to go door to door, and, while osten-sibly it is often nice to get mail, the mailman brings much that is un-pleasant. Kramer even tries to block the delivery of his mail in "The Junk Mail" (season 9, episode 5), much to Newman's chagrin.

Actually, Kramer is friendly with Newman, just as he is often warm toward many of the characters his three friends find so annoying. Un-like Jerry, George, and Elaine, Kramer does not assume the worst in people. Still, he knows Newman well enough to know his neighbor is untrustworthy. In several ways, Newman is Kramer's exact counterpart. Indeed, the visible distinction between the gangly Michael Richards and the short, heavyset (at the time) Knight was one of the reasons David and Seinfeld cast the ubiquitous character actor for the part.[4] Kramer is innocent and vivacious, while Newman is sinister and manip-ulative.

Still, Newman is no more or less dangerous than any of the many recurring characters on the show. As we have seen, the sprawling world of *Seinfeld*'s New York is filled with many kinds of people. From New-man's cartoonish villainy to Sidra's reasonable disgust, they all bring their own troubles to the lives of the four main characters. Or more accurately, as the finale would demonstrate, the four main characters spread their own troubles to the people around them.

# 7

# FAITH, RACE, AND PLACE IN *SEINFELD*'S NEW YORK

**W**hen NBC President Brandon Tartikoff worried, after viewing the pilot, that the show was "too New York, too Jewish," he was approaching *Seinfeld* with the same mindset television programmers had shared for half a century. As NBC's head of entertainment, it was Tartikoff's job to oversee content that was entertaining to as many Americans as possible. Then again, shows about New York, shows made by Jewish creators, and shows that fit into both categories had been successful throughout Hollywood history. Furthermore, it's hard to put a finger on exactly what Tartikoff was sensing in the pilot without resorting to stereotypes about attitude, behavior, and voice.

*Seinfeld* indisputably bears the image of its two creators who grew up in New York City with Jewish families. They also happen to be white men, and while Tartikoff was not worried about *Seinfeld* being too masculine or too white, in retrospect, the show was certainly dominated by white men, both in front of and behind the camera.

*Seinfeld* does lean heavily into its New York setting, albeit a fictionalized vision of the real Upper West Side of Manhattan. New York has been a center of American popular culture for more than 200 years, and throughout that period, Jewish entertainers have been an important part of the city's culture. Given the background of its co-creators, *Seinfeld* is part of that lineage of humor from Jewish American comedians, performers, and writers.

## *SEINFELD* **AND RELIGION**

On *Seinfeld*, Jerry's Jewishness is understated. It is barely a part of his identity and not a guiding system for his behavior at all. It comes up most notably in season 8's "The Yada Yada" (episode 19), when he accuses Dr. Whatley of converting to Judaism so that the dentist can make jokes about Jewish people. However, when Jerry goes to Catholic confession to complain about Whatley's convenient conversion, he tells the priest he is not offended as a Jew, but as a comedian.

George, based on Larry David, might also be expected to be Jewish. However, George is never specifically identified as Jewish on the show, and he does not seem to have been raised Jewish. Frank Costanza's family is from Tuscany, Italy, which might make a Catholic background more likely. As for Kramer, who knows? His nonconformist, antiestablishment positions would make an antireligious worldview unsurprising.

Elaine is apparently not Jewish, either by religious choice or ethnic heritage. Like the other characters, religion plays no discernible part in either her self-identity or her moral code. She does date at least two Christians who are seen as substantially more religious than she is. There is David Puddy who, as revealed in "The Burning" (season 9, episode 16), has a "Jesus fish" on his car and listens to a Christian radio station. And then there is Fred, Elaine's boyfriend in "The Pick" (season 4, episode 13), who Jerry refers to condescendingly as "the religious guy." Elaine, somewhat embarrassed, assures him that Fred is "not THAT religious."

The same episode contains a few clues that hint at Elaine's religious upbringing. With Kramer's photographic assistance, Elaine sends out Christmas cards. After discovering that her nipple is visible in the Christmas card photo, she frantically rattles off a list of people that now have an inadvertently intimate photo of her breast. Besides not-THAT-religious Fred, there is Sister Mary Catherine and Father Chelios, suggesting Elaine was raised Catholic. By "The Burning" she has ceased believing in hell, if she ever did before, and she mocks her boyfriend Puddy for his belief in the concept of eternal damnation.

Many religious figures are mocked throughout the series. In "The Bris" (season 5, episode 5), a Jewish mohel presiding over a circumcision is depicted as an over-the-top caricature, as is the gossipy rabbi who lives in Elaine's building in "The Postponement" (season 7, episode 2). On the whole, religion in *Seinfeld* is seen as silly.

Religion is also seen as arbitrary. In "The Conversion" (season 5, episode 11), George converts to Latvian Orthodox so his girlfriend's parents will approve of him. In a real-life twist that shows how *Seinfeld*'s writers room shared the characters' indifference toward religion, the episode's writer, Bruce Kirschbaum, invented the "Latvian Orthodox Church" for this episode . . . or so he thought until the real Latvian Orthodox Church got in touch with him to thank him for drawing attention to their small denomination.

George does get away with his conversion, convincing the Latvian Orthodox priest he is earnest about the faith, getting a high score on his conversion test, and bumbling his way through the ceremony. Unfortunately, he later discovers his girlfriend is moving to Latvia for a year, so their relationship ends anyway.

Overall, Jerry and his friends are skeptical about the idea that their actions on earth have any cosmic significance. In "The Cadillac" (season 7, episode 14), Jerry talks to Kramer about what he should do with a chunk of money he received for a stand-up gig. After sarcastically suggesting he might give a portion to charity, Jerry says he is thinking about using the money to buy his father a Cadillac—his dream car. Kramer eggs him on, telling him, "You're gonna score some big points with the man upstairs on this one!" Jerry returns to his sarcastic mode and responds, "Oh, isn't that what it's all about?" So, while *Seinfeld* certainly avoided delving into the specifics of Jewish faith, it did express a certain skepticism toward religion seen elsewhere in the works of other entertainers with familial roots in Judaism—yet again, Woody Allen is the quintessential example.

## THE NEW YORK SETTING

Tartikoff's fears about the show's potentially narrow focus did not bear out, as *Seinfeld* became a coast-to-coast hit. This shouldn't have been a surprise because its star was already a coast-to-coast hit. No one had a busier stand-up schedule than Seinfeld, who remains a popular draw decades later.

Seinfeld's comedy brand has been called "observational." Whereas the groundbreaking comedians of the generation before him, like George Carlin and Richard Pryor, established a style of humor through self-confession, Seinfeld's act makes fun of the common and the everyday.[1] His humor is inherently universal, though not universal enough for the show to gain much traction overseas (in complete contrast to its contemporary, *The Simpsons*). The hyperfocus on the nuances of American culture make the jokes in both Seinfeld's act and his television show inherently American.

The show's New York City setting is recognizably American, too. Some of the characters' experiences are unique to their setting, but the vast majority of their problems are relatable to everyone watching. Still, the show does draw from and reveal something about the real New York of the 1990s. That it feels anything like the real place owes something to the show's writing, but the feel of the show is mostly created through its production design, overseen by Thomas "Tho" Azzari.

Azzari had a 40-year career in Hollywood as a designer, but his work on *Seinfeld*, which began in season 2, was his most significant. The autonomy that Larry David fought for extended throughout the show's production, and Azzari enjoyed great independence in bringing the writers' ideas to life. Meanwhile, he quickly earned David's faith that his production team could create anything the writers asked of them, from a set of drawers big and strong enough for three Japanese tourists to sleep in, to the illusion of a multilevel parking garage in a one-level studio building.

The first steps in creating the New York City setting are establishing shots—quick glimpses of the outside of Jerry's apartment, the diner, and other locations. As the show was shot entirely in California, it kept a crew on call in New York City to get any new footage needed for a given episode. After the pilot, the show moved to its permanent home at CBS Studio Center in Studio City, California.[2] Once the show left its tenuous early seasons behind and became established on NBC's schedule, *Seinfeld* moved from Stage 9 to the larger Stage 19, where it remained from season 4 through its final season. Compare the last episodes of season 3 to the first episodes of season 4 and you'll immediately sense that the quality of the production has gone up a notch, from its superior lighting to its greater use of studio space. The only other major change for *Seinfeld* was the addition of a large "New York Street" set by early season 6, allowing more elaborate outdoor scenes.[3]

Within the limits of these studios, the Bronx-born Azzari went to work. Occasionally, he would have a still photographer take a photo of a specific space in New York, but in general, Azzari designed by memory and feel. In creating the set for "The Library" (season 3, episode 5), Azzari says, "I didn't go from research. I went from my perception of what a New York library would be."[4] Thus, Azzari's entire process was based not on specificity and verisimilitude but rather on impression and feel. As a result, the show could appear more New York to non–New Yorkers than it did to natives. In another season 3 episode, "The Subway" (episode 13), the show follows the four characters as they have four separate adventures on the New York subway system. The subway car used for the episode was designed to give the impression of New York rather than mimic a subway car exactly. While New Yorkers would have noticed, Azzari says, "a subway car is a subway car to anybody but a New Yorker."[5]

## NEW YORK IN THE NINETIES

*Seinfeld*'s ascendance corresponded to a transitional moment for the city of New York, and some aspects of this transition are captured within the run of the show. The city was emerging from a decade of decline in the seventies, exemplified in historical memory by twin events in the summer of 1977: the New York City blackout and the "Son of Sam" murders. Though the crime rate remained high in the eighties, the rise of the finance industry brought money back into the city. In the nineties, its crime rate began to improve, mirroring a similar trend across the United States. New York City started to become the tourist haven and the playground for the young and the rich that it has remained into the twenty-first century.

Over the run of *Seinfeld*, these changes are noticeable. We have already discussed Kramer's own transformation. Like Kramer, the nature of the show's peripheral characters went from lots of creepy weirdos to lots of amusingly strange oddballs. "The Subway" is more typical of the show's early years when New York was still perceived as a relatively dangerous and downtrodden place. Elaine's subway breaks down. George, in choosing sex with a beautiful stranger over a job interview, is conned out of $8 (all he has on him) and his only suit. Kramer gets lucky when an overheard horse-racing tip pays off and lucky again when he bumps into an undercover cop just as he is about to be mugged. Jerry's story is the most surprising. He falls asleep on the subway and wakes to find the man sitting across from him has taken off all his clothes (figure 7.1). Jerry is shocked and dismayed, but he rolls with this development because, as everybody knows, there are a lot of weirdos in New York.

In later seasons, the characters' interactions with their fellow New Yorkers were sillier and not so sinister. At worst, the weirdos of the city display an unnerving fascination with Elaine. In "The Cigar Store Indian" (season 5, episode 10), Elaine catches the eye of Ricky, a balding *TV Guide* collector, creepily voiced by ubiquitous character actor Sam Lloyd. After Elaine leaves a copy of the *TV Guide* behind, Ricky shows up unannounced at the address on the magazine—George's parents' house—having shredded and refashioned the issue into a paper bouquet. Five episodes later, in "The Pie," the characters come across a

**Figure 7.1.   Scene from "The Subway," season 3, episode 13 (January 8, 1992).**
*NBC/Photofest*

store mannequin model that looks uncannily like Elaine. At the close of the episode, the audience learns the mannequins are being manufactured by Ricky.

The character and his behavior are undeniably disturbing. But in contrast to the violence and criminality the four characters encounter in "The Subway," Ricky comes off as amusingly creepy. Part of the difference is performance; Lloyd plays Ricky with a certain harmlessness. Moreover, his behavior falls well short of that of the mugger who attacked Kramer, or the con artist who imprisoned George, back in season 3.

## *SEINFELD'S* NEW YORK GEOGRAPHY

*Seinfeld* is based in a particular part of New York City, Manhattan's Upper West Side, where Seinfeld lived when he created the show. The exterior shot of Monk's, the diner where the friends hang out, is Tom's Restaurant in the real world, located on Broadway and West 112th Street. Situated near Columbia University, the restaurant has been owned by the same family since the 1940s.

Seinfeld's apartment and the "coffee shop," as the characters often refer to the diner, are the two central poles of the show's universe. In typical sitcom fashion, they are simultaneously living rooms and meeting spots where the characters regularly converge. Functionally for the show's comedy and storytelling, they work as slightly different systems. For one thing, the apartment allows for much more physical action. At the coffee shop, the characters are generally penned in their usual booth, where they engage in their usual routine of conversation—the lifeblood of the show.

Still, the coffee shop is a crucial site of both drama and comedy. As a public space, the quartet is more likely to run into or be interrupted by a secondary character there. This is where the four characters dissect their many social interactions and, in the next moment, put their discussions into action. Think of George in "The Opposite" (see chapter 5), deciding to do the opposite of every instinct he has ever had, and then rising from his seat in the booth to boldly approach a woman at the coffee shop's counter. The coffee shop is an intersection, both theoretically, in terms of connecting the character's philosophies to their behaviors, and geographically, as other characters are constantly coming and going.

Like the titular bar in *Cheers*, Central Perk in *Friends*, MacLaren's bar in *How I Met Your Mother*, and many other public gathering spots throughout television history, the coffee shop in *Seinfeld* is a "third place"—a public place to meet that is neither home nor work. *Cheers* depicted the healthiest third place in television history, a place where everyone knows your name, and where all could witness and perhaps even be a part of whatever shenanigans were happening in that particular episode. *Seinfeld*'s characters would have hated the bar in *Cheers*. Once Claire, the waitress, was written out the series after the pilot, the characters barely interacted with the diner's waitstaff; if they did, it was usually not out of friendship.

Furthermore, the characters hated it when another acquaintance interrupted their time at the diner. For example, Jerry is visibly annoyed whenever Kenny Bania, an annoying fellow comic, runs into him in the coffee shop. Still, the characters liked the coffee shop well enough to keep coming back, even if it did mean they had to interact with other human beings.[6]

Leaving the coffee shop, the four friends could go anywhere in town, from shops and restaurants within walking distance to more distant parts of the city like George's parents' home in Queens. Typically, they get around the city comfortably, but even within the confines of the show, *Seinfeld*'s New York City could feel massive to the characters. Kramer, the embodiment of New York City himself, even gets lost in a late season 9 episode ("The Maid," episode 19) when, dating a woman who has moved to downtown Manhattan, he finds himself at the intersection of First and First: "the nexus of the universe," he fears.[7]

In the very next episode, the penultimate one of the series, the city gets the best of the four. Foreshadowing "The Finale," the quartet loses everything but each other in "The Puerto Rican Day." Returning from a Mets game, they get caught in traffic caused by the annual Puerto Rican parade. Elaine can't get out of the parade area and misses her beloved *60 Minutes*. And Jerry's car is destroyed by an angry mob after Kramer accidentally burns a Puerto Rican flag. Kramer, who previously had been caught up in the excitement, calls Puerto Ricans "a very festive people" and, remarking on their joyfulness, "It's like this every day in Puerto Rico," repeating the same line as Jerry's car is getting destroyed.

The flag burning made this a controversial episode when it aired in 1998, as the president of the National Puerto Rican Coalition protested the show, declaring, "It is unacceptable that the Puerto Rican flag be used by *Seinfeld* as a stage prop under any circumstances."[8] He added that the episode "crossed the line between humor and bigotry." Ultimately, the episode was not repeated on television for several years. Castle Rock came to the show's defense, pointing out that the National Puerto Rican Coalition seemed overly sensitive, as they started complaining about the episode even before it ran. With the show's finale looming, NBC's response was circumspect: "We do not feel that the show lends itself to damaging ethnic stereotypes, because the audience for *Seinfeld* knows the humor is derived from watching the core group of characters get themselves into difficult situations." Still, we should sympathize with Puerto Ricans who were offended as they were not a group that was often depicted on television. For the Puerto Rican community to finally make an appearance on a massively popular show set in New York, only to be caricatured in a farcical scenario, was understandably disappointing. Indeed, people of color were relegated to the margins of *Seinfeld* throughout its run.

## *SEINFELD* AND RACE

For the most part, the New York City the characters inhabited was overwhelmingly white—yet another characteristic the show shared with the films of Woody Allen. The characters had all white friends and romantic partners, and even their colleagues were almost entirely white. A few characters of color did appear, but the diversity of the world of the show did not resemble the reality of the city at the time, and by the end of *Seinfeld*'s run, it was regularly criticized for this fact.

To the show's credit, *Seinfeld* occasionally referenced this criticism, most notably and self-deprecatingly in "The Diplomat's Club" (season 6, episode 21). In the episode, George is trying to get on good terms with his boss, Mr. Morgan, who is black. Trying to be complimentary, he tells Morgan that he looks like Sugar Ray Leonard. Morgan takes offense to this and accuses George of being racist.

Horrified, George begins an episode-long quest to find a black friend in order to prove to Morgan that he is not prejudiced. As the episode's writers admit, this gave them a thinly veiled excuse to go back and show some of the black characters who had appeared on the show over the course of the season, thus answering critics who had noted the show's lack of black characters and, in effect, *acknowledging* that lack.[9] George's search for a black friend subtly mirrors *Seinfeld*'s own defensiveness about its depictions of minorities. Eventually, George calls Carl, an exterminator who fumigated Jerry's apartment in the previous episode, "The Doodle," into the Yankee offices. Finding Morgan has left for the day, George treats Carl to a meal at the restaurant where he knows Morgan will be. Morgan eventually sees through George's ploy and storms out of the restaurant. Moments later, George's black waiter tells him the bill is on the house for Morgan, whom he has mistaken to be Sugar Ray Leonard.

In "The Wizard" (season 9, episode 15), Elaine presumes that Darryl, the man she is dating, is black, and becomes excited at the idea she is in an interracial relationship. However, she later discovers that Darryl incorrectly thinks she is Hispanic because of her last name Benes. "So, we're just a couple of white people?" Darryl sighs. The two are very disappointed. As in "The Diplomat's Club," this episode is a tongue-in-cheek acknowledgment of the show's lack of black characters, revealing how the pursuit of diversity can be disingenuous.

Here and there, the city depicted on the show could feel cosmopolitan, though its international diversity was usually oversimplified, like Babu Bhatt, a Pakistani immigrant who opens a restaurant near Jerry's apartment in "The Café" (season 3, episode 7). When the restaurant struggles, Jerry suggests that Babu convert the menu to his native Pakistani cuisine. In the years after *Seinfeld*, Pakistani restaurants would become more commonplace in American cities, but in this episode, Jerry admits that he has never tried the food, and the restaurant ends up failing.

The next season, Jerry again tries to help Babu, getting him an apartment in his building and a job at Monk's. But Babu is deported back to Pakistan after his visa renewal form gets mixed up with Jerry's mail. Brian George plays Babu with a thick Pakistani accent, and the character has a cartoonish catchphrase—he calls Jerry a "very bad man" and waves his finger side to side in an exaggerated manner. The character is thus not a well-drawn representation of the extensive Pakistani American community in New York City and across the United States.

On the other hand, as in "The Diplomat's Club," the show signals a recognition of the characters' own shortcomings. Jerry's behavior toward Babu is played as satire, as he is overly prideful and inescapably patronizing. In any event, Babu is an all-too-rare example of a non-white character on a show about white people that was created and written by white people.

## THE NEW YORK NEIGHBORHOOD

Part of Jerry's motivation in these episodes is one of neighborliness; Babu opens his restaurant within sight of Jerry's window, and Jerry watches as the business flounders. Indeed, so much of the New York City life depicted on the show feels more like it is taking place in a neighborhood rather than a metropolis. Part of this comes from filming on a set; no matter how good Azzari was at production design, he could not re-create the actual sense of the monumental city. But another part of the neighborhood feel comes from the behaviors and experiences of the characters on the show; they keep running into people they know. Of course, the main characters, especially Jerry, hate this small-town dynamic. He does not want to constantly run into people he knows; he just wants to be left alone, as he explains to Kramer in "The Kiss Hello" (season 6, episode 16). Kramer collects photos of everyone who lives in the building and labels them with names on a bulletin board in the lobby. The result drives Jerry crazy, as he finds himself receiving a polite kiss hello from every woman who lives in the building.

Elaine has an idea similar to Kramer's in season 5's "The Non-Fat Yogurt" (episode 7), but on a much larger scale. She thinks it would be nice if everyone in the city wore name tags. She proposes the idea to her boyfriend, Lloyd Braun, an advisor to the incumbent mayor, David Dinkins, who is facing an election against Rudy Giuliani. (The election mirrored the real world, as the episode aired within a few days of the 1993 mayoral election. *Seinfeld* prepared two different versions of the episode, ready for either a Dinkins or a Giuliani victory.) Lloyd passes the name tag plan along to Dinkins, who goes public with the idea and is immediately ridiculed, perhaps costing him the election and costing Lloyd his job. Elaine pictures New York turning into a friendly city with a small-town vibe. But the city is more like the antisocial Jerry, who bursts out laughing when he hears the idea.

## LIFE BEYOND THE CITY

As much as certain aspects of New York City life could be annoying to the characters, they were much more comfortable in the city and never contemplated moving away. When they did leave for trips beyond the city limits, their travels almost always went poorly. In "The Bubble Boy" (season 4, episode 7), George and his girlfriend, Susan, are on a trip upstate when they almost kill a sick boy who lives in a protective bubble. Then Kramer accidentally burns down Susan's father's cabin before the other friends even show up to enjoy it. The city, ironically, is the far safer place for these characters. The lesson is repeated one more time in the show's finale, when the characters inadvertently end up in a small town. The civic detachment that helps them survive the social world of New York City ultimately lands them in jail in the world beyond the city.

New York City is the center of the world of the show, and the places beyond the city seem silly, frivolous, and backward to Jerry, Elaine, George, and Kramer. Their New York–centric perspective is reminiscent of the famous *New Yorker* cover from 1976. Drawn by Saul Steinberg, the illustration, known as "View of the World," depicts New York City in some detail in the bottom half of the image, and the rest of the world in exaggerated oversimplification in the top half of the image. *Seinfeld* echoes this mindset in many ways, and yet the show remained appealing to Americans far beyond the Hudson River.

# 8

# JERRY AND COMPANY IN THE WORLD AND IN THE BEDROOM

**B**y now I hope it is clear that *Seinfeld* is not really about nothing. The "show about nothing" label was trumpeted by Larry David and Jerry Seinfeld themselves as they proudly differentiated their show from a typical sitcom. When the show was first evolving, NBC execs thought they knew its premise—a show about how a stand-up comedian draws from his day-to-day life to come up with his material. They underestimated how interested Seinfeld and David were in exploring day-to-day existence.

Many observers have described *Seinfeld* as nihilistic—emphasizing a belief in the meaninglessness of life. Certainly, the "show about nothing" boast seems to support that description. On the other hand, when taken as a whole, the show presents an anti-nihilistic message. While *Seinfeld*'s creators often claimed that it was a show without learning, the characters are repeatedly taught one lesson—don't help others. As we will see, in "The Finale" the characters discover that the way they treat other people does matter. Before we turn, in chapter 9, to the message of *Seinfeld*'s 168th episode, let's explore how the characters treated other people in the first 167.[1]

## *SEINFELD* IN THE NEIGHBORHOOD

*Seinfeld*'s New York is emphasized as an unkind place, a world away from Latham, Massachusetts, where the four characters meet their ultimate fate in "The Finale." New York is where the main characters learn to shirk their social responsibilities. In Manhattan, a good deed is rare, and few of their fellow New Yorkers ever go out of their way to help them. Back-to-back episodes in season 3 help establish the show's anticommunal mindset.

In "The Parking Garage" (season 3, episode 6), the gang gets lost looking for their car at the mall; there is nothing like spending several hours in a parking garage to explore the depths of the human condition. As Elaine, holding a bag of water with some new goldfish, begs various people to drive them around the parking garage so they can look for their car, she ends up encountering an interesting cross-section of America. She approaches a polite, middle-class, middle-aged white couple; two younger white women in leather coats who laugh at Elaine; a white man (played by *Seinfeld* writer Larry Charles) with a scruffy beard and a hat pulled low over thick-framed glasses who completely ignores Elaine; a black man in a colorful baseball hat; and two huge, white bodybuilders who offer token politeness but refuse to help.

The black man's response is the funniest, even as it is ultimately the most honest. "I can't do it," he tells Elaine, who presses him for a reason. He repeats his response and then bluntly confirms Elaine's accusation that he simply doesn't want to do it. She again presses him for an explanation for his indifference, asking if he might get some "satisfaction" for lending a hand. "No. I wouldn't," he replies flatly and continues on his way.

The delivery by actor Gregory Daniel is so stoic it verges on absurdity. He looks Elaine in the eyes as he delivers his final line and then punctuates his words by slamming his car door in her face.

No one is interested in driving four strangers around a parking garage. The mall parking garage is a selfish, self-absorbed world where everyone just wants to quietly get to their car and make their way home without interacting with the people around them, much less offering assistance where it is needed.

Throughout their odyssey, the gang encounters other people acting thoughtlessly. Early on, Elaine is nearly struck by a jeep speeding around the garage. Later, Jerry and George encounter a Mercedes convertible parked across two spaces. Jerry eggs on George to spit on the hood, but just as he is about to hock his loogie, the driver returns. George masks his intentions by asking the man about the car's mileage, but the guy just peels away.

Finally, an attractive woman comes to their rescue. George approaches her and she sympathizes with their plight, cheerfully agreeing to drive them around. She quickly changes her mind when George, unheard by the audience, says something offensive about L. Ron Hubbard. She slams on her brakes and throws them out of her car; apparently, she is a touchy Scientologist.

A few hours later, the parking garage is much emptier when the gang finally locates the car. Elaine's goldfish are dead. George has missed his parents' anniversary celebration. Jerry and George have been ticketed for public urination. And almost no one has offered them any assistance. Of course, would any of them have agreed to drive around someone lost in the parking garage? Kramer maybe.

And yet, these are four characters who *think* they are better than the average person, just as we all like to think we are better than most. In the very next episode, "The Café," Jerry tries to help Babu Bhatt, the Pakistani immigrant who has opened a new restaurant across the street (see chapter 7). The message about human decency is once again cynical. Jerry is nauseatingly smug about his own behavior, and his inner monologue is vocalized to reveal his self-satisfied thoughts as Babu praises him as a kind, smart man. "Very great," he calls himself as the camera frames his head alongside a bust of Julius Caesar decorating the wall of Babu's restaurant. But Jerry's help leads to disaster, and eventually Babu declares that Jerry is a "very bad man."

Babu's enterprise is in shambles, but for Jerry, the consequences for his misguided assistance are a few brief moments of self-doubt before his life continues as normal. Still, the lesson is clear—the potential satisfaction for helping someone out isn't worth the potential aggravation that even a passing relationship with another human being might bring.

## *SEINFELD* OUT OF TOWN

Long before "The Finale," *Seinfeld*'s characters found that, while their worldview often clashed with those of their prickly New York neighbors, they flirted with even more disaster whenever they interacted with Americans outside the city limits. In season 4's "The Bubble Boy" (episode 7), the show returns to the "no good deed goes unpunished" moral. The "good deed gone awry" motif is an old one in comedy, but in *Seinfeld*, things tend to go badly in more twisted ways.

In the episode, Jerry agrees to visit a boy whose ineffective immune system forces him to live his life in a protective bubble. (This condition, which is not made up, had been elevated in public awareness by the 1976 television movie *The Boy in the Plastic Bubble* starring John Travolta in the title role.) The boy happens to live in an upstate town, which is on the way to a cabin owned by the father of Susan Ross, George's then-girlfriend.

Despite this geographic coincidence, the bubble boy visit feels like a complete inconvenience to Jerry. As usual, he is barely affected by the suffering of others. Elaine and the bubble boy's father dab their eyes thinking about the poor child when his condition is first discussed, while Jerry takes a napkin to dab sandwich crumbs from his mouth. Jerry feels compelled to visit the boy not out of personal empathy but because, as always, he feels beholden to the expectations of others.

But Jerry never makes it to the bubble boy's house. George, speeding ahead in a car with Susan, loses Jerry and Elaine on the highway. Jerry ends up at a small-town diner where he is coaxed to make another nice gesture—sign a photo for the diner's wall of famous guests. He attempts to avoid this minor inconvenience with a lie; he claims to have no picture, but Elaine calls him on his fib and rushes out to the car to get a photo. Begrudgingly, he signs, "There is nothing finer than being in your diner." Elaine mocks the line, and Jerry starts to feel self-conscious as he pictures future customers reading it. He tries to take the photo back, but the waitress refuses and a scuffle breaks out.

Jerry never wanted to sign a photo in the first place, but it is not in his nature to stand up for his own discomfort. Or rather, it is more uncomfortable for him to take a stand against a social commitment then it is to give up and give in. He might try to wriggle out of them, but he will never refuse outright, at least not in public.

Meanwhile, George and Susan do reach the bubble boy's house. They find not a meek, sympathetic child but a whiny, aggravating adolescent named Donald. Voiced by *Seinfeld* writer Jon Hayman, Donald is depicted only in the form of a gloved hand sticking out of his bubble. George and Susan can see him, but for the audience he is nothing but a grating, nasally, disembodied voice. As Seinfeld points out, comedy demanded the bubble boy be unlikable. "It really wasn't about making fun of anyone," he says. "The point of the thing is not, 'This poor kid.' In fact, we made him a guy you wouldn't have sympathy for and we made him a guy who you wouldn't see."[2]

The bubble boy was thus intentionally dehumanized; the goal was to leave room for comedy. Some advocacy groups protested against the episode but, for the reasons described above, much of the audience found it hilarious. The bubble boy is so obnoxious and coarse that it is hard to think of him as a helpless innocent when, after George gets into an argument with him over a misprinted Trivial Pursuit card—"Moops" versus "Moors"—his bubble breaks and deflates. Jerry and Elaine arrive at the house just in time to see the bubble boy carted into an ambulance. A posse appears on the scene ready to attack the people who harmed the local hero, forcing the gang to flee town.

In the final moments of the episode, the characters arrive at Susan's father's cabin too late to prevent a fire started by Kramer's negligent disposal of a cigar. The cigars were originally a gift from Susan's father to George; generosity costs the man his beloved cabin. No good deed goes unpunished.

## *SEINFELD* GIVES BACK

The bumbling Kramer is more likely than his friends to be charitable, but his efforts are usually counterproductive. His good deeds include turning his adopted stretch of a four-lane highway into two luxurious, extra-wide lanes; tossing a giant ball of oil out a window to see if it is spillproof; and gifting a faulty wheelchair to a disabled woman. Still, if it is the thought that counts, then Kramer comes out on top. He has a generous spirit and does not resist acts of service the way his three friends do.

Then again, Kramer is not immune from the same rules of punishment for his good deeds. The best example is his participation in an AIDS charity walk in "The Sponge" (season 7, episode 9), which ends with him badly beaten by a mob, furious that he has refused to wear an AIDS ribbon. Ultimately, though, "The Finale" condemns Kramer, too. In Latham, he mocks the mugging victim alongside his friends, and the trial reminds viewers of his many imperfections.

At their most generous, all four characters remain self-serving, even Kramer. After Jerry hurts himself with a kitchen knife in "The Blood" (season 9, episode 4), Kramer donates his own blood to help his neighbor recover. For the rest of the episode, Kramer guilts Jerry, his new "blood brother," into granting him a series of favors. Jerry finds himself shaving his neighbor's neck hair and giving Kramer and Newman permission to make sausages in his kitchen. Jerry's annoyed acceptance of this arrangement is reminiscent of his struggle with Kenny Bania, a fellow comedian who gives him a new suit for "free," only to insist Jerry take him out for a meal as payback ("The Soup," season 6, episode 7). Such rules of social exchange leave Jerry just as unwilling to accept a favor as he is to offer one.

The season 4 episode, "The Old Man" (episode 18), suggests the characters subscribe to the belief that service is inherently selfish. Elaine has signed up with an organization that pairs her with a senior citizen. Her task is simply to go to the senior's house and spend time with her, offering merely the gift of companionship. George is taken aback that Elaine would sign up for such a program but becomes intrigued as Elaine talks about how good it is making her feel . . . and she hasn't even met the woman yet! She is much more concerned with the therapeutic benefits she gets from volunteering than any outcome of her efforts. George is surprisingly enthusiastic about participating, although he is always desperate to try anything that might make him feel better. Jerry resists, but his two friends goad him into it.

Given their selfish motives, their volunteering is doomed from the start. Jerry's guy, Sid, is bitter, crotchety, and paranoid. He is unpleasant to be around, so Jerry vows to dump him. He does go back once more, but only so Kramer and Newman can take Sid's vintage records and George can meet Sid's exotic Senegalese maid. In the course of the visit, Sid's false teeth are shredded in the sink and Sid disappears from his apartment.

Elaine is matched with a woman who, to Elaine's amazement, once had a torrid affair with Gandhi. This story is enough for Elaine to momentarily get over her disgust at looking at the woman's face, which has a large goiter. George's experience is briefest of all. Instead of listening to Ben, George makes the senior feel worse by moaning about his own fear of death. Ben fires George from the volunteer position.

As usual, Elaine, Jerry, and George are trapped in their own self-absorption. They cannot serve the community as long as they are only interested in serving their own immediate interests and desires.

As surprised and confused as Jerry and George are when they hear about Elaine's generosity in this episode, they are even more flummoxed in "The Fatigues" (season 8, episode 6) when they learn about the concept of mentorship. In the episode, Jerry is dating a woman, Abby, who has a mentor. George is baffled to learn Abby does not pay her mentor any money. Brushing off Jerry's suggestion of several intangible benefits a mentor might receive from having a protégé, George tries to deduce some tangible gain. Perhaps, he wonders, the protégé might run errands for the mentor? Jerry laughs George off, but by the end of the episode, he, George, and Elaine have all taken on their own protégés.

Jerry makes the unpleasant discovery that the mentor is dating Kenny Bania, the lousy stand-up comic who once gave him a suit. After the mentor sees her boyfriend's act, Bania gets dumped, and Jerry offers to mentor the struggling comic, helping him improve his routine, perhaps paring down his 12-minute bit on Ovaltine.

Meanwhile, also as a result of seeing Bania perform, Abby loses respect for her mentor and they part ways. Mentor-less, she feels lost. George, seeing an opportunity for personal benefit (namely, he needs someone to write a book report on risk management for him), offers to be Abby's mentor. She eagerly takes up his challenge, though ultimately her book report ends up in the hands of Bania, who mistakes it for Jerry's notes. Somehow, he manages to make the risk management report into a hilarious stand-up set. Over at Yankee Stadium, George finds himself reciting a script about Ovaltine to an office of executives, including his boss, Mr. Wilhelm, who proudly claims George as his own protégé.

Making an effort toward self-improvement is already a foreign concept to George and Jerry, but they are particularly confused by the idea of doing so through a subservient, respectful relationship to another person. George, Jerry, Kramer, and Elaine are too lazy and conceited for self-improvement. Even George, who doesn't think highly of himself, seems to think even less of his fellow human beings. He could never lower himself to ask for help and sees people as obstacles, not allies. This attitude helps breed the isolated, lonely lifestyle of the *Seinfeld* characters.

## *SEINFELD* AND SEX

Though it has nothing to do with the Fifth Commandment, Jerry feels a certain obligation—a filial piety—to look after his parents. Of course, it is an obligation that he finds easier to meet when his parents are far away in Florida. He can tolerate an occasional visit, but the longer his parents are in town, the more they impede his usual pursuits. In season 5's "The Raincoats" (episode 18), for example, Jerry is in a hurry to get his parents out of town so he can have more time with his girlfriend; the only place they can find for romance is at a movie theater in the middle of *Schindler's List*.

As discussed in chapter 6, romantic partners also require a set of obligations that Jerry and his friends must navigate if they want to enjoy the fruits of such relationships—namely, sex. The characters have a lot of sex on *Seinfeld*. But for all the sex that Jerry, Elaine, George, and Kramer are having, there is very little discussion in the show about sexually transmitted diseases.

Though the show fell well within the peak years of the AIDS epidemic, the disease wasn't discussed on the show until Kramer participates in an AIDS charity walk in season 7's "The Sponge," an episode that coincidentally deals with Elaine's and Susan's choice of birth control. *Seinfeld's* rise to prominence coincides with several milestones in popular awareness and understanding of the disease:

- End of 1990 (between *Seinfeld's* first and second seasons): More than 300,000 AIDS cases reported worldwide, though the estimated number of actual cases was closer to 1 million.
- November 7, 1991 (the day after NBC first airs "The Café," season 3, episode 7): NBA star Earvin "Magic" Johnson announces

he has HIV, the virus that causes AIDS. This was a cultural milestone for many reasons, perhaps most importantly because it helped overturn the long-held stereotype that AIDS was a disease limited to the homosexual community.

- April 8, 1992 (about one month before *Seinfeld*'s season 3 finale): Tennis star Arthur Ashe announces he has HIV, which his doctors believed he contracted from blood transfusions. Again, this revelation helped spread awareness of how HIV was contracted.

- 1992: AIDS becomes the leading cause of death for American men aged 25 to 44, the same age range as Jerry, George, and Kramer.

- April 1993 (the end of *Seinfeld*'s fourth season): *Angels in America*, Tony Kushner's play about the AIDS epidemic, wins the Pulitzer Prize for Drama.

- October 28, 1993: AIDS is mentioned for the first time on *Seinfeld* in "The Lip Reader" (season 5, episode 6), when Elaine is pretending to be hearing impaired to avoid having to converse with her driver. He asks her if she has considered a hearing aid. Elaine replies, "Am I fearing AIDS? Oh, yeah sure. Who isn't? But you know you gotta live your life!"

- December 22, 1993 (midway through *Seinfeld*'s fifth season): One of the first Hollywood films about AIDS, *Philadelphia*, hits theaters. It stars Tom Hanks and Denzel Washington. Hanks goes on to win the Academy Award for Best Actor for his portrayal of Andy Beckett, a closeted homosexual attorney who is fired from his firm when he begins to exhibit symptoms of AIDS-related Kaposi sarcoma.

- 1994: AIDS becomes the leading cause of death for all Americans aged 25 to 44.

- December 7, 1995: AIDS is mentioned for the second and final time on *Seinfeld* in "The Sponge" (season 7, episode 9) when Kramer participates in an AIDS walk. The episode is about female birth control, but it does not address issues of STD prevention.

- 1996: The number of new AIDS diagnoses declines for the first time. AIDS is no longer the leading cause of death for Americans aged 25 to 44, though it remains the leading cause of death for African Americans in this age group.

- 1997: AIDS-related deaths decline by 47 percent, largely due to advances in HIV medicine.
- 1998 (*Seinfeld*'s final season): Overall deaths and infections continue to decline in the United States, though the Centers for Disease Control and Prevention reports that African Americans make up almost half of all AIDS-related deaths.[3]

As a network sitcom, *Seinfeld* didn't have much to gain by trying to mine comedy from the AIDS crisis. In 2002, four years after *Seinfeld* went off the air, *South Park* declared "AIDS is finally funny" in a season 6 episode, "Jared Has Aides." Many other envelope-pushing comedies on television and elsewhere have cracked off-color jokes about AIDS, among them Larry David's *Curb Your Enthusiasm*.[4] But *South Park* and *Curb* are cable shows, while *Seinfeld* was on network television and subject to not only FCC regulation but also stricter NBC content control.

On the other hand, *Seinfeld* didn't shy away from parodying other major events, from the Nancy Kerrigan-Tonya Harding figure skating soap opera, to the O. J. Simpson murder trial. And the absence of AIDS on a show like *Seinfeld*, in which its characters had a lot of sex with a lot of partners, is particularly significant. Then again, no other network sitcoms and, indeed, few TV dramas dared to include stories about AIDS throughout most of the nineties. In *Seinfeld*'s final season, an episode acknowledged the promiscuity of one of its characters. Unfortunately, the episode spotlights the sexual activity of the woman in the group.

In "The Apology" (season 9, episode 9), Elaine notices her co-worker, Peggy, is behaving oddly around her. First, Elaine spots Peggy using a toilet bowl cover even though no other women work on their floor. Then Peggy throws out a bottle of water after Elaine touches it with her hand but greedily guzzles down another co-worker's bottle after he has taken a drink from it.

Finally, Elaine goes to Peggy's office to confront her. "You seem to be with a lot of men," Peggy explains. Elaine protests and tries to use her on-again, off-again romance with Puddy as an example of a steady boyfriend. (By this point, their frequent breakups were a running joke in the series.)

Peggy agrees that Elaine's love life is none of her business, but Elaine doesn't leave the office. Instead, to Peggy's horror, she rubs Peggy's keyboard against her butt, sticks Peggy's stapler in her armpit, and coughs on the doorknob.

The next day Peggy calls in sick. Elaine goes to visit her, but it is Puddy who consoles Peggy by admitting that he, too, is disgusted by Elaine's germs. He has struggled to work through his own Elaine-related germaphobia. Peggy feels better, but a furious Elaine breaks up with Puddy "for the day."

Falling into the trap of an old and resilient stereotype, it is the promiscuous female character who is considered dirty, not her male counterparts who engage in an identical lifestyle. To be fair, the series does not typically shame Elaine for her sex life, though this is not the first time a female character is critiqued for having a lot of sex. In "The Sponge," Jerry discovers his girlfriend, Lena, is hoarding a huge supply of female birth control. Relieved to discover this side of his AIDS-walk-organizing girlfriend, he thinks delightedly, "She *is* depraved!"

Lena likes the sponge more than any other form of contraception, a preference shared by both Elaine and Susan, George's fiancée at the time. The sudden news that the sponge is going off the market prompts Lena's hoarding and Elaine's desperate search around the city for any remaining boxes of the contraceptive. Once she has secured her own stash, Elaine realizes she must use them with care, prompting her to institute her own screening process for all potential partners to decide if they are "sponge-worthy."

Why doesn't the guy just use a condom? To his credit, George gets a condom when Susan discovers she is out of sponges. But he struggles getting the condom out of its wrapper before the moment has passed. Ironically, in the second and final time AIDS is mentioned on *Seinfeld*, the use of condoms is criticized.

Early in the episode, Jerry and Elaine discover that George doesn't even know what kind of birth control his fiancée uses. "You don't know?!" Elaine is incredulous. George, flummoxed, replies, "I . . . uh . . . figure it's something." Sex remains a tricky conversation topic in the United States, though hopefully more sexual partners have gotten better than George and Susan about communicating about contraception and birth control in the decades since 1995, when this episode first aired. The question of consent, brought to the forefront of cultural consciousness by the #MeToo movement in 2017, is yet another critical reason for communication before sex. Elaine's "sponge-worthy" conversation with her boyfriend, Billy, is played as humorous and ridiculous, but at the very least, it depicts a woman making a clear decision to consent to sex, and a man completely respecting that woman's right to think about that decision.

Whether or not it is a sitcom's responsibility to educate its viewers on health and sex, *Seinfeld* WAS a source of sex education for its viewers. I had never heard of the sponge nor given much thought to female birth control products before I saw this episode when I was 14 years old.

*Seinfeld* also introduced me to concepts like "ménage à trois" (in "The Switch," season 6, episode 11), and other vaguely described sex acts, referenced obliquely throughout the series. Should I have been watching such a graphic show as an adolescent, and even a pre-adolescent? Maybe not, though there are probably worse ways than *Seinfeld* to gain that kind of exposure. My mother, who worked for nonprofit groups providing education on issues of teen pregnancy and safe sex, was always confident addressing the topic of sex with my brother and me. So I definitely had more contextual understanding than the average 14-year-old viewer. Then again, I still don't know much more than George about what the sponge actually is.

Setting aside the show's influence on my own young mind, the promiscuity portrayed on this popular show was surely influential on American sensibilities about sex in the nineties. Jerry's sexual behavior, along with the comparable sexual behavior of his friends, is presented as normal and acceptable within the world of the show.

I'm not saying impressionable young people decided whether to have sex because of Jerry's or Elaine's behavior. There are complex and multifaceted reasons for when and why a young person first has sex. I'm suggesting *Seinfeld* influenced its viewers in ways that are broad, deep, and less easily observed. *Seinfeld* reflects the way Americans thought about sex in the nineties, but the show also influenced Americans' thinking. It's hard to blame *Seinfeld* for punting on the issue of AIDS, but it's equally hard to say the show's failure to discuss AIDS didn't matter. It absolutely did.

Meanwhile, the characters could be offhand about unplanned pregnancies in general. In season 6's "The Chinese Woman" (episode 4),

Kramer becomes concerned after discovering he has a low sperm count. He asks Jerry if he ever impregnated a woman, but Jerry dodges the question. Kramer says it has never happened to him. "Really?" Jerry responds with surprise. "You never slipped one past the goalie in all these years? Boy, I'm surprised. You've slept with a lot of women!" "A lot of 'em!" Kramer shouts, punctuating his agreement with a full-body twitch. Though neither man has ever been married or even expressed a desire to start a family, their flippant discussion seems to presume that Kramer's failure to impregnate any of his partners signifies he is, in this way, less of a "man" than Jerry.

Uncomfortable in the boxers his doctor suggests he wear to improve his sperm count, Kramer switches to wearing nothing at all under his pants—he is, as he puts it, "out there and loving every minute of it." At the end of the episode this switch has apparently been a success. Kramer appears at his window and shouts down to Jerry, Elaine, and George: "Hey, Jerry! Guess what! The Kramer name might live on! Noreen's late! She's laaaate!!"

Noreen, a recurring friend of Elaine's who just started dating Kramer in the middle of the episode, is much less enthusiastic. The closing scene shows her contemplating suicide on a high bridge until Frank Costanza's cape-wearing lawyer (played by Larry David) arrives to lead her down to safety. Kramer, the would-be father, is nowhere to be seen, and the pregnancy is never mentioned again.

While the episode mines humor from Kramer's despicable treatment of Noreen, "The Chinese Woman" skirts the issue of abortion. But the very next episode, "The Couch," addresses abortion directly. Jerry takes immense pleasure in sparking a near riot at a new restaurant being run by a recurring character, Poppie. Deliberately making trouble, Jerry asks the pro-life Poppie about his views on abortion in front of the pro-choice Elaine. Poppie and Elaine begin shouting at one another, and half of the customers walk out of the restaurant while the other half side with Poppie.

Other than Elaine mentioning the Supreme Court, Larry David's script avoids any real political dialogue, and Poppie's argument relies not on a philosophical argument but a vague personal anecdote about his mother. Elaine is, understandably, offended by Poppie's "no intelligent person can think differently" remark. But her position toward pro-lifers is equally firm. She falls in love with Carl, a mover she meets when he delivers a new sofa to Jerry's. Once again playing the instigator, Jerry spoils the romance when he asks her if she knows Carl's stance on abortion. Elaine is heartbroken to find that Carl is, indeed, pro-life, and the revelation ends their relationship.

Jerry's stance, and the attitude of the show overall, is that political extremity on either side is ridiculous. In reality, that is a tricky argument to make about a divisive issue that can be both emotional and personal. But David's script gives it a shot by making a metaphor out of an argument between Kramer and Poppie about how much freedom to give customers at their planned make-your-own-pizza restaurant. "We can't give people the right to choose any topping they want!" cries Poppie. "It's not a pizza until it comes out of the oven!" Kramer declares. Poppie, of course, completely disagrees. Poppie's refusal to allow customers the right to choose any topping they want makes the "pro-life" side look foolish in this metaphor, but the "when is it a pizza" question is equally absurd on both sides. It is the passion of the abortion argument that this episode teases, not the beliefs of either side.

"The Couch" cleverly captures the extreme polarization of the Culture Wars. In retrospect, it is a shame that Larry David and *Seinfeld*'s other writers failed to engage with the AIDS crisis that loomed so large throughout the decade.

David was not an infinite well of ideas for the show, and he would depart *Seinfeld* after the show's seventh season. He would return to write the show's final episode, taking the opportunity to demonstrate that *Seinfeld*'s characters would, after all, face consequences for their behavior.

# Part III

## After *Seinfeld*

# 9

# THE SPECTACLE, THE DISAPPOINTMENT, AND THE BRILLIANCE OF THE FINALE

Even as *Seinfeld*'s popularity skyrocketed, Larry David would end each season lamenting that he was out of ideas and vowing to leave the show.

"I think that Larry was always hoping the show would get canceled," says Louis-Dreyfus. "He was very up front about that with everybody, hoping that would just happen."[1]

While they worked on the pilot, David lived in Seinfeld's house in Los Angeles. Once the episode was completed, he flew back to New York City, certain that the *Seinfeld Chronicles* project was behind him. David was aghast when NBC purchased a tiny first season. How could he possibly come up with material for four more episodes?! And when NBC ordered a 13-episode second season, David predicted imminent failure—he had no stories left.

"I'll never do another TV show," David said midway through season 4, the second season to get a full order of episodes from NBC. "It's just too hard. I've been praying for the show to be canceled from Day 1. I keep trying to get Jerry to quit with me, but he won't."[2]

We should take these proclamations with a grain of salt given David's lifelong attraction to performance, his self-deprecating public persona, and his post-*Seinfeld* body of work. Still, when David did, finally, fulfill his threat and leave the show after season 7, Alexander mused, "For Jerry, it's fun. For Larry, it's blood and agony."[3]

David's season 7 storyline could thus be read as a metaphor on his predicament: George traps himself in an engagement to Susan (Heidi

Swedberg), a woman he does not care for. According to David, he and Jerry agreed that this seventh season would be the last season (figure 9.1). The other actors were on board with that decision too, but ultimately the four stars decided they were having too much fun to stop. They signed on for one more season (and, eventually, one more after that), but David was done.

"I would have preferred if we had ended this year, yes," David said, when announcing that the show would go on without him.[4] And the show would go on for not one, but two more seasons.

At the end of season 7, Susan dies, poisoned from licking toxic wedding invitation envelopes. David's fictional alter-ego, George, is now unencumbered and liberated. Restraining his jubilation, he reunites with his friends, and the quartet exits the hospital heading for the coffee shop. Their show would go on. So, I guess in this metaphor, David was Susan.

In June 2015, Jason Alexander created a stir after discussing Susan's death on Howard Stern's radio show. According to various media aggregations of the interview, Alexander said the idea to kill off Susan was rooted in an offhand comment by Louis-Dreyfus, who had been finding it difficult to play off Swedberg in their shared scenes. Social media swarmed, and the story evolved into the premise that Susan was killed off on *Seinfeld* because everyone hated working with her.[5] Alexander quickly clarified his comments and jumped to Swedberg's defense, praising her as both a person and a performer. He did admit that he felt, at the time, that there was something "off" about his scenes with Swedberg.

In the aftermath, Alexander took to his own social media account, tweeting, "Oh dear God, leave Heidi alone," and linking to a lengthy explanation: "Heidi would always ask if there was anything in the scenes she could do or if I had any thoughts. . . . If I had had more maturity or more security in my own work, I surely would have taken her query and possibly tried to adjust the scenes with her. She surely offered. But, I didn't have that maturity or security. And, Larry and Jerry would probably have killed me as it was all playing exactly as they wanted. Clearly Susan and George were coming off just the way they wanted."[6]

Indeed, Susan's off-ness, performed so consistently by Swedberg, was perfect for the unease George and the other characters felt around her. Moreover, remember that Swedberg appeared in 11 episodes

Figure 9.1.    Larry David and Jerry Seinfeld on set. *NBC/Photofest*

throughout season 4, and then was brought back for an even larger role in 17 episodes across season 7. If David or any of the stars had had strong feelings about working with Swedberg, they surely would have figured that out in season 4 and avoided bringing her back for the engagement storyline in season 7. They even brought Swedberg back for a brief cameo in season 9's "The Betrayal" (episode 8), the backwards episode. I'm with Alexander. Leave Heidi alone!

Perhaps Alexander is correct, and an offhand comment sparked an idea in David's head that he could kill off the character—not the actress. Once that idea was executed (pardon the word choice), David did depart, leaving it up to someone else to come up with an idea of what to do about the ghost of George's fiancée.

Seinfeld inherited the job of show runner for the final two seasons, taking on a heavy load as an actor, writer, and producer. Seinfeld quickly announced he was ditching the stand-up routines that bookended the show, saying they were too much of an added burden to write. Also, the star couldn't help but delegate more responsibility to the hands of his talented writers. By then, the staff was filled with a new generation of writers replacing the original minds behind the show like David and Larry Charles. Incidentally, when Charles departed the show after season 5, he had more script credits (16) than anyone besides the show's two creators.

Still, the show-runner position was a burden for the stand-up comic. After two seasons at the helm, Seinfeld was ready to call it quits. He wanted to return to his stand-up act, and he wanted freedom to pursue other projects, as did many others associated with the show. NBC threw money at him to keep the show going, offering as much as $8 million per episode—eight times as much as he made for season 9—but Seinfeld turned it down.

In the aftermath of the final season, Seinfeld's agent, George Shapiro, reflected on the hype of that final circuit. "It was overwhelming. In fact, I think it was too much," Shapiro said. "All of us were really happy when it was over."[7]

All?

Certainly not the executives and bean counters at NBC. And not the tens of millions of fans who would keep watching the show in reruns, on DVDs, and via streaming platforms for decades. Many on the show's production crew would have voted to keep the show running—a steady job on a hit TV show can be hard to find. But the writing staff had already turned over several times. David was two years gone. And the stars were ready to move on.

Besides, David's darkest fears always had a ring of truth to them. How long could they keep coming up with new ideas for a show that ran 22 episodes a season, each with two, three, even four storylines apiece? Already, TV critics were writing their "*Seinfeld* is past its creative prime" pieces.

Of course, with nostalgia and money bringing many nineties shows back to television in the late 2010s, David and the cast could take home huge paydays for even a single half-hour reunion special. But by 1998, 180 episodes were already more than enough for them, and, with the important exception of the cast's reunion for *Curb*'s seventh season, the show has remained dormant since the finale.

## CONTEXT

What a cultural moment that finale was! The final episode, called "The Finale," may not have lived up to its hype, but it was a unique moment in time, a snapshot of its context in the television industry, in the nineties, and in American history itself. A brief timeline around the episode reveals *Seinfeld* was not alone in the extreme attention it received, both from the media and the public.

- December 19, 1997: After a tumultuous production, which prompted predictions that the film would bomb at the box office, *Titanic* hits theaters. The film went on to win the Academy Award for Best Picture and eventually earn a record-breaking $2 billion worldwide in ticket sales.
- January 17, 1998: The online gossip and news website, The Drudge Report, breaks the news of President Bill Clinton's relationship with White House intern Monica Lewinsky.
- May 14, 1998: "The Finale" airs at 8:45 p.m. on NBC.
- June 14, 1998: Michael Jordan leads the Bulls to a last-second victory over the Utah Jazz, winning the NBA Championship for the sixth and final time of his career in the highest-rated finals in NBA history.

- September 4, 1998: Google is founded.
- January 10, 1999: The first episode of HBO's *Sopranos* airs, marking the beginning of the end for broadcast television's dominance over scripted television.

This was a time of excess and frenzy in a moment when both the American media and the American audience were more consolidated than they were about to become. Like *Titanic*, you didn't have to watch *Seinfeld* to have an opinion on it. Like Monica Lewinsky or Michael Jordan, *Seinfeld* coverage was almost impossible to avoid.

Soon enough, the television audience would be much more fragmented across a broadening spectrum of options. The continued rise of the internet would spark other communication inventions, each of them seeking to capture the attention of Americans. The *Seinfeld* finale could not happen again. To wit, the much-hyped 2003 *Friends* finale drew about 50 percent fewer viewers than the *Seinfeld* finale had five years before. To date, no episode of scripted television has approached the size of the audience for *Seinfeld*'s "The Finale."

## HYPE

But the hype for the last episode of *Seinfeld* started long before May 14, 1998. For a few years, critics and fans wondered whether each season would be the last for the series. Thus, speculation that the ninth season was indeed the final lap for the show was met with skepticism until Seinfeld himself confirmed the decision. A day after Christmas 1997, the comedian told the *New York Times* that he and the rest of the cast and crew "were all together" on the decision. In truth, though he consulted his co-stars, the decision rested with Seinfeld alone. With ratings still surging, the showman decided to leave on a high note.[8]

In the new year, the show's production would begin to plot their final moves, while NBC executives could drown their sadness by selling ads for "The Finale." Much of the coverage in the months before the episode focused on the price of advertising, which even climbed near Super Bowl levels to an average of $1.5 million for 30 seconds of ad space.[9]

Other networks began planning their counterprograming for May 14. For several seasons, CBS, ABC, and Fox had essentially given up trying to schedule a sitcom against *Seinfeld*'s Thursday-night time slot; they stuck with that strategy for "The Finale." Over on cable, the TV Land network gave up entirely, going dark during the hour-long episode with a notice saying that they were watching *Seinfeld*, too.[10] On the eve of "The Finale," an ABC sitcom, *Dharma & Greg*, paid homage with a storyline about characters having sex in public while the entire city of San Francisco was home watching the final episode of *Seinfeld*.

"Spoiler Alert!" culture is a relatively recent development, born from the post-*Seinfeld* time-shifting technology that allowed viewers to record episodes and watch them at a more convenient time. Still, the plot of "The Finale" was a closely guarded secret, inviting much speculation. The *Boston Globe* was among several newspapers to hold a contest for readers to submit their ideas for the final episode.[11] A script of "The Finale" did appear on the internet, but NBC insisted (truthfully) that it was not accurate—the plot had Jerry and the gang relocating to Beverly Hills. In March, three *Seinfeld* writers appeared on Fox News to tease viewers with made-up excerpts from the episode.[12]

On April 8, most of the episode was filmed in front of a live audience made up of the cast and crew's friends and family, all of whom signed affidavits saying they would keep the plot a secret. Even so, the audience was escorted out before the production filmed the very last scenes.[13] The dozens of recurring actors brought back for "The Finale" also signed confidentiality agreements and only received a portion of the script. "The secrecy. It's unlike anything I've ever experienced," said John O'Hurley, who played Peterman.[14] Despite the show's efforts, by the eve of "The Finale," the bones of the final plot had made its way to the media. A few publications accurately reported the spoilers that the quartet witness a carjacking, get arrested after failing to intervene, and are put on trial.[15]

As the big day approached, speculation began that *Seinfeld* might beat *M\*A\*S\*H*'s mark for 125 million viewers; half the country's televisions were tuned to that finale on February 28, 1983. However, with the rise of cable in the 15 years since that episode, the number of television channels had exploded, and the American television audience had already spread out substantially. NBC research anticipated around 75 million viewers.

Ultimately, just over 76 million viewers watched the *Seinfeld* finale, 14 million less than that year's Super Bowl, and 4 million less than the *Cheers* finale earned in 1993. Other than Super Bowls, the only other program to top *Seinfeld* since that *Cheers* finale were the two nights of the 1994 Winter Olympics when Nancy Kerrigan and Tonya Harding skated—a phenomenon *Seinfeld* parodied in the season 6 finale, "The Understudy."

Even if the final numbers did not meet the expectations of the most ambitious observers, *Seinfeld* did capture the attention of the nation. But before we turn to what the audience saw on that evening in May, we should pause to stress that not *everyone* was caught up in the hoopla. As with the series as a whole, "The Finale" proved to be a phenomenon for a largely white American audience.

## "NO ONE HERE IS REMOTELY INTERESTED"

On New Year's Day, 1998, just a few days after Seinfeld confirmed the end of the series, another classic sitcom aired its series finale. For a certain demographic category, the show was in second place, and yet its network decided to cancel it after five seasons. The show was *Living Single*, and it was in second place among black viewers when Fox pulled the plug.

By contrast, *Seinfeld* was the 54th most popular show for black viewers in its final season. That score actually marked a notable surge—in previous seasons, *Seinfeld* had not even cracked the top 100 among black viewers. [16]

*Living Single*, a sort of Bizarro *Seinfeld*, similarly remained outside the top 100 for white viewers and was low in the overall ratings. Fox decided to pull the plug, along with two other shows that were popular with black Americans: *Between Brothers*, a comedy, and *413 Hope St.*, a drama. More than just a purge of shows that were not bringing in a broad audience, these cancellations marked a change in strategy for the Fox network. Launched in 1986, Fox faced an uphill climb to approach the ratings of the Big Three: NBC, CBS, and ABC. Fox developed shows to counter the programming of the traditional networks, including series that might appeal to an audience—like black Americans— that the Big Three had neglected. By 1998, Fox had made up a lot of ground, thanks in no small part to getting the rights to broadcast NFL games in 1993. Setting its sights on larger audience numbers, Fox dumped *Living Single*.

The fate of *Living Single*, beloved in its time and remembered fondly by fans and critics alike, is a microcosm of network television's trouble with race in the 1990s, a problem that *Seinfeld* personifies. As we have seen in chapter 7, the show depicted four white characters living in an overwhelmingly white New York City. It is thus not surprising that black viewers did not flock to the show. (The show did, in fact, rise to second place among Latinx viewers in its final season, though the number of Latinx characters on television throughout network television in the nineties made the number of black characters look like an army.) Amid the hoopla of the approaching finale, the issue of race and *Seinfeld* was somewhat neglected.

Journalist Amy Alexander brought it up halfway through *Seinfeld*'s final season with an opinion piece in the *Boston Globe*. "I don't think I'm alone among black Americans when I say that 'Seinfeld' was never a 'must-see' proposition for me," she wrote. While applauding several popular dramas, like ABC's *NYPD Blue* and NBC's *Homicide*, for their diverse casts, Alexander correctly observed that *Seinfeld* was typical of the vast majority of network sitcoms in depicting a "World without Blacks."[17]

As "The Finale" loomed, the *Los Angeles Times* sought out opinions on the hype from both the black and Latinx communities. Jannette Dates, dean of the School of Communication at Howard University, a historically black school, called it a "nonevent" for the black community. And while many bars and restaurants were planning *Seinfeld* viewing parties, the manager of a bar in Ladera Heights, a predominantly black section of Los Angeles, said, "No one here is even remotely interested in 'Seinfeld.'"[18]

While race was not a major subject in the coverage of *Seinfeld*'s last episode, its demographics were commonly understood throughout American culture. In the San Francisco of *Dharma & Greg*, with the entire city seemingly deserted during "The Finale," the titular couple prepares to publicly fornicate on the steps of the federal courthouse. Before they can begin, Greg's boss, who is black, spots them. Dharma, flustered, reminds him that he should be rushing home to catch the show. "Yeah, right," says the boss sarcastically, clearly referencing his racial identity. "My whole family is home watching *Seinfeld*."[19]

## ONE WEEK TO GO

A week before the final episode, "The Puerto Rican Day" episode created another talking point for *Seinfeld*'s critics. The exaggerated depiction of New York's Puerto Rican community, discussed in chapter 7, undermines the episode's longevity as a possible classic. That controversy aside, this episode sought to ride the rising excitement with the approaching finale, calling back to a few old *Seinfeld* jokes and referencing nineties popular culture at large.

With David penning the script for "The Finale," the entire season 9 writing staff joined forces writing the script for "The Puerto Rican Day." In retrospect, it was a loaded group of talents, including Jennifer Crittenden (later a writer for *Everybody Loves Raymond* and *The New Adventures of Old Christine*), Dan O'Keefe (writer for *The League* and *Silicon Valley*), Alec Berg (show runner for *Silicon Valley* and co-creator of *Barry*), Jeff Schaffer (co-creator of *The League*), and David Mandel (writer and show runner for *Veep*).

In its ambitious scale, "The Puerto Rican Day" is among the most epic of *Seinfeld* scripts. Elaine's journey is even a parody of epic nineties disaster films; she finds herself leading a group of ragtag survivors lost under the parade bleachers and trying to find a way out of the crowd. Jerry spends much of the episode searching for his MacGuffin— a television set to catch the end of the Mets game—while George pursues his nemesis—a guy following him around with a laser pointer.

"The Puerto Rican Day" is a bottle episode, except the bottle is the crowded, sprawling streets of Manhattan. Unfolding in real time, "The Puerto Rican Day" is thus an inversion of episodes like "The Chinese Restaurant" or "The Parking Garage." This time, instead of waiting for a meal or looking for their car, the gang is simply trying to get home.

The episode also offers a heavy dose of fan service, with an extensive callback to the fake personas Jerry, George, and Kramer have crafted over the years. Jerry fashions himself into Kel Varnsen before he unexpectedly runs into George as Art Vandelay and Kramer as H. E. Pennypacker.

The original idea for "The Puerto Rican Day" production was bold: fly the show out to New York City and, for the first and only time, film on location. Ultimately, with "The Finale" itself looming, that plan was scrapped for time and resources. Still, the episode has a grandiose feel to it. While the episode did not set up any stories for the final episode's plot, it did set the stage for an even more grandiose conclusion.

With "The Puerto Rican Day" in the books, the hype grew higher than ever. The only question was whether David's script could meet the impossibly high expectations.

## LARRY DAVID RETURNS

David's departure after season 7 along with his return for the season 9 series finale brought about a reappraisal of his role in *Seinfeld*'s success. For much of the show's run, Jerry Seinfeld's fame overshadowed David's contributions in the public's mind. If you go back and search newspaper and magazine archives from the early nineties, Larry David profiles are few and far between, while Seinfeld lived at the highest levels of American celebrity culture throughout the decade.

By the time the finale rolled around, fans of the show were more familiar with David's importance to the series, not only as a co-creator, but as the real-life George Costanza and the inspiration for so many of the show's funniest plots. Now, with the anticipated finale approaching, journalists pressed David for interviews. He was as reticent as ever. For a *New York Times Magazine* feature, he tried to steer the writer to his fictional counterpart: "I would say that, knowing George, you know more about me than you do if you speak to me. Because I feel like I'm the phony, I'm the fake. People who are talking to me, they're not getting sincerity, for the most part. They're getting something, they're getting politeness, they're getting a nice person, but it's not real. I think George is much more real than I am."[20]

As far as the fate of George and the rest of the gang at the show's conclusion, David kept that information in the vault. When his own mother begged him not to kill off the main characters, he told her, "That's up to me, not you!"[21] Indeed, it *was* up to David alone. The script for "The Finale" came not out of collaboration with the writers' room but from his own mind, and he returned to both write and produce the final episode. In typical form, he was certain that it would be a failure. The fact that many critics and fans do consider it a failure may explain why David has resisted announcing a final season for his widely loved *Curb Your Enthusiasm*. Understandably, he would like to avoid anything approaching both the pressure and the letdown he must have felt before and after "The Finale."

## RECEPTION

*Seinfeld*'s last episode is remembered as one of the most disappointing series finales in television history. The truth is a bit more nuanced. Among its viewers, the immediate response to the episode was mixed, but leaning positive. One nationwide poll reported 55 percent of respondents rated the episode good or very good, while the other 45 percent said it was disappointing.[22] Not bad, considering another survey reported that half of the show's viewers said they wouldn't miss *Seinfeld* much.[23]

A few television critics responded quite favorably to "The Finale." In particular, the characters' hometown papers loved what they saw. The *New York Times* critic said, "The hilarious final episode was everything *Seinfeld* was at its best: mordant, unsentimental and written by Larry David (who helped create the show and left a few years ago). Wildly self-referential and slightly surreal, the final episode revels in petty details, turns clichés on their heads and reveals why *Seinfeld* worked so well."[24] And the *New York Daily News* reviewer proclaimed that the episode managed to live up to all the hype, and *Seinfeld* "vaulted itself into the very exclusive club of TV series with really great finales."[25]

Perhaps the show did fulfill Tartikoff's pronouncement so many years before that *Seinfeld* was "too New York" because elsewhere across the nation, there were many unfavorable reviews:

- *Orange County Register*: "An uneven, overly contrived anti-climax."[26]
- Associated Press: "Little about the finale's idea or execution was funny. Nor did the creaky setup do justice to a typical air-tight *Seinfeld* script, which braids several stories through a compact half-hour."[27]

- *Baltimore Sun*: "It was static and linear, the exact opposite of the innovative, cross-cutting narrative style that the sitcom introduced to prime time. By *Seinfeld* standards, it was a downright boring kind of storytelling. Seinfeld and David . . . offered lots of fond memories, but no meaningful sense of closure for the nine years of our lives that many of us shared with their show."[28]
- *Los Angeles Times*: "It had its moments, and its concept was clever enough. But it delivered many fewer yucks than yadas. The 45-minute howl of a retrospective that preceded the finale worked against it, in effect, by reemphasizing just how breathtakingly funny and unique *Seinfeld* had been, compared with how meekly it was bowing out."[29]
- *Dallas Morning News*: "No rave review for you!!! For a heartening half minute or so, it looked like the whole miserable, mocking lot of them would go down in flames on a plunging private plane. But the plane righted itself, allowing Thursday's mega-hyped *Seinfeld* finale to instead go up in flames."[30]

Many shows have come and gone since *Seinfeld*, and every series finale proves anew how hard it is to create a finale that pleases everyone. A series finale has a lot to accomplish, and while the *Seinfeld* finale succeeded in offering a final assessment of and fate for its four characters, those accomplishments sidetracked another goal: being hysterically funny.

*Seinfeld* always relied on mining comedy from the minutiae of daily life, but in "The Finale," David's plot goes broad. While the show's many recurring characters always lent a certain realism to *Seinfeld*'s neighborhood, parading those characters through "The Finale," like an impossibly long line of clowns getting out of a clown car, tipped the show into an uncanny valley. What was usually a careful equilibrium of grounded ridiculousness spilled over into a sprawling, unwieldy story.

What was David thinking?

## "THE FINALE" ITSELF

Well, like all writers facing the daunting task of coming up with an ending, Larry David had to be thinking about quite a lot. Even if "The

Finale" was far from the funniest *Seinfeld* episode ever—using one online yardstick, IMDb.com users rate it as the weakest of all episodes from season 4 on—neither the production nor the performances are fatally flawed. The problems are found in the script itself. David's ideas were well thought out and even ingenious. But put together as a final statement, several of his decisions collapsed under the weight of expectations because they betrayed much of what the show had always been.

The plot of "The Finale" is quite straightforward—an immediate red flag, as the best *Seinfeld* plots are delightfully twisted and convoluted. NBC revives George and Jerry's old TV pilot and, as a bonus, gives the gang a chance to take a corporate jet anywhere in the world. En route to Paris, Kramer's clumsiness forces the plane to make an emergency landing in small-town Latham, Massachusetts. While waiting for the plane to be repaired, the quartet observes and mocks an overweight man being mugged. They are arrested under a "Good Samaritan" law that requires a witness to offer reasonable assistance to a person in danger. The subsequent trial takes up most of the episode, becoming a national spectacle as the prosecution brings up witnesses from the foursome's past to prove their antisocial characters (figure 9.2). They are ultimately convicted and sentenced to a year in prison. The series ends with a final scene of Jerry performing stand-up, this time in his orange prison garb, trying out prison-related material on a sullen audience: "What are you in for? Grand theft auto? Don't steal any of my jokes!"

The courtroom trial was the centerpiece of the episode. As a gimmick, the prosecution's strategy of attacking the backgrounds of the four protagonists allowed David to use the finale to bring back as many old characters as he could fit in the courtroom set. Indeed, moments before the verdict is read, the camera pans the courtroom to find familiar faces jammed awkwardly around the room, which is so crowded that many of them are forced to stand. The typical delight the audience might receive from the reappearance of one old familiar face was buried under the avalanche of recurring characters.

The cast and crew had a wonderful time filming this episode—a reunion for so many performers involved with the show over the years. "I felt there were really great things about ['The Finale']," Alexander said nearly a decade after the episode. "We were a really unsentimental group, but we always did love our bench of players. . . . The way Larry David found to get everyone on who had been part of our success over

**Figure 9.2.    Scene from "The Finale."** *NBC/Photofest*

the years was poetic. And the fact we had these four characters who were the most selfish people on the planet getting what they deserved? That was great. But as a story it was a mishmash."[31]

Nostalgia plays an inevitable part of just about every series finale, and this opportunity for a cast reunion made "The Finale" extremely nostalgic, a contradiction for a show that had always been defiantly unsentimental. As multiple reviewers noted, the audience had just sat through a sentimental (and hilarious) 45-minute clip show prior to the finale. Then "The Finale" gradually turned into another, less funny, clip show.

## THE COURTROOM BACKDROP

As the central setting in what was meant to be a grand send-off, the crowded, static courtroom was inherently problematic. However, it was not fatally flawed; quite a few *Seinfeld* episodes over the years had borrowed from the then wildly popular courtroom TV genre.

For example, retired baseball all-star Keith Hernandez, who returned for "The Finale," first appeared in season 3's two-parter, "The Boyfriend" (episodes 17 and 18). That show included a storyline that satirized the courtroom scenes from Oliver Stone's *JFK* (1991), describing Kramer and Newman's accusation that Hernandez spit on them after a game, and flashing back to the "magic loogie" with grainy footage that resembles Abraham Zapruder's 8-mm film of the Kennedy assassination.

In another two-part episode that, in its final moments, references *Nixon*, another of Oliver Stone's presidential biopics, "The Cadillac" (season 7, episodes 14 and 15) depicts the impeachment trial of Morty Seinfeld as his neighbors investigate him and eventually vote to remove him from his position as condo association president.

The show's most famous lawyer (in my opinion, the second funniest lawyer after Frank Costanza's cape-wearing divorce attorney) was Jackie Chiles (Phil Morris), a recurring Johnnie Cochran knockoff who returns for a featured part in "The Finale." "The Caddy" (season 7, episode 12), the second appearance of Chiles, culminates with an extended reference to the 1995 trial of O. J. Simpson, for whom Cochran was a lead defense attorney. Cochran infamously helped goad the Simpson prosecutors into asking the Hall of Fame running back to try on a bloody glove found at a murder scene. On *Seinfeld*, Chiles asks Elaine's nemesis, Sue Ellen Mischke, to try on a bra that she was wearing as a top when Jerry crashed his car.

That had not been the only time *Seinfeld* referenced current events. In fact, it wasn't even the only time the show referenced the story of O. J. Simpson and the events surrounding the death of his ex-wife, Nicole Brown Simpson, which had captivated Americans from the summer of 1993 through the October 1994 verdict. The Simpson trial was on TV in the *Seinfeld* writers room, just as it was on cable news every day throughout the country, marking the rise of courtroom TV as a spectator event. *Seinfeld* satirized this rise throughout its run and one last time in "The Finale."

The media circus that descends on the characters after they are arrested in Latham resembles the type of frenzied coverage surrounding many events throughout the nineties, including both the Simpson case and even the *Seinfeld* finale itself. With the rise of social media still years away, media hype in the nineties was best represented by a crush of television cameras. It was 24-hour news television that led coverage of events like the 1994 Kerrigan/Harding figure skating fiasco, and the 1998–1999 Clinton/Lewinsky scandal. In "The Finale," *Seinfeld*'s quartet finds itself similarly under a national microscope.

## GOING BIG

In the seven seasons he presided over *Seinfeld* as its show runner, David had relied on self-referential humor with great success. *Seinfeld*'s show-within-a-show earned the sitcom its one and only Emmy for Outstanding Comedy Series for its fourth season. The meta joke that year was simply a thread that ran throughout the season, culminating in a season finale that was grand but, in retrospect, not one of the classic episodes of the year. Like "The Finale," "The Pilot" (episode 23) is loaded with callbacks and character returns.

Maybe David learned the wrong lesson from that Emmy? Like "The Pilot," "The Finale" is *broader* than the typical *Seinfeld*. Relying on nostalgia, the jokes are not as clever as usual. And the plot definitely unfolds on a larger scale. Rather than the humorous day-to-day minutiae interfering with, say, a trip to a Chinese restaurant, or a strange character interfering with, say, the attempt to buy soup, the idea itself is the big joke—the characters face a highly public trial and imprisonment for being themselves.

To be sure, big, crazy stuff happened in many episodes of *Seinfeld*. But whether it was George pulling a golf ball out of a whale's blowhole or Kramer rolling a giant ball of oil out a window onto the head of Jerry's girlfriend, those big moments were the culmination—and often the intersection—of little ideas. Kramer hitting golf balls into the ocean + George trying to impress a woman by claiming he's someone he isn't. Kramer trying out another in a long series of inventions + George working at a playground equipment company + Jerry's girlfriend being annoyed at a stupid voice Jerry and his friends had come up with. Those stories found silliness in little things. "The Finale" sought silliness in bigger things.

"There was a lot of pressure on us at that time to do one big last show, but big is always bad in comedy," reflects Seinfeld. "Small and cheap and quick" makes better comedy, he believes. "That's why TV is always funnier than movies, because you don't have that much time and that much money."[32]

The episodic structure of television also allowed *Seinfeld* to reference itself over the years. Occasional self-referential winks were some of the best parts of the show, and self-references are a typical characteristic of any series finale. But "The Finale" was so self-referential that it departed from the familiar, probably right around the moment the characters depart their own familiar stomping grounds and board the NBC jet.

A good series finale also ties up the lives of the main characters in a way that is satisfying. Audiences would like to leave with a sense that the characters they have invested so much time in are going to be okay. While critics pointed out some of the flaws in the structure of "The Finale," many viewers were simply unhappy to see the quartet sent to prison. From its development, *Seinfeld* had been nontraditional and proudly subversive—defiantly *not* a typical sitcom. In sending his characters to jail, David took a chance on subverting expectations one last time. No hugging, no learning, and apparently no happy ending.

## ON THE OTHER HAND . . .

Of course, sending these loathsome characters to jail was *perfect*. They did deserve some reckoning for their behavior, as the trial makes quite clear. These were bad people.

Some critics made this observation while the series was ongoing. With a month to go before "The Finale," *Washington Post* TV critic Tom Shales went against the grain, attacking the show in a piece called "So Long, 'Seinfeld.' Let Me Show You to the Door."[33] Shales calls the show "troubling" and "sour" and blames the series for helping proliferate sitcom characters who are "cold, uncaring, cynical and maybe even misanthropic." He blasts the show for offering mean-spirited caricatures of Jewish characters and tastelessly using the Kennedy assassination for humor. Dismissing the suggestion that *Seinfeld* reinvented the genre, Shales concludes, "What 'Seinfeld' has helped spread through network television is darkness."

After "The Finale," Shales once again went against the grain. This time, his review was extremely positive: "In their misbehavior, we sometimes saw unsettling realities we recognized about ourselves and our own worst instincts. Although the show's creators always eschewed the notion of teaching lessons through a sitcom, the way it ended suggested that 'Seinfeld' was something of a morality play after all."[34]

While "The Finale" failed to approach the show's own comedic standards or meet the impossible expectations for delivering a satisfying experience to its 75 million American viewers, it succeeded in using the series finale to offer a final commentary about itself. Because, of course, it wasn't the prosecutors, judge, or jury of Latham who decided the characters were guilty. It was David and Seinfeld themselves. A happy ending would have vindicated nine years of bad behavior.

Briefly, "The Finale" tantalizes the characters—and their fans—with the possibility of triumph. The NBC deal is a huge career victory for Jerry and George. But it's also an affirmation of all four lives. Their fictional show, *Jerry*, is based on the quartet, so the NBC of this fictional universe is saying, "Your lives are special. People would be interested in you." Nowadays, in the age of "Likes," such an affirmation comes cheap and regularly. At the end of the twentieth century, a few short years before the reality television revolution, there were few higher compliments. On the verge of this achievement, a higher power intervenes. The law, and perhaps fate or God or karma or something else, confirms George's long-held fears—God wouldn't let them be successful. They should be punished for their lives, not rewarded.

The characters' unhappy fate might have soured many viewers, but the conclusion that these four miserable souls should be damned, not praised, might be the most optimistic ending possible. Then again, that faith in a higher moral code was perhaps the most jarring element of "The Finale" and perhaps its most significant betrayal of the hilarious, provocative universe the show typically depicted. For once, the consequence of their actions was not nothing, but something.

## FULL CIRCLE

It is tempting to derive a more layered meaning from the events of "The Finale." Since that May 1998 evening, many fans have sought an existential explanation of the episode. Maybe the characters died in the plane crash after all? Maybe small-town Latham was purgatory, and prison is their eternal punishment? Our last sight of the characters is fitting, as prison offers an abundance of what they supposedly love—a life of nothing.

In fact, David's final message is quite clear.

Jerry's prison stand-up set is the coda for the entire series, added late to the script to ensure the episode ended with a few big laughs. Unfortunately, confined in a women's prison, Elaine is conspicuously absent from the last moments of the series. The last time we see the four characters together is in the Latham lockup, after they have been convicted. This is the best moment of "The Finale" and the true final statement that David would want the show's viewers to take away.

The characters are seated on two hard benches in the cell, Jerry and Kramer facing George and Elaine, an arrangement seen many times before at the coffee shop. It's shot from the same angles: a wide shot picks up the foursome, while two other cameras provide close-ups of each pair. As the camera slowly pulls back, Jerry and George begin discussing the placement of a button on George's shirt. They go back and forth a few times before Jerry starts to wonder if they have had the same conversation before. George isn't sure, but indeed they have. It was a word-for-word reenactment of the first conversation the two characters have in the opening scene of the series pilot.

In jail or in the coffee shop, the characters are exactly the same. Even with their guilt confirmed, these characters cannot and do not learn their lessons. Incapable of change, they fall back into their flawed, unfixable selves.

# 10

# TELEVISION LEGACY

**B**oth Jerry Seinfeld and Larry David have acknowledged and accepted the consensus of disapproval toward "The Finale." Still, they have defended the episode's vision and, gradually, some critics have found it fashionable to take the position: "*Seinfeld*'s last episode wasn't that bad!"

In a 2014 podcast appearance, David was happy to hear the host praise the show for trying to do something different from the typical finale. "I was not interested in an emotional ride, and neither was Jerry," explained David. "No wonder why they [the audience] would dislike it, yeah. But let me toot my own horn for a second. I thought it was clever to bring back all those characters in a courtroom and testify against them for what they did, and then show those clips, and also for why they even got arrested in the first place. And then to wind up— forget the self-aggrandizement here—I thought it was clever."[1]

In *Curb Your Enthusiasm*, David continues to blend his cynical take on day-to-day living with wacky, wild scenarios. Just as in *Seinfeld*'s fourth season, art imitates life in *Curb*'s fourth season; David's character wins a part on Broadway's *The Producers* in what turns out to be a scheme by Mel Brooks to make money off a failed Broadway show—à la the plot of *The Producers*.

And then, of course, the entire seventh season revolves around a *Seinfeld* reunion. David seemed to treat this as an opportunity to correct some of the missteps of "The Finale," and the season includes several references to its poor reception. At the same time, he also took advantage of the chance to create an actual reunion for both cast and crew in the rebuilt set of the show (figure 10.1). Since "The Finale," George has gotten married and made a fortune with an app that finds the closest and best public bathrooms, then lost it in the Bernie Madoff Ponzi scheme, prompting his wife to divorce him. Now living with Jerry, the plot of the reunion episode follows George's efforts to reunite with his wife, just as the Larry character on *Curb* is trying to win back his estranged wife, Cheryl. Even in this universe, Larry borrows ideas from his life to use in *Seinfeld*.

Throughout *Curb*'s long run, David has yet to announce a series finale. Nor has he continued his *Seinfeld* routine of vowing that each upcoming season will be his last. Instead, with HBO's blessing, his show goes on "hiatus" until David comes up with more ideas; the hiatus between seasons 8 and 9 lasted more than six years. David has thus found a loophole to avoid dealing with the pressure he faced in 1998 with *Seinfeld*; if he never announces an end, he never has to face the pressure of a finale.

While many critics and TV fans have argued that *Curb* exceeds *Seinfeld* in quality and humor, even David would admit that his HBO show has a much lower degree of difficulty in several ways. Whereas at *Seinfeld* he was obligated to produce about 24 half-hour episodes of television each year, he only makes 10 episodes of *Curb* per season. *Curb* episodes run a little longer because HBO does not have commercials, but HBO also grants its creators some flexibility in the timing of their episodes; *Seinfeld* had to adhere to a precise network schedule, leaving time for commercials. As a broadcast network, NBC is regulated by the FCC, a handicap *Seinfeld* cleverly dealt with through innuendo and metaphor. *Curb* is explicit in both language and content, and a typical episode would garner FCC fines within its first moments if it appeared on NBC.

Still, both shows unmistakably descend from David's brain. Taking the reins of the show as he did with minimal television experience, David learned many lessons from his work on *Seinfeld*. In its comedic tone, its worldview, and even its premise, *Curb* is unmistakably *Seinfeld*'s descendant. *Curb* is *Seinfeld*, only more so.

Just as Seinfeld played a fictional version of himself in *Seinfeld*, David plays a caricature of himself on *Curb*. The Larry David on the show is a wealthy comedian famous for co-creating *Seinfeld*. Here, the

**Figure 10.1.** The cast of Seinfeld reunited in 2009 for the seventh season of *Curb Your Enthusiasm*. *HBO/Photofest*

style of *Curb* starts to diverge from its predecessor, as the specificity of Larry's achievement immediately creates the impression that *Curb* is more realistic than *Seinfeld*. Other details further emphasize that realism.

David has many famous friends, and throughout the years, many of these celebrities have appeared as themselves on the show. Again, *Seinfeld* did the same thing, with appearances by pro athletes (Keith Hernandez, Derek Jeter), politicians (Rudy Giuliani), and famous actors (Jon Voight, Bette Midler), all playing themselves on the show. *Curb* takes these cameos further, making the celebrity culture of Larry's life in Los Angeles an essential aspect of the show. Larry routinely hangs out with Richard Lewis (34 appearances through nine seasons) and Ted Danson (21 appearances). Most of the regulars on the series play characters that share their first name. Cheryl Hines plays Larry's wife, Cheryl David. Jeff Garlin plays Larry's manager, Jeff Greene. And Susie Essman plays Jeff's wife, Susie Greene.

Given the tight parallels to the real world, viewers can be forgiven for making the understandable mistake of thinking everyone on the show is playing a version of themselves. When I first watched the show, even while I understood I was watching a work of fiction, I remember being confused about whether Hines was married to David in real life. Don't scoff at my stupidity! Apparently, after the series began, one of Hines's real-life friends was offended to have not received an invitation to their wedding.[2]

More than the casting, the show's dialogue further adds to the illusion of realism. Here again, David seems to have found a way to make *Curb* with much less stress than *Seinfeld* gave him. His trick: no scripts! Instead, he creates a rough outline of every episode and scene, and the actors ad lib through their interactions. David will shoot a scene multiple times to see what improvised comedy might ensue each time, but as long as the actors hit the precise plot points he has laid out, he doesn't care what words they use to get there. In this way, even though the characters do not acknowledge the cameras, *Curb* can often feel even more like a mockumentary than *The Office*, which first appeared in its British iteration on BBC about a year after *Curb*'s first episode on HBO.

In fact, *Curb* did start as a mockumentary, a one-hour HBO special about Larry planning a one-hour HBO special. David says he got the idea when, after leaving *Seinfeld*, he started working on stand-up material and a friend suggested he have a film crew follow him around as he prepared his return to the stage. The always reticent David balked at that idea. Instead—and this might sound familiar—he started coming up with some ideas for a made-up story to intersperse within his comedy routines.[3]

It is worth pausing to reflect on how important this special was for David's career. Besides leading to one of the greatest comedy series of the new century in *Curb*, it cleared the slate for David, who had just suffered two perceived failures: the *Seinfeld* finale, and *Sour Grapes*, the only feature film David has written to date.

Unlike "The Finale," the reviews for *Sour Grapes* were not mixed—everyone hated it. "I can't easily remember a film I've enjoyed less," said Roger Ebert. "The material, the dialogue, the delivery and even the soundtrack are labored and leaden. How to account for the fact that Larry David is one of the creators of 'Seinfeld'? Maybe he works well with others."[4] It's a brutal review, but without the success of *Curb*, that very well could have summed up David's legacy, and Seinfeld would have carried much more of the lasting credit for the show they both created.

Fortunately for David, an old friend from his early stand-up days, Chris Albrecht, had risen to president of original programming at HBO. There, Albrecht was in the process of revolutionizing television, having just launched *The Sopranos* and *Sex and the City*. Despite the lingering aftertaste from *Sour Grapes*, Albrecht gave the go-ahead for the HBO special, called *Larry David: Curb Your Enthusiasm*. It aired October 17, 1999, and the new series began almost exactly a year later.

David's other masterpiece, *Seinfeld*, will never return, while *Curb* might never end. Beyond this most obvious descendant, *Seinfeld* launched a subgenre of sitcoms that tread in its wake, occasionally expanding on its brilliance in different ways.

## FRIENDS AS FAMILY

"It's about sex, love, relationships, careers, a time in your life when everything's possible. And it's about friendship because when you're single and in the city, your friends are your family."

If you squint, that could be a description of *Seinfeld*. The show didn't think much about love, but *Seinfeld* was certainly about sex, relationships, and careers. And the four friends were certainly each other's family, more close-knit than their actual family members.[5]

In fact, that quote is from a 1993 pitch for a new show that was trying its own twist on *Seinfeld*'s success. *Seinfeld* imitators began to appear as soon as the show became a hit. Some of the imitators were on NBC, and some were even paired with *Seinfeld* on Thursday night, as NBC tried to use *Seinfeld*'s success to buoy other new sitcoms. This particular knockoff was the best of the bunch: *Friends*.[6]

*Friends* is a lot like *Seinfeld* except its cast is younger and sexier. More of a serialized romantic comedy than an existential social satire, *Friends* nevertheless could approach both the goofiness and cynicism of *Seinfeld*. The *Friends* pilot tested almost as poorly as *Seinfeld*'s, but *Friends* was an immediate hit, and by its second season it found a permanent home on NBC at 8:00 p.m. on Thursdays, an hour before *Seinfeld*'s time slot. The two shows came to be seen as prototypical fictionalizations of American single life in the city at the turn of the century. They also share a common theme in the idea that friendships have become more meaningful than either family or career.

This was a key shift from the first four decades of television sitcoms, when the nuclear family—a married woman and man, often with one or more kids—had been the basic building block for scripted comedies. By the 1970s, workplace sitcoms had emerged. The parting message of the last episode of *The Mary Tyler Moore* show encompasses the theme of so many workplace sitcoms throughout American TV history, as Mary Richards tells her co-workers, "Thank you for being my family."[7] By the end of the seventies, the life of single people in the city became an increasingly popular theme on sitcoms. *Cheers*, technically a workplace sitcom, anticipates the hang-out culture of *Seinfeld* and *Friends* as well as the long-running "will they/won't they?" romance in *Friends* (a trope that *Seinfeld* defiantly avoided).

What did the rise of the friends-as-family sitcom mean? This commonality of both *Seinfeld* and *Friends* is directly related to a few key themes of twentieth-century American history. The post-1970s rejuvenation of American cities led to the rise of the young urban professional (see chapter 5). And, not unrelated, Americans were getting married at a later age. Decades later these trends remain, and thus the legacy of these two great friends-as-family sitcoms remains apparent throughout television. Whenever a character goes on an awkward date, then meets up with her friends at a coffee shop to tell the story . . . whenever a character has a rough day at work, then heads to a bar to commiserate with his friends . . . you're watching a show that has its roots in NBC's Thursday night.

Two other successful shows that, briefly, ran on NBC's Thursday night in the 1990s are interesting contrasts. *Mad About You* was a rare example of a show that NBC successfully replanted on a different night after incubating it on Thursdays for its first two seasons. Created by and starring Paul Reiser, opposite co-star Helen Hunt, the show was about two newlyweds. While *Mad About You* was ultimately sentimental toward marriage, *Seinfeld*, in contrast, was disdainful toward the institution. Marriage is a prison, Kramer warns Jerry, and George learns this lesson all too well when he gets engaged to Susan. By the end of the episode, Susan is snuggling up to a miserable George as the recognizable theme to *Mad About You* plays on their bedroom television set. For George, it seems, the only thing worse than watching *Mad About You* is watching *Mad About You* with a woman he is going to spend the rest of his life with.[8]

*Frasier* also briefly aired on Thursday, taking *Seinfeld*'s 9:00 slot for two seasons after "The Finale." A spin-off of *Cheers*, *Frasier* is likewise a bit difficult to categorize. It is about a father and two brothers, but it also includes regular workplace scenes. With the amount of time the main characters spend in their favorite coffee shop, *Frasier* often looks a lot like *Seinfeld*. More than *Cheers*, *Frasier* leaned into the kind of comedy of conversation that *Seinfeld* emphasized. Even Dr. Frasier Crane's catchphrase is "I'm listening," although the self-absorbed lead is not quite as good a listener as he thinks he is.

Despite its similarities to *Seinfeld*, *Frasier* is definitely not a friends-as-family show. It actually depicts two adult sons overcoming the kind of generational gap with their father that was so often a source of comedic exasperation for Jerry and George. Like *Friends* and *Cheers*, *Frasier* has a long-running "will they/won't they?" story. Like *Friends*, the conclusion of that story ultimately upholds marriage as the romantic ideal.

Over on Fox, a few of *Seinfeld*'s contemporaries were arguably just as ambivalent about marriage. *The Simpsons* satirized the very idea of the nuclear family as the linchpin of American life. Social conservatives of the early nineties criticized the show as being anti-family. Ultimately, over the long run of *The Simpsons*, it has become perhaps the most pro-family and pro-community show on television, even while remaining a consistent parody of American culture.

That leaves only one other sitcom that matched—and even surpassed—*Seinfeld*'s anti-marriage, anti-family position. Fox's *Married . . . with Children* was arguably the most subversive comedy of its moment. While the Simpsons seemed to stay together because they loved each other despite their flaws, the Bundys seemed stuck together despite the fact that they didn't even like each other. *Married . . . with Children* is perhaps the alternate future for George, the hell he faced if Susan did not poison herself with envelope glue.

Most of the rest of the characters across the television sitcom landscape were, despite their flaws, good people. It is hard to find any characters in the nineties who arguably deserved to go to jail by the end of their series. That changed in the new millennium as *Seinfeld*'s legacy penetrated into the very soul—and souls—of television sitcoms.

## THE GANG GETS EMPOWERED

"It isn't really a show about anything. It follows these young guys, who you don't want to like because they're sort of despicable but you can't help but like."

That's not Larry David describing the Elaine-less pilot of *Seinfeld* in 1989, but Rob McElhenney explaining in 2005 the premise of a sitcom he had co-created, *It's Always Sunny in Philadelphia*, which was about to debut its first episode, "The Gang Gets Racist," on FX.[9] McElhenney stars as Mac, alongside co-creator Glenn Howerton (Dennis), Charlie Day (Charlie), and Kaitlin Olson (Dee). After a low-rated first season prompted FX to insist the show add Danny DeVito to its cast, *Sunny*—slowly, gradually, eventually—caught on, even as it pushed the envelope with its coarse humor. Over the show's long run on FX and into syndicated and streaming riches, it has managed to disprove its early critics who thought it was too vulgar and mean-spirited to actually be intelligent.

Emily Nussbaum, the *New Yorker* critic and, for me, the "poet laureate" of the post-2000 television landscape, celebrated *Sunny*'s 50th episode in 2013: "It looks stupid but is in fact smart. It seems cruel but is secretly compassionate. Mostly, it is very, very funny. Laugh-out-loud funny. At its finest moments, cackling-in-the-basement-while-huffing-glue funny."[10] *Sunny*'s bleak brashness makes it uneasy to love, but as Nussbaum points out, that's the way the gang likes it:

> It's not as if dark shows can't be popular: "Seinfeld" was a hit, after all. Yet, as impressive as "Seinfeld" was, it had no muck in it. It was icy and calculated, with its anger banked. In part, this was because of who the members of the "Seinfeld" gang were: educated Manhattanites with safety nets. In contrast, the "Always Sunny" characters are gutter punks—mostly Irish-Catholic drunks, although the twins [Dennis and Dee] grew up rich, with a Nazi grandfather—with no skills, intractable addictions, terrible families, and little capacity to get anywhere except the Jersey Shore, where they end up fighting over a "rum ham."[11]

As *Sunny*'s second season began, *Philadelphia Inquirer*'s Jonathan Storm called it, lovingly, "Seinfeld on crack."[12] That review has stuck, and FX has even used it to promote the show. Indeed, the premise—three men and a woman mistreat each other and those around them—is identical to *Seinfeld*. From there, the shows vary by only a few degrees. Instead of hanging out in a coffee shop, the *Sunny* gang hangs out in a bar (which they own). Their get-rich-quick schemes are more likely than Kramer's to cross into criminal behavior (though Kramer was known to flaunt interstate bottle deposit laws in his day). Their parents are frequently involved, but in much more grotesque and dysfunctional ways than in *Seinfeld*. Most prominently, DeVito's brilliant, appallingly base Frank Reynolds, father of Dennis and Dee (and, probably, Charlie), makes George's father (also a Frank!) look like a saint. While *Seinfeld*'s four characters were never quite as smart as they thought they were, *Sunny*'s four idiots think they're the smartest people in the world, despite all evidence to the contrary.

*Sunny* thus takes *Seinfeld*'s framework one step further into darkness. At the same time, when it is at its most brilliant, *Sunny* occasionally dares to dabble in political and social satire, something that *Seinfeld* tended to avoid. For example, *Seinfeld* never tried to parody the Israeli-Palestinian conflict, as *Sunny* did in season 2's "The Gang Goes Jihad." In this way, *Sunny* is at least a notch above the rest of the shows in the "friends acting nasty" subgenre that proliferated after *Seinfeld*.

There is one more apt comparison between *Sunny* and *Seinfeld*, involving the relationship between show and network. Just as NBC did with *Seinfeld*, FX's chief John Landgraf stuck with the show through its barely rated first few seasons. Like *Seinfeld*, *Sunny*'s creators were unproven but, like *Seinfeld*'s backers at NBC, Landgraf liked what they were doing and believed the rest of the world would, too, when they discovered the show. Indeed, Landgraf's strategy throughout his long, successful run at FX has been based on giving free rein to creative people.

Since *Seinfeld*, and in light of FX's successes, creative freedom has become more typical in the traditionally fraught relationships between networks and the people who actually make their shows. Not that *Seinfeld* is the sole reason for this change—the industry has evolved so much, in so many ways, since "The Finale"—but Larry David's insistence on autonomy from NBC laid the groundwork for many independent-minded show runners that followed him. In terms of television output in the twenty-first century, the quality of FX's programming has been second only to HBO, the subscription-based cable service that led the way into a new Golden Age of television. Since *Curb Your Enthusiasm*, HBO's most critically acclaimed comedy has been *Veep*, another show about bad people that traces its roots back to *Seinfeld*.

## VEEP

"There is an authority to this character that I feel I have because I've been doing this a long time," Julia Louis-Dreyfus once said. "There's also an insecurity underneath that authority, and that's something I'm very comfortable with. I don't feel that secure, you know."[13]

As you've probably guessed, Louis-Dreyfus was not talking about Elaine, but rather her character, Vice President Selina Meyer, ahead of *Veep*'s debut in April 2012. The role ultimately confirmed her as one of the greatest comic actors of her time.

Louis-Dreyfus is the only woman to win an acting Emmy for three different comedy series, having taken the award in *Seinfeld*, *Veep*, and *The New Adventures of Old Christine*. The latter ran for five acclaimed seasons on CBS. In that sitcom, Louis-Dreyfus plays "Old" Christine, a divorced mother whose ex-husband has coupled up with a younger woman, "New" Christine. "Old" Christine is a bit of a lovable mess, swilling wine while she juggles her parenting responsibilities, her work at a fitness center she co-owns with her friend, and her brother who lives in her guest house.

Never quite in control of her busy life, Christine takes even more ribbing from the other characters on the show than Elaine did from her snarky friends. Christine is a lot like Elaine, as the character plays into Louis-Dreyfus's ability to perform unearned self-confidence. With Christine, however, Louis-Dreyfus lets a lot more desperation bubble to the surface. As the title cruelly point out, Christine is not as young as she used to be, and her life has not become what she hoped it would be.

These are themes that Elaine occasionally referenced, especially late in *Seinfeld*'s run, when she often expressed a desire to break free from her life of nothingness. On *Old Christine*, this Louis-Dreyfus character did get to the other side, only to discover the grass was no greener.

These character themes continue into an entirely different context in *Veep*, where Louis-Dreyfus plays a politician, Meyer, who has ascended to the verge of the most powerful job in the world. The role fits Louis-Dreyfus's talents perfectly. Like Elaine and Christine, Selina is never quite as great as she thinks she is.

*Veep*'s creator, Armando Iannucci, is a Scottish comic writer with a penchant for political satire. *Veep* is adapted from his BBC series *The Thick of It*, which, for four seasons (or "series," as the Brits say), follows mid-level, political machinations within the British government. Iannucci also received an Academy Award screenplay nomination for his film *In the Loop*, a satirical movie about an Anglo-American push for war in the Middle East. These political comedies are not primarily about corruption, extremism, or incompetence (though there is plenty of incompetence to laugh at). For Iannucci, politics is a catch-22. The nature of the political games and the nature of the power-hungry people who seek to play them dooms any chance of developing good policy. Serving the public good is too far down the list of leaders' priorities.

The office of the vice president of the United States, so close to and yet so far from the pinnacle of power, is the perfect embodiment for Iannucci's ideas. For Louis-Dreyfus's Selina, that frustration is the story of her life, and the office of vice president, where she toils for a distant, unseen president, epitomizes the dead-end cycle of her own life's pursuits. Selina is unlike Louis-Dreyfus's other characters; it is hard to imagine Elaine running for office. And yet Selina's characterization is very similar to Elaine. Selina is deeply flawed but not lacking in intelligence, utterly cynical but not without a hint of idealism, selfish and vain but not completely unlikable.

While *Seinfeld* is built around its creators' senses for finding comedy in the minutiae of everyday American culture, in *Veep*, Iannucci flexes his strength in mining comedy in the minutiae of America's power culture. The episode-to-episode disasters that Selina and her staff face are not world-threatening debacles but the kinds of gaffes that the American 24-hour news cycle adores. As Iannucci explains, "If something awkward is happening, my instinct is to make fun of it."[14] Neither Iannucci nor David and Seinfeld invented that approach to comedy, but all three seem to have a microscopic vision for locating comically awkward moments in their particular field of focus.

Iannucci steered *Veep* for four seasons before David Mandel, who worked on both *Seinfeld* and *Curb Your Enthusiasm*, took over as show runner for the final three, just as life in America increasingly seemed to imitate the art of *Veep* with the rise of Donald Trump. As Louis-Dreyfus said in her fifth-straight Emmy acceptance speech in 2016, a couple of months before election day, "Our show started out as a political satire, but it now feels more like a sobering documentary."

One major difference between Louis-Dreyfus's work on HBO's *Veep* and her previous work on network television: she gets to swear a lot. Iannucci is the Van Gogh of comical cussing, and the sprawling cast of *Veep* gets to curse fast and often. Though the halls of Washington, DC, are a long way from the back alleys of Philadelphia or the sunny streets of Los Angeles, both the language and the behavior of the characters in the classic cable comedies of the early 2000s—*Veep, It's Always Sunny in Philadelphia*, and *Curb Your Enthusiasm*—are often equally filthy.

Once upon a time, Larry David won his second Emmy for Outstanding Writing for a *Seinfeld* script that never used the word "masturbation," even though it was the subject of the entire story. In "The Contest" (season 4, episode 11), after George's mother catches him in the act, the four friends have a bet on who can go the longest without masturbating. Throughout the episode, David writes a variety of creative euphemisms to avoid upsetting NBC executives or FCC regulators. The genius of "The Contest" comes from the many clever ways the show discusses sex without being too explicit. Even without using naughty language, *Seinfeld* created a world of naughty characters. Subsequent sitcom characters in the *Seinfeld* tradition have gotten naughtier and naughtier.

## JERRY SEINFELD AND THE STARS

As the television industry changed with more channels and more options, the opportunities for comedians expanded. Larry David was one of the first to capitalize on this shift with *Curb* on HBO. More than a decade later, Jerry Seinfeld also found his way to success in the new media landscape with a show that was innovative in its own way.

*Comedians in Cars Getting Coffee* began as an independent venture. Using the internet itself as a distribution platform, Seinfeld sought out sponsorship and put together a small crew to help produce his idea for a talk show. Sony hosted the series for a while on its streaming platform, Crackle, but episodes were eventually available for free on YouTube before Netflix bought the archive and funded new episodes of the show.

The title, *Comedians in Cars Getting Coffee*, is the show. Seinfeld picks up a famous comedian or other celebrity and takes them to a coffee shop. Their conversation is filmed and edited into a 10- to 20-minute episode. Seinfeld, who has been linked to late-night talk show hosting gigs since the NBC execs brought him in for that first meeting, thus found a way to build his own talk show. But it is a talk show that looks more like *Seinfeld* than Letterman or Leno. It resembles what *Seinfeld* fans might imagine the co-creators' conversations looked like—the very thing that inspired the show in the first place. Fittingly, David himself was Seinfeld's very first guest on the show's first episode, released on July 19, 2012. In it, David observes, "You have finally done the show about nothing."

Since then, Michael Richards, Julia Louis-Dreyfus, and Jason Alexander have all appeared on the show. The latter appeared in character as George in the sixth episode of the show's third season. A portion of the episode aired during coverage of the 2014 Super Bowl. David wrote and directed that episode, which finds George and Jerry (also in character, though who can tell?) discussing Super Bowl party etiquette. George was not invited back to a certain party after "over-cheering" for

the Giants and using the master bathroom. Their conversation is interrupted by Wayne Knight, in character as Newman. For their transpor-
tation in the episode, Jerry drives the AMC Pacer, a two-door car from
the seventies that was marketed as "the first wide small car." Infamously
unreliable, it is the George Costanza of cars. The two make their way to
Tom's Restaurant in Manhattan's Upper West Side. This time, they
actually go into Tom's, not a studio somewhere in Los Angeles.

In the final moments, Jerry can't get the Pacer to start, leading
Alexander to break into laughter. The moment is reminiscent of season
3's "The Parking Garage" (episode 6), when the quartet spent the entire
episode wandering a mall garage in search of their car. That episode
also ends with the car not starting, an unplanned but serendipitous
moment that prompted the weary performers to break into laughter—
all except the always-on Michael Richards, who struggles at the wheel,
trying unsuccessfully to get the engine to turn over before the episode
fades to black.

The appearance in the final episode of the first season of *Comedians
in Cars Getting Coffee* was a rare one for Richards, whose comedy
career all but ended after an infamous outburst at a Los Angeles comedy club. Upset about the noise and heckling from a group in the audience, he responded by shouting racial epithets at them from the stage.
Someone else in the audience recorded a video of the scene, which was
subsequently posted on the gossip website TMZ.com. It was 2006
(about a year after YouTube was founded), and the clip went viral, an
early example of a celebrity scandal in a new era of technology.

A few days later, Seinfeld was a guest on *Late Night with David
Letterman* when Richards appeared via satellite to offer an apology.
Despite Seinfeld doing his best to serve as, essentially, a mediator between Richards and the public (a role he would fill on *Comedians in
Cars Getting Coffee*, albeit in lighter circumstances), the apology was
awkward and unsuccessful. The incident will forever be a part of Richards's bio, and the video remains the first thing that appears if you
search "Michael Richards" on YouTube. The performer's career has
never recovered, although he poked fun at the incident on *Curb* during
the *Seinfeld* reunion season, and, in a more genuine tone, admitted its
haunting resonance in his life during his appearance in *Comedians in
Cars Getting Coffee*.

Seinfeld himself has managed to avoid the minefield of American celebrity for several decades now. His romance with 17-year-old Shoshanna Lonstein is a distant memory. Few can recall the more recent lawsuits he and his wife, Jessica, faced after she was accused of plagiarizing another author in her cookbook *Deceptively Delicious: Simple Secrets to Get Your Kids Eating Good Food* (2007); the lawsuits were eventually dismissed. Jessica and Jerry met while she was engaged and started dating right *after* the honeymoon for her first marriage. The two have now been married for two decades and have three kids. None of these prickly issues have stuck to Jerry Seinfeld. He continues to sell out his tours, while *Comedians in Cars Getting Coffee* can probably continue on Netflix as long as he wants it to.

Seinfeld is the Michael Jordan of comedy. Though they are separated by almost a decade in age, both rose to fame in the eighties and ascended to the heights of their professions in the nineties. Both have their public blemishes, but they have shaken off any permanent stains by remaining defiantly nonpolitical. They both symbolize a certain era of celebrity, now passed. They are more self-aware than prior generations of celebrities but much less accessible or active than younger celebrities of the social media era. Both attained an impossibly larger-than-life persona while somehow maintaining a reputation of authenticity without ever really letting the public in behind their shell.

All this helps to make Seinfeld the perfect host for a talk show wherein two celebrities act as though they are normal people having a normal conversation. While *Comedians in Cars Getting Coffee* is groundbreaking in its own way, it is not a particularly creative show in terms of comedy or storytelling. Aside from his moderately successful animated film, *Bee Movie* (2007), Seinfeld has avoided the sort of fictional storytelling that made him a television legend. Other comedians have used the opportunities in television for innovative and acclaimed storytelling, daring to engage with both their own inner persona and the world around them with a vulnerably confessional style—a mode Seinfeld has always resisted. Nevertheless, many of these shows bear a clear resemblance to *Seinfeld*.

## LOUIE

For a brief moment, Louis C.K. was perhaps the biggest comedian in America, reaching a consensus of critical acclaim that even his friend, Jerry Seinfeld, had not quite attained. Finally, in 2017, with the explosion of the #MeToo movement, long-whispered rumors became public when the *New York Times* reported on five women who had accused the comedian of sexual misconduct. All of the women had met C.K. through the stand-up industry, and many of them cited C.K.'s behavior as a defining moment—an encapsulation of the seedy obstacles female comics face—that ultimately drove them out of show business. C.K. quickly responded with an acknowledgment: "These stories are true."[15]

Immediately, his film, *I Love You, Daddy*, about an older film director who seduces the teenage daughter of C.K.'s character, was shelved indefinitely. In distressing echoes of C.K.'s behavior, the film included scenes of a character simulating masturbation in front of others, as well as people dismissing rumors of the character's sexual misconduct. Many other appearances and projects were canceled, and C.K. disappeared from the public view. About a year later, he returned to the comedy circuit with new material. While many criticized his reappearance, Seinfeld was among many comedians who defended his comeback.

*Seinfeld* depicted bad people who, despite ultimately facing punishment for their actions, nevertheless seemed unwilling and unable to learn and grow. Indeed, "no learning" was a mantra of the show. Louis C.K.'s comedy has always been built on his own frankness in admitting his flaws. He even alluded to his misconduct for years in his act and his other creations, long before 2017. Public confession has long been a strain of some of the best stand-up comedy, and his self-deprecation helped give C.K. a pass for years in pushing the envelope in the graphic content of his humor.

We might imagine C.K., somewhere out there, shouting, "I've been telling the world I'm not a good person for my entire life! Why are you all acting so shocked?" But confession alone does not excuse the act. Self-deprecation can be funny, but it can also risk sidestepping the destruction left behind. It can distract from the need for real personal transformation and growth.

The cynicism of *Seinfeld*—the argument for the impossibility of human change—seems to carry over into the story of Louis C.K. It *is* hilarious to watch characters be bad people and do bad things. Taken to the extreme, however, that message excuses bad behavior as inevitable and bad people as unchangeable. C.K. embodies the darkest reading of *Seinfeld*. He watched four TV characters laugh their misbehavior away on the most popular show on television and subsequently built a career out of laughing his own, even worse behavior away.

The public persona of Louis C.K. is inextricable from the art he created, all the more so because he performed a version of himself in so much of his creations, from the comedy club to television. While acknowledging that the man looms inevitably over his work, let's turn, finally, to that work and its many connections to *Seinfeld*. Interestingly, the best of *Louie* refutes the darkest side of *Seinfeld* by suggesting that personal growth is possible, even if it is only incremental.

The similarities between *Louie* and *Seinfeld*, both about a stand-up comic with the same name as the star who plays him, are immediately obvious. The introduction places him in New York City, making his way through town until he eventually descends into a ground-level comedy club. The intro immediately suggests something similar to *Seinfeld*'s original premise—a show about how a stand-up comic gets his ideas from his life.

Like C.K., the Louie character is divorced with kids and lives and works in New York. Bits of stand-up are often interspersed within the show, including the very first episode, as if to acknowledge immediately the inspiration of *Seinfeld*.

Balding and stocky, C.K. looks vaguely like a tall, red-haired George Costanza. Completely lacking the sarcastic confidence of the Jerry character, Louie leans into a morose hopelessness; like George, he is resigned to the inevitability of failure and disaster. Even as *Louie* is more cringe-inducing than *Seinfeld* in depicting the title character's many flaws and failures, Louie remains likable because he gets himself out of bed each morning even when he lacks any conceivable reason for doing so. From the opening sequence throughout his many misadventures, he plods on, and the character's steadfastness once in a while leads him to rare moments of happiness and personal growth.

In its serialized storytelling and self-referentiality, *Seinfeld* nudged forward the possibilities of storytelling within the sitcom genre. Still, as a multi-camera sitcom within a strict network framework of both content and time, *Seinfeld* now looks old-fashioned in many ways. *Louie*, like *Curb Your Enthusiasm*, is done in a single-camera style, meaning the show is typically shot on location. *Louie* also took advantage of FX's freedom for both explicit content and flexible time—not every episode fits into a neat half-hour on the network's schedule.

The character, Louie, can be just as frank as the real-life comic, but C.K.'s brashness is even more apparent in the many ways the show confronts social norms, holding them up, as a good comic does, to reveal their inherent absurdity. What *Seinfeld* did for dinner parties with your future in-laws, barbershop loyalties, and made-up belly-button voices, *Louie* tried to do for cultural standards of female beauty, Christian rules about sex, and early-morning garbage men.

The best stretch of the series comes in the last few episodes of the show's third season—the three-part story, "Late Show" (episodes 10 through 12), plus the denouement of the "Late Show" plot—the season finale, "New Year's Eve" (episode 13). Louie has a life-changing opportunity to take over for the retiring David Letterman and host his own late-night talk show on CBS. We know, of course, that he is doomed to failure. The show knows it too, as Louie is repeatedly told that he is not going to get the job. The white-haired network men that guide Louie through his futile quest are played by two of television's greatest auteurs—one from the world of sitcoms, Garry Marshall (*Happy Days*), and one from the world of dramas, David Lynch (*Twin Peaks*). Their casting evokes the ways *Louie* itself has blended the two genres. Their characters tell Louie straight to his face that he is only being brought in as negotiating leverage for CBS to use against the shoo-in for the position, a far more famous and successful comedian: Jerry Seinfeld, playing himself as always. Much discussed as Louie's nemesis throughout the storyline, Jerry makes only a brief appearance (his first of two in the series), attempting to sabotage Louie right before his big audition. Louie ultimately delivers a great performance but loses out to Seinfeld anyway, just as he was told he would. He celebrates, however, when he learns that CBS used him as leverage to cut Seinfeld's deal by $20 million.

In the season finale, Louie's exuberance has worn off as he finds himself depressed and, through a series of sad and tragic events, completely alone on New Year's Eve. He is eventually invited to spend the holiday with his sister and her family. He heads to the airport but instead of flying to Mexico to be with his family, he is suddenly inspired by the Christmas present he gave to his daughters—a classic children's book *The Story about Ping*. He buys a ticket for China.

The final minutes of the episode are actually filmed in China where Louie begins a quixotic search for the Yangtze river. He is eventually led to a small burbling brook, not a mighty river. Some locals invite him into their small home for a meal, where he connects—meaningfully and happily—with a group of strangers, despite the language barrier. The final moments of the third season thus leave the audience with a sense of the beauty of nature exceeded only by the warmth of human love—a mysterious yet powerful force leading strangers to extend neighborly care to a sad-sack loser from the other side of the planet. It's a far cry from the treatment the *Seinfeld* quartet both gave and received on their own final trip out of town.

## *SEINFELD'S* CONTINUED LEGACY

*Louie*'s success sparked its own wave of imitators, as high-profile stand-ups were increasingly given the opportunity and freedom to build a series in their own voice. In the *Seinfeld* tradition, these series typically contain autobiographical elements. *One Mississippi*, which ran for two seasons on Amazon, stars Tig Notaro as a fictional version of herself. The show listed C.K. as an executive producer even as Notaro was a leading voice calling for a public examination of C.K.'s past behavior, well before the *New York Times* reported on that behavior.[16]

Another *Louie* imitator, Netflix's *Master of None*, also intersects with C.K. beyond the show's content. Creator and star Aziz Ansari was himself accused of sexual misconduct in 2018.[17] He apologized after the allegation surfaced, corroborating its substance, which resembled the gender-based power imbalance that typified C.K.'s behavior. Ansari found more defenders than C.K. To date, only one person has publicly raised allegations about Ansari's behavior, compared to the multiple accusations and years of whispers about C.K. The specifics of their actions also differ substantially.

Ansari says he and the woman (who has remained anonymous) "ended up engaging in sexual activity, which by all indications was completely consensual."[18] Their interaction stopped short of actual sex, but the woman, who says she both nonverbally and verbally indicated her disinterest, felt violated and uncomfortable. She texted him the next day to express her feelings, and she says Ansari did respond at that point with an apology.

In the moment, Ansari stepped back from the public, but has since returned to the stand-up circuit. He released a new special on Netflix, which begins and ends with a seemingly heartfelt and vulnerable speech about how he has dealt with the allegations. Ansari is trying to get on the right side of post-#MeToo American culture. Both his words and his behavior will determine how successful that effort is.

A cockeyed optimist, I'd like to think Americans are finally changing the way we talk about sex—or rather, the way we avoid talking about sex. I'd like to think we are seeing the beginning of the end of an era of innuendo and euphemism—an era that *Seinfeld*'s own interaction with sex exemplifies more than any other show. No television show was better—and funnier—at talking about sex without talking about sex. But that approach is no longer healthy.

From Jerry and George fretting about their preference for sitting on a certain side of the couch ("The Implant," season 4, episode 19) to Frank Costanza intentionally stopping short while driving to initiate physical contact with a woman ("The Fusilli Jerry," season 6, episode 20), the show was both symptomatic of and fed into a culture that emphasized the role of the male in instigating sex, more through physical action than verbal communication.

The increase in sexual content on television has offered more opportunities for explicit dialogue that shows, often with great humor, how words are an important part of initiating sex. A final comparison between *Seinfeld* and *Master of None* reveals how much further television can now go in addressing sexuality, safe sex, and much more.

In "The Sponge" (season 7, episode 9), George is forced to use a condom for sex with his fiancée when Susan's preferred birth control is discontinued. He fumbles with opening the package, and eventually he gives up. The moment has passed. Using a condom actually costs him the chance to have sex.

Exactly 20 years later, *Master of None*'s very first episode begins with a scene of Ansari's character, Dev, having sex with a woman, Rachel. His condom breaks during intercourse, and the couple frantically searches the internet to learn whether she could become pregnant, and then they go to the pharmacy, where Dev buys Rachel a box of Plan B birth control pills—"My treat," he tells her. In a subsequent *Seinfeld*-like scene, Dev recaps the incident to his friends, and the gang discuss safe sex, condoms, STDs, and much more in a scene that never could have aired on NBC.

We can quibble over the nuance of the entire story in the episode—the "condom breaking" twist is not particularly original for a comedy—but the frankness with which the characters in *Master of None* talk about sex is representative of television's creeping progress.

In general, *Seinfeld*'s many descendants offer a more nuanced appraisal of human behavior. True to the self-deprecating nature of the comedians who star in the shows, their main characters are flawed, though likable. Despite the inability of characters like *Louie*'s Louie to ever truly come out on top, there are moments of sunny optimism that break through the clouds. Unlike *Seinfeld*'s final message—and against the grain of the real world's headlines—these comedies are often hopeful, suggesting the possibility of redemption. It is in television drama, rather than comedy, where we find more examples of *Seinfeld*'s ultimate cynicism toward human nature in some of the most acclaimed shows of the twenty-first century.

## *SEINFELD* AND TV'S ANTIHEROES

The age of the antihero was heralded by the *Seinfeld* finale, which, even as it condemned its characters for their actions, confirmed a change in TV sensibility that *Seinfeld* anticipated. Television didn't have to be all roses and sunshine. After all, life isn't that way.

*The Sopranos* and its central character, mob boss Tony Soprano, began a run of now-classic dramas focusing on a male antihero, a central protagonist defined by his own misdeeds. The roster of these antiheroes includes *Mad Men*'s Don Draper, *Breaking Bad*'s Walter White, *The Shield*'s Vic Mackey, and *Deadwood*'s Al Swearengen. Is Walter White's construction of a methamphetamine empire really so different from Jerry's theft of a marble rye from a little old woman?

OK, maybe that's a stretch. But *Seinfeld* is also a part of this phenomenon of building good shows around bad people.

From the post-apocalyptic hopelessness of *The Walking Dead*, to the nasty, brutish world of *Game of Thrones*, *Seinfeld*'s cynical worldview seems rampant in the most popular dramas of the new millennium. Even its existential questioning, exemplified in the finale's callback to the button conversation scene in the pilot, filtered into *Lost* and other shows that used their own finales for existential pondering.

As blockbuster films have increasingly turned to the high-flying heroes of comic books, TV has taken a ground-level view of humanity, moving inward—not upward—to explore the human psyche. Since *Seinfeld*, what television has revealed about humanity has not always been pretty.

# 11

# CRITIQUES AND MISSTEPS

The first episode of *Seinfeld*'s tiny first season, "The Stakeout," opens with Jerry running through a stand-up routine about paying for groceries. He mocks two women who, in front of him in line, paid for their small bags of groceries with checks. The check, as a method of payment, is one of many details here and there throughout the show that now feels ancient. As the routine progresses, however, the jokes begin to feel subtly dated in another way. After mocking them for paying with checks, he notes that women have trouble finding their keys in their purses, and he concludes by musing on why it isn't masculine to pay with a check.

If you decide to watch the series in order, you might be surprised to find yourself cringing at the stand-up segments more often than the main show. Gender difference has been a quintessential subject for comedians before and after *Seinfeld*, though our conception of gender has become significantly more complex a quarter-century on. There is nothing overwhelmingly offensive about Jerry's observations, and certainly the gender-based humor on other shows—most notably another hit nineties sitcom over on ABC, *Home Improvement*—could be a bit more egregious to viewers today, just as gender difference was even more central to the schticks of other comedians, like *Home Improvement*'s star, Tim Allen. Still, the joke of a woman's disorganized purse as a metaphor for the stereotype that women tend to be more scatter-brained is what we now might call a microaggression—a tiny slight,

often unintended, that subtly puts down a certain group, usually stem-
ming from a racial or gendered stereotype.

Aside from a reference to junk mail stating, "You may have already
won!" or TV shows that finish with a "to be continued" caption, Jerry's
bits hold up fairly well. And when it comes to gender, *Seinfeld* was
ahead of its time in many ways. The character of Elaine, in particular,
has been upheld as a notable advancement for female characterization
on TV. Setting aside my own critiques of the character's deeper flaws
(see chapter 5), Elaine is strong and independent. She is also sexual
without being overly sexualized. Julia Louis-Dreyfus deserves the legendary status she has received for her portrayal of Elaine, not only
because the performance was so great, but because she helped craft
such a multidimensional female character on a show that was written
mostly by men.

## SEINFELD AND GENDER

Forty-one men were credited or co-credited for the script of at least
one episode of *Seinfeld*. Here is the full list of women credited or co-
credited with a script on *Seinfeld*:

- Carol Leifer: six episodes, and a producer for *Seinfeld*'s Emmy-
  nominated seventh season
- Jennifer Crittenden: five episodes, and a producer for *Seinfeld*'s
  Emmy-nominated final season
- Marjorie Gross: four episodes, and a producer for *Seinfeld*'s
  Emmy-nominated seventh season
- Elaine Pope: three episodes, including (with Larry Charles) the
  Emmy-winning script for season 3's "The Fix-Up," and a producer
  for *Seinfeld*'s Emmy-nominated third season
- Jill Franklyn: one episode (with Peter Mehlman), the Emmy-
  nominated script for season 8's "The Yada Yada"

I should note that several other women worked on the production
side of *Seinfeld*, including, for most of the series, Suzy Mamann-Green-
berg and Nancy Sprow. Also, both Leifer and Crittenden worked in the
writers' room for multiple seasons and thus influenced more scripts

than that count would imply. Still, Leifer, an ex-girlfriend of Seinfeld, did not join the show until season 5. And Crittenden, who had previously written for *The Simpsons*, did not come on to *Seinfeld* until season 8. The female voice was far from dominant behind the scenes of *Seinfeld*.

True to form, David and Seinfeld showed they were aware of this issue in a season 4 episode they co-wrote, "The Shoes" (episode 16). Jerry and George are struggling to finish the pilot script for their show about nothing. They run into a snag when, trying to figure out what the Elaine character says when she enters a scene, they realize they don't know how to write lines for a woman. Later, Elaine gets angry after discovering she has not yet been written into the pilot. "Well, we tried," says Jerry. "We couldn't write for a woman. We didn't know what you would say. Even right now, I'm sitting here, I know you're going to say something, I have no idea what it is."

Later, Jerry observes another ex-girlfriend, Gail, interact with Elaine. Gail compliments Elaine's shoes. (Women talking about shoes . . . what a novel concept!) When Elaine reports that she bought the shoes from Botticelli's, Gail feigns amazement. Elaine is miffed at her sarcasm, but Jerry can't grasp why. "That bothered you?" he asks, and when Elaine is frustrated at his lack of sensitivity, he points out that this is the exact reason why her character is not in the pilot. Once again typical for the hyperconscious season 4, the joke works on multiple levels: Elaine *wasn't* in the *Seinfeld* pilot.

Given the opportunity, women contributed to some of *Seinfeld*'s best episodes. Writers like Leifer could add great insight about the woman's side of a romantic relationship, as she did in her last episode before departing the show to create and star in her own sitcom on the WB network, *Alright Already* (1997–1998). "The Rye" (season 7, episode 11) finds Elaine in a relationship with a jazz saxophonist, John. Everything is going great, except . . . Elaine isn't completely satisfied with their sex life. In Larry David–like fashion, Leifer's script dances playfully around the issue. "He . . . um . . . doesn't really like to do . . . everything," Elaine explains to Jerry who, after a beat, understands; to put it far more bluntly than Leifer's script does, John won't perform oral sex. Eventually Elaine, in her own words, "gets the little squirrel to come over to her." John senses his first attempt was not entirely successful, though. Plus, with a gig coming up, his mouth is tired. He ends up bombing a big performance, leading Elaine to quietly slip away.

We can easily imagine an alternate script, written by one of the male writers on the staff, that focused on George finding himself in the position of John in this story. "The Rye" and its focus on Elaine's perspective in the story seems more layered and perceptive because it was written by a woman. Elsewhere, the episode also includes the memorable scene of George reeling in a marble rye that Jerry had just stolen from an old woman. This has little to do with gender norms, but it is hysterical—and it was Leifer's idea.[1]

Another season 7 episode illustrates pitfalls of a male-dominated writers' room as a script credited by two men falls into a narrow and stereotypical depiction of a woman. In "The Calzone" (season 7, episode 19), Jerry is dating Nicki, a woman who uses her physical appearance to get all sorts of advantages.

"You know, they could get away with murder," George explains, ranting about good-looking women. "You never see any of them lift anything over three pounds. They get whatever they want, whenever they want it. You can't stop them." Indeed, using Nicki's looks, Jerry gets out of a speeding ticket.

Meanwhile, Elaine has several outings with a guy named Todd Gack, though he insists their excursions don't qualify as dates. To pay for betting that Dustin Hoffman was in *Star Wars*, Todd takes Elaine to the movies—they are stuck seeing *Blame It on the Rain* while, thanks to Nicki's charm, she and Jerry enjoy the supposedly sold-out *Means to an End*. Jerry rightly suspects that Todd is purposely throwing bets to get dates without having to ask women out. Todd gets another date, which he again insists isn't a date, to give Elaine cigars to give to Jerry. The third time they go out together, Todd takes Elaine to dinner with his parents. Still insisting it is not a date, Todd tries to kiss Elaine goodnight. That's their final date, though, as Todd steals Nicki away from Jerry by betting Nicki that Nixon's middle name was "Moe."

These two storylines explore two sides of gender behavior in romantic relationships. Nicki exerts power through her body. Even after she and Jerry break up, Jerry still finds himself offering to walk her dog, thus proving George's thesis about beautiful women. Todd, on the other hand, wins Elaine and then Nicki through deception. As a man, he cannot rely on his body to seduce women, so he tries to outwit them while simultaneously protecting his own ego by insisting that these outings are not dates.

"The Calzone" was written by Alec Berg and Jeff Schaffer, two writers that have produced some otherwise brilliant comedy, both in *Seinfeld* and in their future work. In this episode, however, the Nicki character draws from old-fashioned female characterizations with an overly simplistic conception of female beauty and its supposed power. Rather than unpacking these conceptions, as *Seinfeld* would do at its best, the episode merely affirms them.

Jerry points out several times on *Seinfeld* that society expects men to be more superficial than women. Because of this double standard, Elaine feels compelled to disguise her superficial attractions. In fact, Elaine is just as superficial as her friends. "The Stall" (season 5, episode 12) illustrates Elaine's problem perfectly. She is dating Tony, a handsome younger man with a passion for extreme sports. Immediately, Jerry accuses her of being superficial, but Elaine insists she would be interested in Tony "no matter what he looked like." Jerry declares Tony to be a "a male bimbo . . . a mimbo," but Elaine refuses to relent, calling Tony "exciting" and "charismatic," though she does admit he has a "perfect face."

But Elaine is not the only person interested in Tony. George thinks Tony is "such a cool guy" and starts to act like Tony's sidekick. He accepts an invitation to go rock climbing with Tony but is upset when Kramer also gets an invitation. George's jealously turns to embarrassed discomfort when Kramer suggests George is in love with Tony. (This is not the first time one of the male leads has a "man crush." Jerry develops a similar infatuation with Keith Hernandez, the baseball all-star who dates Elaine in "The Boyfriend," season 3, episodes 17 and 18.)

On the rock-climbing outing, George's inexperience leads to an accident that wrecks Tony's perfect face. Elaine is forced to admit that, indeed, her interest in Tony *was* purely superficial. George, on the other hand, is devastated when Tony refuses to see him after the accident. Though he acts a bit childish in his pursuit of Tony, George really does love Tony in a more meaningful way than Elaine ever could.

In one season 9 episode, *Seinfeld* offers a more insightful take on gender norms. The aptly-named episode 12, "The Reverse Peephole," flips gender markers around by giving men fashion items that are normally viewed as feminine. Typical for *Seinfeld*, the plot is so mixed-up that it is hard to explain a few storylines without describing the whole tied-up ball of yarn: George helps buy a massage chair as an apartment gift for the gang's mutual friend, Joe Mayo, but secretly keeps the chair for himself to help soothe his back, which is sore from carrying an extremely overloaded wallet. To keep Newman from being evicted, Kramer helps cover up the postman's affair with the landlord's wife by pretending that a fur coat the landlord, Silvio, found wasn't given to his wife by Newman but was actually left in the laundry by Jerry who, according to Kramer, is a fancy boy. The fur coat *originally* belonged to David Puddy until Elaine, disgusted with his fashion choices, threw it out the window at Joe Mayo's party, only to have Puddy mistake Joe Mayo's fur coat for his own, leading Elaine to get blamed for losing Joe Mayo's coat since she was responsible for the coats at the party. And Jerry starts using a European carry-all to carry around his and his girl-friend's belongings. This accessory, along with the fur coat Kramer makes him wear to back up Newman's story, leaves Jerry open to mock-ery.

The deep-voiced, muscular Puddy looks ridiculous wearing the fur coat, but nobody ever calls Elaine's big boyfriend a woman. Elaine just thinks he looks like an idiot. When Jerry puts on the coat and grabs his purse-like carry-all to strut around in front of Silvio and help Kramer clear Newman's name, no one says he looks like a woman. They do use some words that are code for "homosexual" (dandy, fancy), but their critique is more about Jerry's fame going to his head, turning him into an effete elitist.

Ultimately, though, Silvio is the real laughingstock of this episode, as both his paranoia about his wife's relationship with Newman and his taunting of Jerry become increasingly absurd. Thus, the reliance on things like clothing and accessories as gender markers is also made to seem absurd.

## WORST EPISODE EVER?

We have already discussed the episode of *Seinfeld* that was the most controversial in its moment, "The Puerto Rican Day" (see chapter 7). That episode and its reaction received extensive coverage because it was the penultimate episode of the series. A few episodes before, *Seinfeld* included a line that was even more egregious; in "The Bookstore" (episode 17), Peterman, Elaine's boss, refers to opium as "the Chinaman's nightcap." A watchdog group, the Media Action Network for Asian Americans, pointed out what should have been obvious to both *Seinfeld* and NBC—"Chinaman" is an offensive term on its own, and linking the word to heroin made the line even more demeaning. NBC did not offer an apology, but it did cut the line in reruns.[2]

On one occasion, *Seinfeld* scrapped an episode because its content was both edgy and unfunny. Back in season 2, Larry Charles wrote a script called "The Bet" (aka "The Gun"), in which Elaine purchases a gun and, at one point, points it to her head and references the Kennedy assassination. Julia Louis-Dreyfus expressed her discomfort to Jason Alexander, who approached the producers. The episode was nixed 20 minutes into rehearsal, forcing David and Seinfeld to rush the script for "The Phone Message" (season 2, episode 4) into production.[3]

In retrospect, the episode with some of the worst jokes the show ever aired was part of season 5. In "The Masseuse" (episode 9), Elaine dates a man who unfortunately shares his name with a New York City serial killer, Joel Rifkin. Kramer, apropos of nothing, shares an ill-conceived theory about the infamous murderer: "You know why Rifkin was a serial killer? Because he was adopted. Just like Son of Sam was adopted. So apparently adoption leads to serial killing."

Yikes! NBC received a number of complaints for this line. However, no one at the time seemed to mind Jerry parodying the behavior of a date rapist in his efforts to pressure the masseuse he is dating into giving him a free massage. The girlfriend, Jodi, asks Jerry if he wants to go out, but he has other ideas. He positions himself in front of her and puts her hands on his shoulders, then gradually tries to maneuver over to her massage table. Jodi, for reasons that are never completely clear, resists the implication. "No," she repeats several times, but Jerry continues to pressure her for the massage. "Come on! I know it's something you want to do!" Jodi finally pulls away, and Jerry falls off the table.

I now find that scene almost unwatchable. But it wasn't the first time a massage prompted behavior from one of the main characters that now feels a bit extreme. In season 3's first episode, "The Note," George is horrified—and horrifically homophobic—before, during, and after receiving a massage from a man. His interactions with Raymond, the tall, trim, blond masseur, play a bit better than Jerry's massage/date-rape gag, mainly because the script and the performance make George's homophobia seem ridiculous to the point of absurdity. Still, both Jerry and George reveal homophobic inclinations throughout the series that feel increasingly insensitive by today's conventions.

## WAS THERE SOMETHING WRONG WITH THAT?

"Not that there's anything wrong with that" is yet another *Seinfeld* catchphrase, but one that is particularly loaded with connotations specific to its context. The phrase is repeated throughout "The Outing" (season 4, episode 17) when George and Jerry are mistaken for a homosexual couple in an episode that blends both political correctness and the inner homophobic anxieties of heterosexuals in the early nineties when it first aired.

George, Jerry, and Elaine are seated at their usual booth in the coffee shop where Jerry is waiting to meet a writer for an interview. Noticing a woman in the booth behind them listening in on their conversation, Elaine tries to take advantage of the eavesdropper with a spur-of-the-moment joke—she tells George and Jerry that they should come out of the closet as an openly gay couple. George plays along with the gag for a bit, but Jerry is resistant. The eavesdropping woman gets up to make a phone call, and at this point the audience learns what Jerry and George will not discover until later in the episode—she is the reporter Jerry was scheduled to meet.

Later, she comes to Jerry's apartment for the rescheduled interview, finds George there too and immediately recognizes him from the diner. Failing to realize who she is, the two friends bicker in their usual manner, and to the reporter, they sound like a homosexual couple. Only as the reporter presses them for details of how they met does Jerry realize she was the woman from the diner. Frantically, Jerry and George try to explain that they are not really gay . . . "not that there's anything wrong with that." Their protests are to no avail, and the report that the two men are gay is printed, picked up by the Associated Press, and publicized around the country.

Now the two friends have to deal with the fallout. Strangers approach Jerry to thank him for coming out of the closet. Their parents call, frantic for an explanation. Each time they profess their straightness, George and Jerry include the addendum, "Not that there's anything wrong with that." Other characters also repeat the refrain throughout the episode.

The joke, emphasized by Jerry's and George's agonized protestations, is that while the two men are doing their liberal-minded, politically correct duty in acknowledging that they accept homosexuality without protest, they are clearly afraid of being thought of as homosexuals. The refrain itself adds a crucial layer to the episode's underlying message. Without the repeated line, Jerry and George would merely be desperate to not appear gay. With the line, that desperation remains, but it is acknowledged as ridiculous.

In fact, the line was not in the script at the first table read. NBC executives were left with grave concerns about the episode, worrying how it would be received by gay and lesbian viewers. The biggest problem, according to Castle Rock's Glenn Padnick, was that the episode was "unfunny and unhappy."[4] For once, NBC leaned on the show—ultimately with positive results. The episode's writer, Larry Charles, continued to tinker with the script and eventually came up with the now-famous line. So, the next time you watch "The Outing," imagine how unfunny and unhappy the episode would be without that phrase.

Charles's script ultimately earned him an Emmy nomination, only losing out to Larry David's script for the equally catchphrase-laden "The Contest." "The Outing" did win an award from GLAAD (the Gay and Lesbian Alliance Against Defamation), cementing its status at the time as an episode that advanced representations of sexuality and gender issues on television. The script is particularly clever at illuminating the arbitrary nature of stereotypes. Jerry tells Elaine and George that he is often mistaken for being gay because he is thin, neat, and single, and his stand-up set at the end of the episode jokes that it is a bit rarer to find a gay man who is fat, sloppy, and married. Jerry's birthday falls during the episode and otherwise harmless gifts become loaded with irony. He gets a Bette Midler album from Elaine and tickets to see *Guys and Dolls* with George, who quickly points out that the show is not called *Guys and Guys*.

Still, while the episode invites a heterosexual audience to identify with Jerry and George and, hopefully, recognize their own inner anxieties about homosexuality, many scholars argue the episode falls short of forcing its audience to confront those inner anxieties.[5] The over-the-top reactions from Jerry and George in "The Outing" now feel dated, especially within the series as a whole, which regularly dipped into the duo's latent homophobia.

In the first episode of season 2 ("The Ex-Girlfriend"), George comes right out and admits his homophobia. George and Jerry are picking up Elaine, who refuses to sit in the backseat because she'll have to lean forward to be a part of their conversation. George doesn't want to sit in the back either, but when Elaine asks him to slide over and sit in the center (A bench seat! The cars are dated, too!), he refuses. "It doesn't look good: boy-boy-girl." Elaine scoffs as George gets out so she can sit in the middle, and she accuses her friend of being homophobic. "Is it that obvious?" he asks with sarcasm.

Jerry's homophobia can be even worse. In "The Jimmy" (season 6, episode 18), he squirms at the mere thought of watching a man sing a song. In that same episode, both George and Jerry become uncomfortable when Elaine asks them if they've noticed a particularly handsome man at their gym. The fitness center is often a site for sexual discomfort; in another episode, "The Pool Guy" (season 7, episode 8), Jerry and Newman both refuse to administer mouth-to-mouth resuscitation to an unconscious man purely out of their own homophobia.

George's homophobia reaches a new level of insanity in "The Cartoon" (season 9, episode 13) when his friends point out that his new girlfriend looks exactly like Jerry. As with the male masseur in "The Note," George once again panics about his own sexuality. Maybe this episode plays to my own preference for surreal comedy, but I find "The Cartoon" to be one of the most riveting explorations of George's twisted psyche. Like "The Outing," "The Cartoon" may fall well short of leading the audience to healthy self-examination, but it does push George's homophobia to preposterous, hysterical conclusions. George's best friend is Jerry. George is a heterosexual. Why shouldn't he be attracted to a woman who has every physical attribute Jerry has, plus a vagina?

One of my favorite scenes in the entire series holds up well in the way it addresses homophobia, as it shows Jerry in a rare moment of sexual woke-ness. In "The Wig Master" (season 7, episode 18), George and his then-fiancée Susan host Susan's friend, Ethan, at their apartment for two weeks. Ethan is the titular wig master, touring with *Joseph and the Amazing Technicolor Dreamcoat*. He is, as the audience soon discovers, effeminate in his speech and mannerisms, presenting as stereotypically gay. Toward the end of the episode, Jerry meets up with

Kramer, Ethan, and the show's costume designer at an outdoor café, where they are enjoying champagne coolies—another feminine marker. Abruptly, Kramer leaves with the costume designer; he wants to borrow her backup dreamcoat. Jerry and Ethan are left alone together with their matching champagne coolies.

When the episode cuts back to the duo, they are still enjoying their drinks while gossiping about George and Susan. Another man arrives, recognizes Ethan, and eventually asks him out on a date. Jerry cuts the man off and ultimately chases him away, offended that the guy would see the two of them together, laughing and drinking champagne coolies, and *not* presume they were a couple! "It's very emasculating!" cries Jerry, as the befuddled man wanders off.

This moment is something of a redemption for Jerry's distress back in "The Outing." Just as he was upset at being mistaken as gay in "The Outing," he is now furious at *not* being mistaken as gay in "The Wig Master." For once, sexual orientation is beside the point; Jerry is mad about assumptions, stereotypes, and the mistaken behaviors they can lead to.

But let's not praise Jerry *too* much. The always self-possessed character's behavior in "The Wig Master" is driven not by an interest in uprooting gender stereotypes but a far more selfish desire to protect his own pride; earlier in the episode, a man had asked Elaine out right in front of Jerry without considering the possibility that the ex-couple might actually be a current couple. Ultimately, Jerry's chief concern is the image he presents to the world. In this way, *Seinfeld* isn't merely a quintessential representation of nineties culture with resonance a few decades later on; it is a show that encapsulates better than perhaps any other sitcom the facets and flaws of life in our modern age.

# 12

## *SEINFELD* TODAY

In one season 8 episode, "The Comeback" (episode 13), Jerry finds himself in what George describes as a "medieval sexual payola" scheme. Jerry has discovered that Milos, the equipment salesman at his tennis club, has a terrible secret: He's really bad at tennis. Having just taken Milos's advice in purchasing an expensive racket, Jerry is upset, but he is distracted from his annoyance by an attractive woman in the store. Later, the woman shows up unexpectedly at his apartment and begins to seduce him before abruptly pulling away and bursting into tears. She is, it turns out, Milos's wife, and her husband has sent her to sleep with Jerry in exchange for keeping the secret of Milos's lack of tennis talent. Jerry does not accept this twisted bribe, much to the chagrin of George, who was hoping to hear more from this salacious tale. "Because of society, right?" scoffs a disappointed George.

Society. As much as *Seinfeld* poked fun at the unwritten rules that make up society, as much as the show held society up to the light of its mockery, society remained the real prison from which the characters could not escape. Despite his sarcastic detachment, Jerry is always a man who finds comfort in the order imposed by society's norms and expectations. George laments the same set of unwritten rules but is himself too cowardly to break them. Elaine, ever-focused on climbing society's ladder, seems the least concerned by the fact that the ladder is an artificial creation of society. Only Kramer seems liberated from many of society's conventions. Still, he can't drift too far from those norms. Otherwise, he'll be deemed insane and thus rejected from society, and he already is a pretty bizarre dude.

Social conventions are strong and, as much as *Seinfeld* pokes fun at them, the show also acknowledges that social conventions keep everyone in line, living within a narrow range of acceptable behavior. Act too far and too often outside that range and there will be social consequences. Jerry is already weirded out by Milos's behavior. If Milos starts sending his wife to sleep with every customer who suspects he stinks at tennis, he will probably be fired and his wife will probably leave him. She'd be crazy to stay.

Other episodes explore the concept of insanity directly. In another season 8 episode, "The Pothole" (episode 16), Elaine warns Jerry that his anal-retentive behavior may become a serious concern if he cannot find the strength to kiss his girlfriend after she brushed her teeth with a toothbrush he knocked into the toilet. In season 7's "The Gum" (episode 10) George spends the entire episode trying to convince an old friend that he is not crazy, despite the fact he rants with paranoia about a woman on a horse and prances around town wearing a King Henry VIII costume.

Lloyd Braun, a recurring character and nemesis for George, is the embodiment of the show's interest in insanity. The character had a breakdown and entered a mental institution after failing to lead Mayor David Dinkins to an election victory. When he returns in "The Gum," Kramer insists that the other characters treat Lloyd gently to reassure him that he is not crazy. Ultimately, this means cushioning the character from society's harshness. Kramer essentially creates an artificial society around Lloyd, with its own rules and its own version of reality. In this society, Jerry wears glasses, Kramer loves eating really old movie theater hot dogs, and all the guys enjoy sitting around chewing Chinese gum together. It's hilarious to the viewers, but, on Kramer's word, Lloyd Braun is reassured that it's not crazy. The society Kramer is shaping around Lloyd deems this behavior to be perfectly sane. Of course, the same is true about our real-world society; behavior is deemed sane or insane by tacit agreement.

No comedy before *Seinfeld*—and few after—explored the artificiality of society so well. *Seinfeld*'s hyperawareness of society is one of the things that make it a postmodern sitcom. Indeed, whatever else the complex idea of postmodernity means, a hyperawareness of social conventions might be one of its defining characteristics. Hyperawareness is a key ingredient in the heavily ironic sense of humor that began to emerge in the United States somewhere around the time Bill Murray joined the cast of *Saturday Night Live* and David Letterman got his first network show, blossomed in the nineties with *Seinfeld* and *The Simpsons*, and now thrives in its natural habitat that is the internet where the serious becomes a meme in an instant. *Seinfeld* did not create this Age of Irony, and it certainly did not inaugurate postmodernity, but it did nudge these characteristics of American society along. From *The Seinfeld Chronicles* to "The Finale," the world had changed, and in a few ways, *Seinfeld* drove some of these changes.

## CULTURE OF NARCISSISM

Twenty-first century viewers have suggested that the cell phone made the plots of most episodes of *Seinfeld*, along with many other old shows and films, obsolete. A cell phone certainly would have helped Jerry meet up with the interviewer in "The Outing" long before she overheard him and George pretending to be gay. On the other hand, I still have to wait for a table in busy restaurants and forget where I parked my car at the mall. Both *Seinfeld*'s plots and its characters continue to ring true in the digital age.

In late 2012, in the midst of another busy Festivus season, two writers launched an account on Twitter called Modern Seinfeld, with the handle @SeinfeldToday.[1] They quickly demonstrated how easily the quirks and worries of the four main characters translated into a new technological reality, gaining around a million followers in the few years the account was active. A few examples:

- May 14, 2014: Jerry's gf [girlfriend] dumps him for not wishing her happy bday on Facebook. J:"I said it to her face!" E:"But her friends can't see that & get jealous."
- July 3, 2014: Kramer rents out his apartment every night on Airbnb & lives in the hallway. K:"I'm making cash hand over fist, Jerry!" J:"You're homeless!"

- January 26, 2015: After Elaine's BF [boyfriend] logs into his email on her computer, she makes the mistake of searching her name & seeing everything he's said about her.

As Modern Seinfeld proves, though the context has changed drastically, the characterizations ring as true as ever, capturing the narcissism that remains persistent in American society—an "exquisitely minute concern with our own psyches," as *New York Times* columnist Maureen Dowd put it in a 1997 column criticizing the show alongside the news of the cast's considerable raise.[2] (Years later, having developed a deep fondness for the show, Dowd called this column her one and only regret.)[3]

Christopher Lasch argued that American culture could be described as a "culture of narcissism" in his best-selling and award-winning 1979 book of that title.[4] In the nineties, *Seinfeld* seemed to epitomize Lasch's assessment—that the rise of a consumer society had created a nation of individuals seeking to polish their own self-image above all other social considerations. Now, when celebrities are famous for being famous and everyone posts selfies in the hopes of earning likes, Lasch's diagnosis seems only more justified.

Lasch and others influenced by his writings have observed a strong "therapeutic" sensibility in this narcissistic culture. Our minute concerns about our own psyches are driven by consumer culture. The same advertising industry that paid so many millions of dollars for precious seconds of time during *Seinfeld* episodes has tricked us all into thinking that self-healing is just a new product or a new experience away. We're like Jerry, thinking we should upgrade our significant other at the first sign of imperfection, or Elaine, thinking fair recognition and compensation at work is just around the corner. As we are continually disappointed, we spiral into a nation of Georges, convinced that, in every way, we cannot possibly achieve the happiness advertising tells us is a step away. In this nation of Jerrys, Elaines, and Georges, no wonder the self-improvement industry continues to thrive in its many variants: diet, exercise, self-help, and more.

*Seinfeld* itself poked fun at the futility of self-help pursuits in "The Serenity Now" (season 9, episode 3). Jerry's new girlfriend, Patty, tells him that she has never seen him mad. She suspects he is suppressing his true feelings, and, with her help, he starts to let his emotions out. He seems to feel good, but everything else falls apart around him. Patty soon breaks up with him when she gets tired of his yelling. His best friend, George, is uncomfortable with Jerry's expressions of affection. Jerry admits he is no longer funny, so theoretically his career is over, too. And he even asks Elaine to marry him, a request she flees from. Finally, Jerry convinces George to let out his emotions, too. George does, revealing his darkest thoughts and fears. Jerry, horrified, is shocked out of his emotional state and quickly gets up to leave George behind until his friend has similarly returned to normal.

Meanwhile, George's father, Frank, is experimenting with a new method to expel his own stress. As instructed by a cassette tape his doctor gave him, when he feels his blood pressure rise, Frank yells, "Serenity now!" It's a method designed to offer catharsis, to relieve inner stress by transforming it into a physical and vocal act, expelling the bad emotion from the body. Unfortunately, this practice doesn't work, as George is warned by Lloyd Braun. Having overcome a nervous breakdown, Lloyd has what passes for mental health expertise on the show. "Serenity now, insanity later," he warns George.

Like so many misguided fixes in the self-help era, yelling "serenity now" is a temporary, surface-level fix. The mantra makes Frank feel better in the moment but fails to address the underlying causes of his stress. It's an appealing method for the quick-fix sensibility of this therapeutic age, but as Lloyd knows, it will ultimately fall short of giving Frank true satisfaction. Indeed, by the end of the episode, both Frank and Kramer, who has adopted the mantra himself, suffer their own breakdowns.

We might think the healthier alternative would be to actually engage with their stress and talk it out, fully expressing their inner emotions . . . except Jerry's story shows us that doesn't work either. The world doesn't want people who express their emotions so freely. The more Jerry expresses his emotions, the more he drives people away. Perhaps social media has led us to a third way—now we can post our emotional outbursts on Twitter or Facebook. We seem to give our mediated selves more permission for expression than we allow in our face-to-face interactions.

## *SEINFELD* **AND SOCIAL MEDIA?**

Social media epitomizes our culture of narcissism, encouraging our most narcissistic tendencies to fret about all aspects of our outward appearance. So, it is easy to imagine the *Seinfeld* quartet wholeheartedly embracing the practice of using social media to craft their online identity and curate a version of the person they want the world to see.

Berated in "The Finale" for her poor phone etiquette as she tried to reach her sick friend, Elaine would have been disgusted with the new etiquette of both texting and social media, even as she simultaneously embraced social media's power to confirm her self-image of beauty and success. Social media would give George just another realm of existence to fret about; he'd be regularly caught in his own web of online lies. Even as Jerry would remain outwardly dismissive of social media, he would probably be the most hyperaware of his online identity. After all, this is the same guy who is so vain that he scratches out the size 32 on his jeans and writes in 31 ("The Sponge," season 7, episode 9). Imagine how long Jerry would obsess over choosing the right Instagram filter!

I worry about Kramer in this age, with his dark distrust of the wider world and his tendency toward paranoia. Would he fall down a YouTube rabbit hole into its endless tunnels of conspiracy theories and anti-science bunk? Is it so crazy to think that the same character who once protested the U.S. Postal Service ("The Junk Mail," season 9, episode 5) and chased evidence of a genetically mutated "pigman" in a hospital ("The Bris," season 5, episode 5) might start to believe the countless hours of YouTube cases for flat-earth theory, climate-change conspiracies, and worse? Might this kind of distrust in mainstream news and information channels drive Kramer into the conspiracy-laden world of alt-right politics? Yikes!

In fact, *Seinfeld* already has an unexpected connection to the alt-right by way of Steve Bannon, the former chairman of the extreme right-wing Breitbart News and former chief strategist to President Donald Trump. Prior to his rise to prominence as a global proponent of nationalist populism, Bannon was an investment banker and Hollywood producer. By chance, opportunity, and a bit of foresight, Bannon managed to get what Jason Alexander, Julia Louis-Dreyfus, and Michael Richards never could—a share of *Seinfeld*'s endless syndication profits.

How Bannon got his share of *Seinfeld* is as convoluted as a Larry David plot. As *Seinfeld* reached its third season (its first full order of episodes), its production company, Castle Rock, was put up for sale. As co-founder Rob Reiner explains, a handful of successful films as well as a few solid TV shows had made Castle Rock profitable, but the studio was finding it increasingly hard to compete with the larger production companies. Media mogul Ted Turner would ultimately buy the company and its holdings, including *Seinfeld*, just as the sitcom was on the cusp of its breakout, Emmy-winning fourth season.

A few years before the deal, Castle Rock was looking for an influx of cash, so a share of the company was sold to Westinghouse. With Turner set to purchase that asset, Westinghouse wanted to figure out how to maximize its own profits and brought in a small but well-regarded investment group to consult on their negotiations: Bannon & Co. Steve Bannon advised Westinghouse to retain its share of a handful of Castle Rock's TV shows, suggesting that one or more of the shows might hit pay dirt in the syndication market. Westinghouse essentially countered with, "Well, if you like these TV shows so much, why don't *you* take the rights in lieu of a payment for your services." Yada, yada, yada . . . and decades later, *Seinfeld*'s profits have helped fund some of the racist and anti-Semitic messaging of Breitbart and other Bannon projects.[5]

"It's horrible," says Rob Reiner, who comes from a Jewish family. "When I first heard about it, it made me sick. It makes me sick. Because I had no idea. I didn't know who he was, or that he was representing Westinghouse."[6]

*Seinfeld* writer Peter Mehlman, who was credited with more scripts than anyone not named Larry David, says its "galling" that Bannon, a "raging anti-Semite," has made "all this money off a show that's associated with Jewish humor."[7]

Bannon's financial might is one of the show's darker legacies. Happily, *Seinfeld* has already made its way into Washington, DC, in a far more lighthearted manner. The puffy shirt Jerry wears in season 5's second episode, "The Puffy Shirt," was donated to the Smithsonian in 2004. In that episode, Jerry accidentally agrees to Kramer's low-talking girlfriend's request that he wear the shirt she designed on the *Today Show* (figure 12.1). The frilly shirt makes him look like a pirate, and he lambasts the shirt's style on national television, much to the designer's fury.

As Jerry boasted when the shirt was donated, "This might be the first joke that is inducted into the Smithsonian Institution!"[8]

## FESTIVUS FOR THE REST OF US

So much of *Seinfeld*'s humor was intended to *deconstruct* culture, mocking traditional behaviors and undermining everyday life. Yet, through the sheer power of the show, it frequently managed to *construct* culture anew, introducing powerful new language and even new modes of behavior into American life. Festivus is a lasting example.

The show introduced the invented holiday to the world on December 18, 1997, in "The Strike" (season 9, episode 10), but it was actually started by the father of one of Seinfeld's writers, Dan O'Keefe. "It did not have a set date," O'Keefe told *Mother Jones* in 2013 in the middle of a Fox News–led uproar against the secular holiday. "We never knew when it was going to happen until we got off the school bus and there

**Figure 12.1.   "The Puffy Shirt," season 5, episode 2 (September 23, 1993). NBC**
*Photographer: Michael Yarish/Photofest*

were weird decorations around our house and weird French '60s music playing."⁹

O'Keefe explained the tradition to his fellow writers one day. Over his objections that the idea wasn't that funny, Alec Berg and Jeff Schaffer put it into the show via the eccentric Frank Costanza, adding details like the Airing of Grievances, the Feats of Strength, and the aluminum pole in place of a Christmas tree. They did keep the spirit of the O'Keefe family Festivus as an anti-holiday—a tradition that made fun of traditions. In this way, despite O'Keefe's misgivings, Festivus was the perfect fit for *Seinfeld*.

It was the perfect fit, too, for American culture at the turn of the millennium, and it has been embraced for its anti-religion and anti-consumerism messages. The holiday remains popular and, if you want to throw your own party, you can find a dozen or so aluminum Festivus poles available for order on Amazon.

More than the pole, it is the Festivus spirit—or anti-spirit—that continues to resonate for Americans uncomfortable with and tired of the annual Christmas slog. Festivus is safely secular, and its anti-commercial essence—Festivus pole manufacturers notwithstanding—is baked into its origin story. As George's father explains, one Christmas season he found himself raining blows down on a customer who dared reach for the last doll on the shelf that Frank was eying for his son.

Festivus, as Frank Costanza practices it in "The Strike," captures the essence of the entire series of *Seinfeld*. Airing of Grievances? Feats of Strength? What do Jerry, George, Elaine, and Kramer do every week other than complain about the minutiae of their lives and come up with schemes to get a leg up on those around them?

Festivus survives along with so many other *Seinfeld* ideas because it celebrates the attitude of the show. During Festivus, not only is it okay to complain about and demonstrate superiority over others but such expressions are celebrated. The *Seinfeld* quartet may find Frank's holiday insane, but if they looked a little closer, they'd realize it was their perfect holiday.

## *SEINFELD*'S CULTURAL THESAURUS

Besides Festivus, many other *Seinfeld* terms have similarly entered the American lexicon, and are, no doubt, used by people who have never watched the show. *Seinfeld* has given us a "cultural thesaurus," as television scholar Robert Thompson calls it—a list of terms that we can and now do apply throughout everyday life.[10] In other words, *Seinfeld* was creating internet memes a decade before internet memes became a thing. Now that memes *are* a thing, it only takes a quick Google search for "*Seinfeld* memes" to confirm that the show's catchphrases and caricatures continue to thrive in all sorts of new, twenty-first-century contexts.

The first *Seinfeld* line listed on *Seinfeld*'s page on knowyourmeme.com (a rich, crowdsourced compilation of internet meme history) is "No soup for you," the catchphrase for the titular character in "The Soup Nazi" (season 7, episode 6). Besides being many fans' pick as the best *Seinfeld* episode ever, "The Soup Nazi" is a prime example of how *Seinfeld* has influenced American language. Based on a real, ultra-serious soup chef in New York City, the Soup Nazi character runs a no-nonsense restaurant that offers the best soup in town but only for customers who follow his rigorous system of etiquette for ordering, paying for, and collecting the soup. As much as "No soup for you" remains in usage in the age of memes, it is the moniker Soup Nazi that has had the deepest cultural penetration. "He's a real (blank) Nazi" remains in broad circulation as a put-down for anyone upholding a strict set of rules. For better or for worse, *Seinfeld* helped undermine the inherent sense of evil in the word "Nazi," creating a new, ironic use for what had been a deeply unironic term.

*Seinfeld* also gave labels to various phenomenon that lacked a culturally agreed-upon name. For example, when a man goes swimming in cold water, he may experience "shrinkage," as George did in "The Hamptons" (season 5, episode 20). George's problem is that he fears Rachel, Jerry's girlfriend who accidentally walked in on him naked after his swim, may not understand the concept of shrinkage. Worse, she may report an unfair assessment of George to his girlfriend, Jane, who has not yet seen him naked. Jerry is more confident that women understand shrinkage, but when the two quiz Elaine, she proves to be unaware of this peculiar facet of the male anatomy. George's worst fears are realized when Jane leaves the house in the Hamptons in the middle of the night. She didn't know about shrinkage either.

What's amazing about the ignorance the female characters display toward shrinkage in this episode is that their confusion was dated as soon as the episode aired. Twenty million people watched it live, and thus a new definition of "shrinkage" was cast into the American language. Before that evening, May 12, 1994, most American women probably did not know about shrinkage. We can even imagine that many American men perhaps feared that their post-swim shrinkage was a unique problem rather than a normal occurrence. After that date, the phenomenon became more widely understood and now had a handy label to go with it. If Jane had only seen this episode, she might have given George the benefit of the doubt until he had dried off and warmed up.

Jane did not get a nickname in this episode (late-night-leaver?), but many of the gang's girlfriends and boyfriends did. Over the years, Jerry dated a woman with "man hands" and a "two face." Kramer dated a "low-talker." Elaine dated a "close-talker" and a "bad breaker-upper."

*Seinfeld* put a label on all sorts of people and behaviors. Elaine dealt with a "sideler" at work and pondered whether new boyfriends were "sponge-worthy." George pursued "make-up sex," "conjugal visit sex," and "fugitive sex." Kramer discovered a Latvian Orthodox nun was attracted to his Kavorka, "the lure of the animal," while Elaine fended off Jewish men attracted to her "Shiksa appeal." Jerry and the gang held a contest to see who could remain "master of their domain."

Two other examples have become so widespread that *Seinfeld*'s role in bringing them to prominence is easily forgotten. "Yada, yada, yada" was not coined on *Seinfeld*, but "The Yada Yada" (season 8, episode 19) added an ironic connotation to the phrase as it was used to obscure potentially embarrassing information in the episode.

In "The Implant" (season 4, episode 19), George is caught double-dipping a chip at a funeral reception, but rather than hide his guilt, he proceeds to triple-dip a chip, prompting a scuffle. Since then, the supposed health risk of double-dipping has been debated and even studied; a 2009 Clemson University study found that double-dipping did increase the bacteria in the bowl, though the amount of additional bacterial measured depended on the type of dip. On the other hand, the study concluded that you're highly unlikely to get sick from a double-dipped chip.[11]

## SEINFELD'S FUTURE

Like a delicious dip, it remains enjoyable to return to *Seinfeld*, again and again. It is also easier than ever to return to, again and again. The show is currently on Hulu, but, as Disney, NBC, and other content creators have begun building their own streaming platforms, many wondered if *Seinfeld* would find a new home after 2021 when Hulu's rights expired. Warner Bros. was an obvious destination, as the company controls Castle Rock, co-owns the show, and could use *Seinfeld* as a centerpiece for its own new streaming platform, HBO Max.

Then, in September 2019, another platform sidled in—a company founded a few weeks before *Seinfeld*'s final season began. Now the "elder statesman" of streaming platforms, Netflix, had long benefited from the rights to *Friends* and *The Office*, two other sitcoms that remained popular after first airing on NBC. With the rights to both shows approaching their expiration date, Netflix was looking for a proven show to bolster its ever-growing library of original programming. So, Netflix reached an agreement to buy the global streaming rights for *Seinfeld*. As of this writing, the terms of the deal have not been disclosed. Considering the rights for *The Office* and *Friends* both went for about half a billion dollars apiece for five years of U.S.-only streaming rights, it's safe to say Seinfeld and David can expect another big check. And in moving to Netflix, *Seinfeld* will be viewed in a way no one ever could have imagined in 1988 when Seinfeld had his first meeting with NBC.

I would like to think subsequent generations will fall in love with *Seinfeld*, and the show will keep resonating long into the future. But part of me hopes that some aspects of the show eventually feel dated. As hysterical as the show remains, its characters are not great people. Even when *Seinfeld* was on, many people disliked the show because they disliked the characters. If and when *Seinfeld* does finally fade out of cultural relevance, I hope it is because viewers increasingly find the characters' behavior too repellent to enjoy.

For now, I hope the show's attention to the minutiae of daily life continues to help its viewers identify their own repellent behaviors as they navigate the intricacies of society. I hope audiences see Jerry, George, Elaine, and Kramer not as exemplars of how to treat others but as cautionary figures with a tragic inability to express love. But I also hope that a Titleist in a whale's blowhole or a Junior Mint in an open body cavity remains just as hysterical for decades to come.

# THE RANKINGS

Every Episode, from Best to Worst

**B**elow are my rankings for every *Seinfeld* episode (with season and episode numbers noted). This list is indisputable, in the sense that no one can dispute the fact that these are my personal rankings. In creating this list, I asked myself, "Which episode would give me more joy to rewatch?" So, while factors like "historical significance for television," "quotability," and "popularity" might play some part in my thinking, this list ultimately rates how funny and pleasurable I find each episode. In the episode descriptions, rather than recapping the complex plot of each episode, I have merely gestured toward my favorite parts. Note: two clip shows are not ranked: "Highlights of a Hundred" (6:14), and "The Chronicle" (9:21).

1. "The Opposite" (5:21): The pinnacle of *Seinfeld*'s construction of its main characters. George ignores every instinct as his life hits a new high point, while Elaine bottoms out. Kramer promotes his coffee-table book.
2. "The Bizarro Jerry" (8:3): The best of several "meta" episodes in *Seinfeld*'s post–Larry David era. Elaine finds a new group of friends. Jerry dates a woman with "man hands." Kramer accidentally gets a job.
3. "The Marine Biologist" (5:14): George weaves a tangled web of lies. Kramer tries to hit golf balls into the ocean. The episode culminates in

the coffee-shop booth with perhaps the most thrilling collisions of story-lines the show ever pulled off.

4. "The Invitations" (7:22): A sick yet hysterical conclusion to George's relationship with Susan. Jerry gets engaged, too! Kramer doesn't get a "hello" at the bank.

5. "The Secret Code" (7:7): Peterman's mother dies after George tells her his secret bank code is "Bosco." Jerry's leg keeps falling asleep.

6. "The Merv Griffin Show" (9:6): Kramer hosts his own talk show in his apartment. Jerry's girlfriend won't let him play with her collection of antique toys. Elaine deals with a "sideler" at work.

7. "The Barber" (5:8): Set to some of Seinfeld's best use of music, Jerry gets a bad haircut before Elaine's charity bachelor auction. Kramer falls off the auction's catwalk. At his new job, George works on the Penske file in a small office.

8. "The Non-Fat Yogurt" (5:7): Another wonderful collision of story-lines as the episode crosses into the reality of the 1993 New York City mayoral race. Elaine dates George's nemesis, Lloyd Braun. Jerry keeps cursing in front of a neighbor's kid.

9. "The Puerto Rican Day" (9:20): Elaine leads an escape party. George eludes a laser pointer. Kel Varnsen threatens an all-out bidding war with H. E. Pennypacker and Art Vandelay, leaving no one to watch the Saab factory.

10. "The Junior Mint" (4:20): Jerry and Kramer have a snack during Elaine's boyfriend's operation. Jerry tries to remember his girlfriend's name. (Hint: It's not "Mulva.")

11. "The Gum" (7:10): Jerry, Kramer, and Lloyd Braun chew gum together. Elaine loses a button. Ruthie Cohen rides a horse. George's old friend, Deena, thinks he is crazy, especially when he essentially tries to explain the plot of the episode to her.

12. "The Glasses" (5:3): After losing his glasses, George spots dimes and eats onions. Kramer helps Elaine with a dog problem.

13. "The Puffy Shirt" (5:2): Kramer dates a "low talker" who gets Jerry to dress like a pirate on The Today Show. George becomes a hand model.

14. "The Postponement" (7:2): George tries to convince Susan to postpone their wedding. Elaine confides in a gabby rabbi. Kramer burns himself sneaking a caffè latte into the movies.

15. "The Engagement" (7:1): George has a deep conversation with Jerry, shakes his friend's hand, and then gets engaged to Susan. Kramer and Newman help Elaine with another dog problem.

16. "The Rye" (7:11): Using a fishing pole and a hansom cab, Jerry and Kramer help George sneak a marble rye into Susan's parents' home. Elaine dates a sax man.

17. "The Foundation" (8:1): Susan's parents put George in charge of a foundation in her memory. Peterman heads to Burma, leaving Elaine in charge. Kramer dominates the dojo.

18. "The Summer of George" (8:22): George vows to make the most of his three months of severance pay from the Yankees. Jerry's girlfriend lives with a dude. Elaine's co-worker doesn't move her arms when she walks. After Kramer gets a Tony, he parties all night and watches the sun come up at Liza's.

19. "The Pitch/The Ticket" (aired as a one-hour episode, 4:3–4): Jerry and George pitch a show about nothing to NBC, where they see "Crazy" Joe Davola and meet Susan.

20. "The Maestro" (7:3): Elaine dates Bob Cobb, an orchestra conductor. The Maestro, as Bob prefers to be called, gives Kramer a balm and tells Jerry there are no houses to rent in Tuscany.

21. "The Chinese Restaurant" (2:11): Jerry, Elaine, and George wait for a table.

22. "The Doll" (7:16): One of Susan's dolls looks exactly like George's mother. Frank Costanza invites Kramer and the Maestro to check out his new billiards room, where the three men take their pants off.

23. "The Betrayal" (9:8): The backwards episode ends with the first time Jerry met Kramer.

24. "The Frogger" (9:18): George enlists Kramer, Slippery Pete, and Shlomo to help him preserve his high score on a Frogger machine. Elaine eats an expensive slice of wedding cake.

25. "The Raincoats" (5:18): Jerry's parents visit New York, and they meet Elaine's boyfriend, a "close talker." Jerry makes out with his girlfriend during *Schindler's List*.

26. "The Pen" (3:3): While visiting his parents in Florida, Jerry gets a pen that can write upside-down from one of their friends.

27. "The Soup Nazi" (7:6): A strict soup chef causes problems for the gang. Kramer fails to protect Elaine's new armoire.

28. "The Dealership" (9:11): Jerry buys a car from Puddy. After losing a Twix, George organizes a candy-bar lineup. Kramer takes a test drive.

29. "The Soup" (6:7): Bania gives Jerry a suit for free, but there are strings attached.

30. "The Pledge Drive" (6:3): Elaine's friend is dating a "high talker." Elaine discovers Mr. Pitt eats his Snickers with a knife and fork.

31. "The Lip Reader" (5:6): George asks Jerry's deaf girlfriend to eavesdrop on the woman who just dumped him. Kramer becomes a ball boy at the U.S. Open. Elaine gets caught hearing.

32. "The Wig Master" (7:18): Jerry has champagne coolies with the wig master from *Joseph and the Amazing Technicolor Dreamcoat*. Kramer borrows the dreamcoat.

33. "The Little Kicks" (8:4): Elaine dances. Jerry bootlegs *Cry, Cry Again*.

34. "The Voice" (9:2): Kramer gets an intern and the two come up with an idea to solve the world's energy problems. Jerry pretends his girlfriend's belly button speaks with a silly voice.

35. "The Comeback" (8:13): George comes up with a great comeback. Elaine rents movies based on the picks of a mysterious video store worker named Vincent.

36. "The Strike" (9:10): The gang celebrates Festivus.

37. "The Slicer" (9:7): Elaine borrows Kramer's new meat slicer to feed the cat in the apartment across the hall. George is worried his new boss will remember him from a previous run-in.

38. "The Switch" (6:11): Jerry's girlfriend doesn't laugh at his jokes, so he and George come up with a plan that will allow Jerry to date his girlfriend's roommate. The gang finally learns Kramer's first name is Cosmo.

39. "The Wink" (7:4): A squirt of grapefruit pulp causes problems for George. Jerry is dating Elaine's cousin who invites the two over for mutton.

40. "The Pick" (4:13): Jerry's girlfriend mistakes a scratch for a pick. Elaine's nipple is visible in the Christmas card photo Kramer took for her.

41. "The Pothole" (8:16): Jerry knocks his girlfriend's toothbrush into the toilet. Elaine pretends to live in a janitor's closet so she can order Chinese food.

42. "The Face Painter" (6:22): Jerry doesn't want to call his friend to thank him for giving him hockey tickets. Elaine discovers Puddy is a rabid hockey fan.

43. "The Cartoon" (9:13): George's girlfriend looks like Jerry.

44. "The Soul Mate" (8:2): George bugs his briefcase to see if the board of Susan's memorial foundation thinks he killed Susan.

45. "The Kiss Hello" (6:16): Kramer's idea to put everyone's photo up in the building's lobby forces Jerry to give a "kiss hello" to all his neighbors. Jerry's Nana discovers her bank burned down.

46. "The Parking Space" (3:22): George gets into a standoff over a parking space.

47. "The Susie" (8:15): Elaine's co-worker thinks Elaine's name is "Susie."

48. "The Bottle Deposit" (aired as a one-hour episode, 7:20): Kramer and Newman hatch a Michigan bottle-return scheme on the Mother of All Mail Days. Wilhelm sends George downtown on a job.

49. "The Alternate Side" (3:11): Kramer gets a line in a Woody Allen movie.

50. "The Watch" (4:6): Elaine's therapist refuses to stop dating her, so she enlists Kramer to pretend to be her boyfriend. Jerry builds a web of lies after discovering his Uncle Leo found a watch he threw out that was a gift from his parents.

51. "The Wallet" (4:5): Jerry's dad thinks his wallet was stolen at the doctor's office. "Crazy" Joe Davola threatens Jerry.

52. "The Mom and Pop Store" (6:8): George buys John Voight's LeBaron. The owners of a local shoe-repair store run off with Jerry's shoes, leaving him with nothing but a pair of cowboy boots. Jon Voight bites Kramer.

53. "The Reverse Peephole" (9:12): The gang buys a massage chair for Joe Mayo, but George likes it so much, he keeps it. Jerry starts using a "European carryall" and wearing, at Kramer's behest, a fur coat.

54. "The English Patient" (8:17): A beautiful woman mistakes George for Neil, her boyfriend. Izzy Mandelbaum, an 80-year-old fitness enthusiast, hurts his back after challenging Jerry to a weight-lifting competition.

55. "The Mango" (5:1): Jerry discovers Elaine faked her orgasms while they were dating. Kramer gets banned from a produce stand.

56. "The Hot Tub" (7:5): Kramer gets a hot tub. Elaine looks after a marathon runner from Trinidad and Tobago. George starts cursing like his new friends at the Houston Astros.

57. "The Checks" (8:7): Jerry collects royalties for a brief appearance on a Japanese television show. Three Japanese tourists end up sleeping in Kramer's drawers. George and Jerry pitch their sitcom to Japanese TV executives but are told, "You must go now."

58. "The Café" (3:7): Jerry helps a Pakistani restauranteur. Elaine helps George cheat on an IQ test.

59. "The Calzone" (7:19): Kramer warms his clothes in a pizza oven. George gets Steinbrenner hooked on calzones.

60. "The Burning" (9:16): Kramer "gets" gonorrhea. Jerry's girlfriend has a mysterious tractor story. George tries to leave on a high note.

61. "The Contest" (4:11): The gang competes in a contest to see who can be "master of their domain."

62. "The Dinner Party" (5:13): En route to a dinner party, Jerry and Elaine stop for babka while George and Kramer buy wine. George wears a puffy Gore-Tex coat.

63. "The Stakeout" (1:1): Jerry and George pretend to have a meeting with importer/exporter Art Vandelay.

64. "The Van Buren Boys" (8:14): George picks a George-like underachiever to receive a scholarship. Kramer sells his life stories to Peterman for the publisher's autobiography, including one about falling in mud while wearing pants he was about to return.

65. "The Race" (6:10): Jerry races his high school archnemesis. Elaine dates a communist.

66. "The Abstinence" (8:9): Abstaining from sex makes George smarter but Elaine dumber. Kramer looks hideous after turning his apartment into a smoking lounge.

67. "The Parking Garage" (3:6): The gang can't find Kramer's car.

68. "The Butter Shave" (9:1): Newman wants to eat Kramer because he is using butter as body lotion.

69. "The Boyfriend" (aired as a one-hour episode, 3:17–18): Jerry and Elaine become interested in Keith Hernandez. George spins lies at the unemployment office.

70. "The Fusilli Jerry" (6:20): The DMV mistakenly gives Kramer a vanity plate that reads "ASSMAN." Frank Costanza falls on a sculpture of Jerry that Kramer made out of pasta.

71. "The Muffin Tops" (8:21): George dresses like a tourist. Elaine helps Lippman with his new muffin-top business. Kramer launches "The Real Peterman Bus Tour."

72. "The Nap" (8:18): George starts taking naps under his desk. Jerry gets new kitchen cabinets. Kramer and Elaine start a fad of swimming in the East River.

73. "The Little Jerry" (8:11): The gang gets involved in cockfighting. George discovers the pleasures of "conjugal visit sex" and "fugitive sex."

74. "The Andrea Doria" (8:10): When she breaks up with him, Elaine's boyfriend says she has a big head. Jerry delivers the mail for Newman.

75. "The Hamptons" (5:20): Jerry, Kramer, and Elaine see George's girlfriend topless. Jerry's girlfriend sees George naked. George sees Jerry's girlfriend naked.

76. "The Chinese Woman" (6:4): Jerry's girlfriend, Donna Chang (née Changstein) seems to like tricking people into thinking she is Chinese. Kramer is out there and loving every minute of it. Frank Costanza's lawyer wears a cape.

77. "The Chicken Roaster" (8:8): Jerry and Kramer swap apartments. George steals his ex-girlfriend's clock.

78. "The Finale" (9:22): The gang is delayed on their way to Paris.

79. "The Blood" (9:4): George adds food and TV to sex.

80. "The Pie" (5:15): Kramer discovers a mannequin that looks just like Elaine. Jerry discovers that Poppie is a little sloppy.

81. "The Cigar Store Indian" (5:10): Jerry tries to be politically correct in front of Elaine's Native American friend. On the subway, Elaine meets a man who collects *TV Guides*.

82. "The Movie" (4:14): The gang goes to the movies where Kramer sees *CheckMate* while the others watch *Rochelle, Rochelle*.

83. "The Doodle" (6:19): George's girlfriend doesn't care what he looks like. Newman gives Jerry fleas, and Kramer gets fumigated.

84. "The Seven" (7:13): Susan's cousin steals George's idea for a baby name. Jerry's girlfriend seems to own only one dress.

85. "The Fatigues" (8:6): The gang gets into mentorship. (I docked this episode 10 spots in the rankings because it should have been called, "The Mentor.")

86. "The Wizard" (9:15): Kramer moves to the retirement community where Jerry's parents live. George drives Susan's parents out to the Hamptons.

87. "The Package" (8:5): George plays a game of seduction with a photo-store clerk. Uncle Leo burns his eyebrows off.

88. "The Chaperone" (6:1): Kramer chaperones Jerry's date with Miss Rhode Island. Elaine becomes Mr. Pitt's personal assistant.

89. "The Wait Out" (7:21): A couple separates after George jokingly tells a married woman she could have done a lot better than her husband. Kramer can't get his slim-fit jeans off.

90. "The Yada Yada" (8:19): Jerry thinks Whatley converted to Judaism for the jokes.

91. "The Serenity Now" (9:3): Frank Costanza hires George and Lloyd Braun to sell computers out of his garage. Jerry lets out his emotions.

92. "The Maid" (9:19): Jerry sleeps with his maid, who stops cleaning his apartment but still takes his money. George tries to get his co-workers to call him "T-Bone."

93. "The Pez Dispenser" (3:14): Elaine bursts into hysterical laughter when Jerry puts a Pez dispenser on her lap at George's girlfriend's piano recital.

94. "The Implant" (4:19): Jerry wonders if his girlfriend's breasts are real. George double-dips a chip.

95. "The Couch" (6:5): Poppie pees on Jerry's new couch. George crashes a random family's apartment to watch *Breakfast at Tiffany's* before his book-club meeting.

96. "The Sponge" (7:9): Kramer refuses to wear an AIDS ribbon at a charity walk. Elaine devises a "sponge-worthy" test.

97. "The Shower Head" (7:15): Elaine tests positive for opium. George tries to get his parents to move to Florida, while Jerry tries to get his parents to return there.

98. "The Bookstore" (9:17): Jerry turns in Uncle Leo for shoplifting. Newman and Kramer start a rickshaw business. George takes a book for a wild ride.

99. "The Keys" (3:23): A fight with Jerry prompts Kramer to move to Los Angeles.

100. "The Millennium" (8:20): George tries to get fired from the Yankees so that he can work for the Mets. Elaine enlists Kramer to help sabotage a clothing store. Jerry fights for speed-dial supremacy on his girlfriend's phone.

101. "The Gymnast" (6:6): Jerry hopes his gymnast girlfriend will use him as a pommel horse. George eats garbage. Mr. Pitt gets ink on his face.

102. "The Visa" (4:15): Jerry pretends to be unfunny in front of George's new girlfriend.

103. "The Opera" (4:9): "Crazy" Joe Davola acts crazy at the opera.

104. "The Pilot" (aired as a one-hour episode, 4:23): Jerry and George produce their NBC pilot. Elaine files a complaint about the buxom waitresses at Monk's. George has a spot on his lip.

105. "The Jimmy" (6:18): Jerry worries Whatley took advantage of him while he was knocked out with gas for a dental operation. The gang encounters a man who speaks in the third person.

106. "The Cadillac" (aired as a one-hour episode, 7:14): Jerry buys his father a Cadillac. Morty Seinfeld faces impeachment from his position as condo president. George has a crush on Marisa Tomei. Kramer avoids the cable guy.

107. "The Money" (8:12): Jerry's parents think he needs money. George thinks Elaine is showing off how much money she makes.

108. "The Secretary" (6:9): Elaine has trouble with skinny mirrors. Jerry thinks his dry cleaner is wearing his clothes. Bania buys a suit off Kramer . . . literally.

109. "The Junk Mail" (9:5): Jerry gets a van. George dates his cousin. Elaine dates "The Wiz." Kramer boycotts mail.

110. "The Library" (3:5): Lt. Bookman, a library detective, investigates Jerry for a long-overdue book. George runs into his old gym teacher.

111. "The Pony Remark" (2:2): Manya, an elderly relative who grew up with a pony, dies shortly after Jerry says he hates anyone who had a pony growing up.

112. "The Caddy" (7:12): George Steinbrenner thinks George is dead.

113. "The Virgin" (4:10): Jerry dates a virgin. George thinks being a sitcom writer is a great way to meet women, but he can't break up with Susan because then he wouldn't be a sitcom writer.

114. "The Outing" (4:17): The gang insists there is nothing wrong with being gay.

115. "The Apology" (9:9): Kramer schemes to stay in the shower most of the day. Elaine's co-worker thinks Elaine is gross. George anticipates an apology from an old nemesis.

116. "The Doorman" (6:17): Kramer and Frank Costanza invent a bra for men. Frank sleeps over at George's place.

117. "The Label Maker" (6:12): Whatley regifts a label maker. George's girlfriend has a roommate who looks just like him. Newman and Kramer play Risk.

118. "The Conversion" (5:11): Jerry finds a tube of fungicide in his girlfriend's bathroom. George converts to Latvian Orthodox for a woman.

119. "The Big Salad" (6:2): George buys Elaine a salad, but doesn't get a "thank you" when his girlfriend hands over the salad. Jerry discovers his girlfriend once dated Newman. Elaine buys a pencil for Mr. Pitt.

120. "The Diplomat's Club" (6:21): George tries to convince his boss, who is black, that he is not racist. Mr. Pitt thinks Elaine and Jerry are conspiring to murder him.

121. "The Friars Club" (7:17): Elaine thinks her co-worker is faking deafness to get out of work. After reading a book about Leonardo da Vinci, Kramer tries to sleep 20 minutes every three hours. Jerry loses a jacket he borrowed.

122. "The Pool Guy" (7:8): George's worlds collide. Kramer takes calls as Moviefone.

123. "The Sniffing Accountant" (5:4): George interviews for a job as a bra salesman. Elaine's boyfriend neglects to use an exclamation point for an important phone message.

124. "The Shoes" (4:16): George and Jerry don't know how to write the woman's part in their pilot script. The president of NBC catches George looking at his daughter's cleavage.

125. "The Jacket" (2:3): Jerry and George hang out with Elaine's father while Elaine does a "solid" for Kramer.

126. "The Wife" (5:17): Jerry and his girlfriend pretend to be married to get a dry-cleaning discount. George pees in the shower at his health club. Kramer falls asleep in a tanning bed on the eve of meeting his girlfriend's parents, who are black.

127. "The Smelly Car" (4:21): A valet leaves the smell of body odor in Jerry's car. George discovers his ex-girlfriend, Susan, is dating a woman.

128. "The Trip, Parts 1–2" (aired over two weeks, 4:1–2): Jerry and George look for Kramer in LA.

129. "The Beard" (6:15): George, wearing a toupee, is uninterested in a woman because she is bald. He also tells Jerry how to beat a lie detector.

130. "The Bubble Boy" (4:7): Susan and George visit a boy whose medical condition requires him to live in a plastic bubble. Kramer burns down Susan's family cabin.

131. "The Fire" (5:19): Kramer is dating Toby, Elaine's overenthusiastic co-worker. Toby heckles Jerry during his act. Jerry retaliates by heckling her at work.

132. "The Old Man" (4:18): Jerry, Elaine, and George try charity work. A housekeeper puts oil on George's bald head.

133. "The Subway" (3:13): The gang encounters a mugger, a nudist, a con artist, and a homophobe on the subway.

134. "The Stall" (5:12): George is infatuated with the "mimbo" Elaine is dating. Kramer thinks the woman Jerry is dating works for a phone sex line.

135. "The Heart Attack" (2:8): George tries a holistic healer. Jerry can't read a note he wrote.

136. "The Strongbox" (9:14): George's girlfriend refuses to break up with him. Jerry refuses to let a stranger into the apartment building, only to discover the guy lives down the hall.

137. "The Scofflaw" (6:13): Elaine sticks it to her ex-boyfriend by getting the same glasses frames he has.

138. "The Understudy" (6:23): Jerry dates Bette Midler's understudy for the Broadway adaptation of *Rochelle, Rochelle.*

139. "The Nose Job" (3:9): George dates a woman with a large nose.

140. "The Bris" (5:5): Kramer thinks he saw a pigman at the hospital.

141. "The Cheever Letters" (4:8): Trying to match his date's dirty talk, Jerry makes an odd remark, which he fears will get back to Elaine. Susan's father learns the family cabin burned down.

142. "The Stand-In" (5:17): Jerry performs for a sick friend and kills . . . literally.

143. "The Airport" (4:12): Kramer somehow convinces George that if he buys airline tickets and returns them, he'll keep the frequent flyer miles.

144. "The Tape" (3:8): George's head stinks after he gets a cure for baldness from China.

145. "The Deal" (2:9): After sleeping with Elaine, Jerry gives her $182 cash for her birthday.

146. "The Good Samaritan" (3:20): A woman sneezes and, seeing her husband remain silent, George says, "God bless you!" Then George and the woman have an affair.

147. "The Masseuse" (5:9): Jerry tries to force his girlfriend to give him a massage. George becomes infatuated with the same woman because she hates him.

148. "The Note" (3:1): A man gives George a massage. Kramer sees Joe DiMaggio dunking a donut.

149. "The Red Dot" (3:12): Looking for a gift for Elaine, George gets a discount on a sweater with a red dot on it.

150. "The Handicap Space" (4:22): George parks his father's car in a handicap space, and an angry mob destroys the car. As punishment, Frank Costanza makes George his butler.

151. "The Suicide" (3:15): After his neighbor attempts suicide and goes into a coma, Jerry starts dating his girlfriend. Kramer plays nude backgammon with swimsuit models.

152. "The Letter" (3:21): A couple buys a painting of Kramer. Elaine wears an Orioles cap to the owner's box at Yankee stadium.

153. "Male Unbonding" (1:3): Jerry tries to break up with an old friend. Elaine and Jerry make plans to sit in a coffee shop.

154. "The Statue" (2:6): A young actor apparently stole a statue while doing a really good job cleaning Jerry's apartment. This plot makes no sense, but Kramer gets a fun scene at the end.

155. "The Baby Shower" (2:10): Elaine throws a baby shower at Jerry's apartment for a woman who once dumped chocolate sauce on George.

156. "The Truth" (3:2): Jerry gets audited.

157. "The Busboy" (2:12): A busboy runs into Elaine's boyfriend in the hall.

158. "The Fix-Up" (3:16): Jerry and Elaine arrange a blind date for George.

159. "The Stranded" (3:10): Jerry and Elaine get stuck at George's office party on Long Island.

160. "The Stock Tip" (1:4): Jerry and George play the market.

161. "The Phone Message" (2:4): George refuses an offer of coffee at the end of a good date.

162. "The Limo" (3:19): Jerry and George pretend to be white supremacists.

163. "The Robbery" (1:2): Everyone wants to move, but no one does.

164. "The Revenge" (2:7): George gets Elaine to help him poison his boss. Kramer and Jerry put concrete in a machine at the laundromat.

165. *The Seinfeld Chronicles* (pilot): George and Kessler help Jerry decipher signals.

166. "The Apartment" (2:5): Jerry prevents Elaine from getting an apartment in his building.

167. "The Dog" (3:4): A drunkard's dog causes problems for Jerry.

168. "The Ex-Girlfriend" (2:1): George asks Jerry to help get his books back from his ex-girlfriend, prompting Jerry to start sleeping with her.

# NOTES

## 1. JERRY AND LARRY

1. Fred Schruers, "Jerry Seinfeld: King of Prime-Time Comedy," *Rolling Stone*, September 22, 1994, https://www.rollingstone.com/tv/tv-news/jerry-seinfeld-king-of-prime-time-comedy-47034.

2. Billy Rennison, "Seinfeld Comes Home, Performs at Alma Mater Queens College," *Queens Courier*, October 23, 2012, https://qns.com/story/2012/10/23/seinfeld-comes-home-performs-at-alma-mater-queens-college.

3. Seinfeld's first appearance on television came in 1978 in an episode of Jack Linkletter's daytime talk show *America Alive!* Bob Hope happened to be one of the other guests in that episode.

4. *Jerry Seinfeld: Stand-Up Confidential* was co-written by Joel Hodgson, who went on to create *Mystery Science Theater 3000*. The cast members included Seinfeld's pal, Larry Miller, and future *Seinfeld* writer, Carol Leifer.

5. Charlie Rose, "Who Is Larry David?" *60 Minutes*, CBS, March 1, 2015.

6. James Kaplan, "Angry Middle-Aged Man," *New Yorker*, January 19, 2004, https://www.newyorker.com/magazine/2004/01/19/angry-middle-aged-man.

7. Kaplan, "Angry Middle-Aged Man."

8. David Noonan, "The Power of Self-Loathing," *New York Times Magazine*, April 12, 1998, https://www.nytimes.com/1998/04/12/magazine/the-power-of-self-loathing.html.

9. David worked with Gottfried for two Cinemax comedies in 1987: *The Original Max Talking Headroom Show* and *Norman's Corner*. The same year, he was credited with one episode of Showtime's *It's Garry Shandling's Show*.

10. "How Larry David Earned Your Enthusiasm," *Rolling Stone*, July 20, 2011, https://www.rollingstone.com/movies/movie-lists/how-larry-david-earned-your-enthusiasm-17626/saturday-night-live-1984-1985-20225.

11. Sara Vilkomerson, "When Woody Met Larry," *Independent*, May 8, 2009, https://www.independent.co.uk/arts-entertainment/films/features/when-woody-met-larry-1680901.html.

12. Castle Rock officially appointed David as show runner after he fixed a story issue on the fly during the production of "The Robbery" (season 1, episode 2).

13. Jesse David Fox, "Talking to the *Seinfeld* Writer behind 'Yada Yada Yada' and 'Double-Dipping,'" Vulture, July 2, 2014, https://www.vulture.com/2014/07/classic-seinfeld-episodes-writer-peter-mehlman-yada-yada-shrinkage-double-dipping.html; Jeremy Hobson, "One Former 'Seinfeld' Writer Reflects on the Show's Impact, 20 Years after Its Finale," *Here & Now*, WBUR, May 14, 2018, https://www.wbur.org/hereandnow/2018/05/14/seinfeld-finale-20-years-later.

14. Fox, "Talking to the *Seinfeld* Writer."

15. "Notes about Nothing: 'The Dog,'" *Seinfeld: The Complete Series, Vol. 2: Season 3* (Culver City, CA: Sony Pictures Home Entertainment, 2004), DVD, disc 1.

## 2. A GUY WALKS INTO NBC . . .

1. Joseph J. Darowski and Kate Darowski, Frasier: *A Cultural History* (Lanham, MD: Rowman & Littlefield, 2017).

2. To mention a few examples, *The Simpsons* was co-created by James L. Brooks, who also co-created *The Mary Tyler Moore Show*. Ed. Weinberger also worked at MTM in the 1970s before going on to help create *The Cosby Show*, where he worked with Tom Werner and Marcy Carsey who went on to create several other hits, including *Roseanne*. And John Wells was the show runner for *ER* after working on *China Beach*, where he worked closely with Mimi Leder, who broke into television working on *Hill Street Blues*.

3. David Itzkoff, "Julia Louis-Dreyfus on Clinton, Trump and an Election-Year 'Veep,'" *New York Times*, April 14, 2016, https://www.nytimes.com/2016/04/17/arts/television/julia-louis-dreyfus-on-clinton-trump-and-anelection-year-veep.html.

4. Itzkoff, "Julia Louis-Dreyfus."

5. Chris Smith, "Jerry Seinfeld: Making Something out of Nothing," *New York*, 30th Anniversary Issue, April 6, 1998, http://nymag.com/nymetro/news/people/features/2430.

6. Lee Goldberg, *Unsold Television Pilots: 1955–1989* (Calabasas, CA: Adventures in Television, 2015).

7. Smith, "Jerry Seinfeld."

8. David Noonan, "The Power of Self-Loathing," *New York Times Magazine*, April 12, 1998, https://www.nytimes.com/1998/04/12/magazine/the-power-of-self-loathing.html.

9. Smith, "Jerry Seinfeld."

## 3. WHO (ALMOST) KILLED THE PILOT?

1. William Goldman, *Adventures in the Screen Trade: A Personal View of Hollywood and Screenwriting* (New York: Warner Books, 1983).

2. Stephen Battaglio, "The Biz: The Research Memo That Almost Killed *Seinfeld*," *TV Guide*, June 30, 2014, https://www.tvguide.com/news/seinfeld-research-memo-1083639.

3. Rick Kogan, "Short and Funny 'Seinfeld Chronicles' Stands Out as Standup Sitcom," *Chicago Tribune*, July 5, 1989, https://www.chicagotribune.com/news/ct-xpm-1989-07-05-8902140989-story.html.

4. Ray Richmond, "Seinfeld Special Brightens Up Boring Summer Fare," *Orange County Register*, July 5, 1989, L10.

5. Ken Tucker, "White House Showcase, Jerry Seinfeld Sitcom," *Philadelphia Inquirer*, July 5, 1989, E1.

6. *Wings*, which ran for eight seasons, was the only other new NBC sitcom to last more than two seasons. NBC's eight failed comedies from the 1989–1990 season included seven sitcoms—*The Nutt House, Ann Jillian, Down Home, A Family for Joe, FM, Grand, Sister Kate*—and a comedy anthology starring Carol Burnett called *Carol & Company*.

7. Battaglio, "The Biz."

8. Ibid.

9. Tom Green, "Comic Seinfeld Stands Up for His Personal 'Chronicles,'" *USA Today*, July 3, 1989, 3D.

10. Harry E. Waters, "Can Tinker Save NBC?" *Newsweek*, no. 99 (June 14, 1982): 97. (See chapter 2.)

11. *Down Home* was one of the few new sitcoms to last into a second season, perhaps because NBC's golden boy, Ted Danson, was a co-producer.

12. Kate Stanhope, "Former NBC Execs Look Back on the Births of 'ER,' 'Seinfeld,' and 'Will & Grace,'" *Hollywood Reporter*, February 7, 2017, https://www.hollywoodreporter.com/live-feed/nbc-execs-look-back-er-seinfeld-will-grace-973094.

13. "Forever *Seinfeld*," *People*, Special *Seinfeld* Farewell Issue, May 14, 1998, https://people.com/archive/cover-story-forever-seinfeld.

14. Reed Dunlea, "The Wolff of 116th Street: How Seinfeld's Theme Song Was Created," Noisey: Music by Vice, March 17, 2015, https://www.vice.com/en_us/article/689n7a/how-seinfelds-theme-song-was-created.

15. "Inside Look: 'The Stakeout,'" *Seinfeld: The Complete Series, Vol. 1: Seasons 1 & 2* (Culver City, CA: Sony Pictures Home Entertainment, 2004), DVD, disc 1.

16. Larry David and Jerry Seinfeld, "DVD Commentary: The Stakeout," *Seinfeld: The Complete Series, Vol. 1: Seasons 1 & 2* (Culver City, CA: Sony Pictures Home Entertainment, 2004), DVD, disc 1.

17. "How It Began," *Seinfeld: The Complete Series, Vol. 1: Seasons 1 & 2* (Culver City, CA: Sony Pictures Home Entertainment, 2004), DVD, disc 1.

18. Larry Getlen, "The Backstage Drama That Nearly Brought Down 'Seinfeld,'" *New York Post*, July 10, 2016, https://nypost.com/2016/07/10/the-backstage-bickering-that-almost-brought-down-seinfeld.

19. Duane Dudek, "Seinfeld Is Moving Up in NBC's Stable of Top-Seeded Comics," *Milwaukee Journal Sentinel*, June 12, 1991, D6.

20. Jack Major, "TV Highlights: What's Funny These Days? Try 'Seinfeld,'" *Providence Journal*, May 23, 1991, E5. This piece ran the day "The Chinese Restaurant" aired. Other TV critics around the country gave their hometown audiences a similar heads-up, which helped spread the word in this pre-internet era.

21. Warren Littlefield and T. R. Pearson, *Top of the Rock: The Rise and Fall of Must See TV* (New York: Doubleday, 2012).

## 4. ENSEMBLE ALCHEMY

1. "Inside Look: 'The Busboy,'" *Seinfeld: The Complete Series, Vol. 1: Seasons 1 & 2* (Culver City, CA: Sony Pictures Home Entertainment, 2004), DVD, disc 4.

2. "Inside Look: 'The Busboy.'"

3. Tom Cherones directed most of the episodes in seasons 1 through 5, and Andy Ackerman took over from season 6.

4. Barry Koltnow, "It's OK to Call Him George," *Orange County Register*, October 9, 2000, F01.

5. Ian Goldstein, "Steve Buscemi: Seinfeld Audition Never Happened," *Entertainment Weekly*, August 8, 2015, https://ew.com/article/2015/08/08/steve-buscemi-seinfeld-audition-never-happened; Bradford Evans, "The Lost

Roles of *Seinfeld*," Vulture, April 14, 2011, https://www.vulture.com/2011/04/the-lost-roles-of-seinfeld.html.

6. Austin Siegemund-Broka, "Larry David's Best Advice on Dealing with Network Execs: 'Just Say No,'" *Hollywood Reporter*, September 29, 2014, https://www.hollywoodreporter.com/news/larry-davids-best-advice-dealing-736325; "How It Began," *Seinfeld: The Complete Series, Vol. 1: Seasons 1 & 2* (Culver City, CA: Sony Pictures Home Entertainment, 2004), DVD, disc 1.

7. Susan King, "Alexander's Big-Time Band of Characters," *Los Angeles Times*, March 27, 1994, https://www.latimes.com/archives/la-xpm-1994-03-27-tv-38811-story.html.

8. King, "Alexander's Big-Time Band of Characters."

9. "How It Began," *Seinfeld: The Complete Series*.

10. "Michael Richards," *People*, May 14, 1998, https://people.com/archive/michael-richards.

11. David Kronke, "Kramer Gets Serious: Michael Richards of 'Seinfeld' Reveals Another Side in 'Unstrung Heroes,'" *Los Angeles Times*, September 20, 1995, https://www.latimes.com/archives/la-xpm-1995-09-20-ca-47891-story.html.

12. Bill Zehme, "Jerry & George & Kramer & Elaine: Exposing the Secrets of Seinfeld's Success," *Rolling Stone*, July 8, 1993, https://www.rollingstone.com/music/music-news/jerry-george-kramer-elaine-162060.

13. Steve Inskeep, "Interview: Michael Richards Discusses 'Seinfeld,'" *Morning Edition*, National Public Radio, November 23, 2004.

14. Brian Cronin, "TV Legends Revealed: Why Did 'Seinfeld' Replace Its Original Female Lead?" CBR.com, August 3, 2016, https://www.cbr.com/tv-legends-revealed-why-did-seinfeld-replace-its-original-female-lead.

15. Rick Lyman, "Touching Moments with Leifer? Get Real!" *New York Times*, September 7, 1997, https://www.nytimes.com/1997/09/07/tv/touching-moments-with-leifer-get-real.html.

16. Lacey Rose, "Julia Louis-Dreyfus Reveals Awkward Fan Letter from Hillary and Her Panic on That 'Last F—able Day,'" *Hollywood Reporter*, April 20, 2016, https://www.hollywoodreporter.com/features/julia-louis-dreyfus-reveals-awkward-885385.

17. Ariel Levy, "Julia Louis-Dreyfus Acts Out," *New Yorker*, December 17, 2018, https://www.newyorker.com/magazine/2018/12/17/julia-louis-dreyfus-acts-out. Warner Bros. would eventually get to work with Louis-Dreyfus when they produced *The New Adventures of Old Christine*.

18. Rose, "Julia Louis-Dreyfus."

19. Levy, "Julia Louis-Dreyfus Acts Out."

20. Geoff Edgers, "How Julia Louis-Dreyfus Quietly Became the Most Successful Sitcom Star Ever," *Washington Post*, October 17, 2018, https://www.

washingtonpost.com/entertainment/tv/how-julia-louis-dreyfus-quietly-became-
the-most-successful-sitcom-star-ever/2018/10/16/b434a03a-ce2e-11e8-a3e6-
44daa3d35ede_story.html.

21. Levy, "Julia Louis-Dreyfus Acts Out."

22. "Inside Look: 'The Little Kicks,'" *Seinfeld: The Complete Series, Vol. 7: Season 8* (Culver City, CA: Sony Pictures Home Entertainment, 2007), DVD, disc 1.

23. Ross Johnson, "Getting a Piece of a DVD Windfall: Sales Are Soaring and Hollywood Is Split over Dividing Profits," *New York Times*, December 13, 2004, https://www.nytimes.com/2004/12/13/business/media/getting-a-piece-of-a-dvd-windfall.html.

24. Matthew Kalman, "Pact Brings Peace to the Seinfeld Cast," *Globe and Mail*, February 27, 2004, https://www.theglobeandmail.com/arts/pact-brings-peace-to-the-seinfeld-cast/article4087758.

25. "Salaries Reported in Deal for Cast of 'Seinfeld,'" *New York Times*, May 12, 1997, https://www.nytimes.com/1997/05/12/us/salaries-reported-in-deal-for-cast-of-seinfeld.html.

26. Kalman, "Pact Brings Peace."

27. Johnson, "Getting a Piece of a DVD Windfall."


## 5. THE FOUR

1. John Freeman, "Subtle 'Seinfeld' Succeeds by Refusing to Try Too Hard," *San Diego Union-Tribune*, March 24, 1992.

2. Steve Inskeep, "Interview: Michael Richards Discusses 'Seinfeld,'" *Morning Edition*, National Public Radio, November 23, 2004.

3. Bill Zehme, "Jerry & George & Kramer & Elaine: Exposing the Secrets of Seinfeld's Success," *Rolling Stone*, July 8, 1993, https://www.rollingstone.com/music/music-news/jerry-george-kramer-elaine-162060/.

4. Ibid.


## 6. THE PEOPLE IN THEIR NEIGHBORHOOD

1. For the record, I am not including two-part episodes, as well as episodes like the season 4 finale, "The Pilot," and the series finale, which included brief, uncredited cutaways to characters from previous episodes.

2. Daniel Kreps, James Montgomery, David Fear, Kory Grow, and Gus Wenner, "And They're Spectacular! 10 Actors on Their Memorable 'Seinfeld'

Roles," *Rolling Stone*, July 8, 2014, https://www.rollingstone.com/tv/tv-lists/
and-theyre-spectacular-10-actors-on-their-memorable-seinfeld-roles-17322/
teri-hatcher-sidra-115186.

3. Whatley appeared in four more episodes of *Seinfeld*, helping Cranston
land a lead role in Fox's hit sitcom, *Malcolm in the Middle*. Before that show
aired, Cranston appeared in another Fox hit, *The X-Files*, in an episode written
by Vince Gilligan. Gilligan recalled Cranston's versatility when he was creating
*Breaking Bad*, and Cranston would thus land his signature role. So, basically, if
NBC never picked up *Seinfeld*, the world misses out on both one of the best
shows of the end of the twentieth century *and* one of the best shows of the
beginning of the twenty-first.

4. Glenn Esterly, "Sweating It Out with Newman: Here's What *Seinfeld*,
*Jurassic Park* and *Basic Instinct* Have in Common," *St. Louis Post-Dispatch*,
November 30, 1995.

# 7. FAITH, RACE, AND PLACE IN
## *SEINFELD*'S NEW YORK

1. Francis Davis, "Recognition Humor," *Atlantic*, December 1992, https://
www.theatlantic.com/past/docs/issues/92dec/seinfeld.htm.

2. Why was an NBC show filmed at a CBS studio? Remember that Castle
Rock, not NBC, was the show's producer, so there was not necessarily a benefit, economically or otherwise, to making the show at the home network's
studio. In the mid-1990s, the FCC relaxed restrictions on how many of their
own programs a network could produce and thus control. This created an
increase in vertical integration in the television industry, allowing a network
like NBC to both produce and distribute its own shows.

3. The first episode to utilize the New York Street set was "The Big Salad"
(season 6, episode 2).

4. John Calhoun, "Seinfeld," *Theater Crafts International* 26, no. 7 (August 1992): 44.

5. Ibid.

6. For more on the concept of the "third place," see Ray Oldenburg, *The
Great Good Place: Cafés, Coffee Shops, Community Centers, Beauty Parlors,
General Stores, Bars, Hangouts, and How They Get You through the Day*, 2nd
ed. (New York: Marlowe, 1997). And if you have read this far, you may as well
check out my book on nineties television, which includes a whole chapter
about *Seinfeld*'s coffee shop and other television third places: Paul Arras, *The
Lonely Nineties: Visions of Community in Contemporary US Television*
(Cham, Switzerland: Palgrave Macmillan, 2018).

7. For several years after the show ended, there was a night club called "The Nexus" at this intersection.

8. Associated Press, "NBC Apologizes for 'Seinfeld' Episode on the Puerto Rican Day Parade," *New York Times*, May 9, 1998, https://www.nytimes.com/1998/05/09/nyregion/nbc-apologizes-for-seinfeld-episode-on-the-puerto-rican-day-parade.html.

9. "Inside Look: 'The Diplomat's Club,'" *Seinfeld: The Complete Series, Vol. 5: Season 6* (Culver City, CA: Sony Pictures Home Entertainment, 2005), DVD, disc 4.

## 8. JERRY AND COMPANY IN THE WORLD AND IN THE BEDROOM

1. As with the rankings at the end of this book, that tally of 168 does not include two clip shows, and it counts most of the hour-long episodes as single episodes. *Seinfeld* actually aired 180 half-hours of television.

2. "Inside Look: 'The Bubble Boy,'" *Seinfeld: The Complete Series, Vol. 3: Season 4* (Culver City, CA: Sony Pictures Home Entertainment, 2005), DVD, disc 2.

3. "A Timeline of HIV and AIDS," HIV.gov, U.S. Department of Health and Human Services, n.d., https://www.hiv.gov/hiv-basics/overview/history/hiv-and-aids-timeline.

4. For example, Larry jokes that heterosexuals can't get AIDS in season 5's "The Freak Book" (episode 6, first aired October 7, 2007), an episode that happens to be a critic and fan favorite.

## 9. THE SPECTACLE, THE DISAPPOINTMENT, AND THE BRILLIANCE OF THE FINALE

1. David Noonan, "The Power of Self-Loathing," *New York Times Magazine*, April 12, 1998, https://www.nytimes.com/1998/04/12/magazine/the-power-of-self-loathing.html.

2. Jefferson Graham, "Seinfeld's Oddball Alter Ego: Series Co-Creator Larry David Adds His Own Twists," *USA Today*, February 4, 1993, 3D.

3. Lisa Schwarzbaum, "'Seinfeld' Is Back, Baby! The Show Gains an 8th Season, but Loses Larry David," *Entertainment Weekly*, February 2, 1996, https://ew.com/article/1996/02/02/seinfeld-back-baby.

4. Ibid.

5. Ryan Gajewski, "Jason Alexander: 'Seinfeld' Killed Off Susan Because Actress Was 'F—ing Impossible' to Work With," *Hollywood Reporter*, June 4, 2015, https://www.hollywoodreporter.com/live-feed/jason-alexander-seinfeld-killed-susan-800031.

6. Jason Alexander, "Oh Dear God, Leave Heidi Alone," @IJasonAlexander, June 4, 2015, https://twitter.com/IJasonAlexander/status/606414256427442176.

7. Jim Schembri, "Seinfeld's Legacy," *Sydney Morning Herald*, November 9, 1998, 14.

8. Bill Carter, "Seinfeld Says It's All Over, and It's No Joke for NBC," *New York Times*, December 26, 1997, https://www.nytimes.com/1997/12/26/us/seinfeld-says-it-s-all-over-and-it-s-no-joke-for-nbc.html.

9. Dottie Enrico, "'Seinfeld' Finale Advertisers Put on Game Faces," *USA Today*, April 29, 1998.

10. Richard Huff, "Competing Networks Plot Countermoves for 'Seinfeld' Finale," *Dallas Morning News*, April 5, 1998.

11. Matthew Gilbert, "Endgame: Dreaming of a 'Seinfeld' Finale," *Boston Globe*, March 1, 1998.

12. Dusty Saunders, "Plot Thickens over 'Seinfeld' Finale," *Rocky Mountain News*, March 30, 1998.

13. Lynn Elber, "'Seinfeld' Creators Beg Audience to Keep Quiet," Associated Press, April 10, 1998.

14. Pamela Mitchell, "Peterman Mum on 'Seinfeld' Finale," *Hartford Courant*, April 13, 1998, https://www.courant.com/news/connecticut/hc-xpm-1998-04-13-9804110044-story.html.

15. Gayle Fee and Laura Raposa, "Ssssshhhhh! Secret's out on 'Seinfeld' Finale," *Boston Herald*, May 13, 1998.

16. Jennifer Hickey, "Knowing Who Watches What," *Insight on the News* 14, no. 21 (June 8, 1998): 12–13.

17. Amy Alexander, "Not Everyone Will Miss 'Seinfeld': Some Resent Paucity of Black Faces," *Boston Globe*, January 30, 1998, C1.

18. Greg Braxton, "For Many Black Viewers, 'Seinfeld's' End Is Nonevent," *Los Angeles Times*, May 12, 1998, F9.

19. "Much Ado During Nothing," *Dharma & Greg*, season 1, episode 22 (ABC, May 13, 1998); Braxton, "For Many Black Viewers."

20. Noonan, "The Power of Self-Loathing."

21. Ibid.

22. Gail Pennington, "'Seinfeld' Finale Draws Mixed Reviews, OK Ratings," *St. Louis Post-Dispatch*, May 16, 1998.

23. David Bauder, "'Seinfeld' Finale," Associated Press, May 15, 1998.

24.  Caryn James, "'Seinfeld' Goes Out in Self-Referential Style," *New York Times*, May 15, 1998, https://www.nytimes.com/1998/05/15/arts/television-review-seinfeld-goes-out-in-self-referential-style.html.

25.  David Bianculli, "'Seinfeld' Delivers Finale," *New York Daily News*, May 15, 1998, 4.

26.  Kinney Littlefield, "Sein-off, Alas, Was Nothing Much," *Orange County Register*, May 15, 1998, F01.

27.  Frazier Moore, "No Laughs for You! 'Seinfeld' Finale Turned Out to Be a Real Stinker," Associated Press, May 15, 1998. Printed in the *Sheboygan Press* (WI), May 16, 1998, 19.

28.  David Zurawik, "Not His Finest Hour," *Baltimore Sun*, May 15, 1998, https://www.baltimoresun.com/news/bs-xpm-1998-05-15-1998135029-story.html.

29.  Howard Rosenberg, "Past Comes Back to Haunt 'Seinfeld,'" *Los Angeles Times*, May 15, 1998, https://www.latimes.com/archives/la-xpm-1998-may-15-mn-49999-story.html.

30.  Ed Bark, "Nothing Doing—As Elaine Would Say, 'Seinfeld' Finale Just Wasn't Spongeworthy," *Dallas Morning News*, May 15, 1998, 1G.

31.  Louis Carlozo, "Alexander Revisits 'Seinfeld' Finale," *Chicago Tribune*, November 6, 2007, https://www.chicagotribune.com/news/ct-xpm-2007-11-06-0711020445-story.html.

32.  David Remnick, "Interview with Jerry Seinfeld," New Yorker Festival, October 6, 2017, https://www.newyorker.com/culture/new-yorker-live/videos-from-the-2017-new-yorker-festival.

33.  Tom Shales, "So Long, 'Seinfeld.' Let Me Show You to the Door," *Washington Post*, April 16, 1998, https://www.washingtonpost.com/archive/lifestyle/1998/04/16/so-long-seinfeld-let-me-show-you-to-the-door/ced8dc1a-a8af-42ad-8dd9-75965ab15b22.

34.  Tom Shales, "Guilty Pleasures: 'Seinfeld' Goes up the River," *Washington Post*, May 15, 1998, https://www.washingtonpost.com/archive/lifestyle/1998/05/15/guilty-pleasures-seinfeld-goes-up-the-river/ea8fa5d7-93ec-47ed-9543-6274a5d785df.

## 10. TELEVISION LEGACY

1.  Bill Simmons, "Larry David on the Future of 'Curb Your Enthusiasm' and the 'Seinfeld' Finale," *B.S. Report*, ESPN, December 16, 2014, http://grantland.com/hollywood-prospectus/b-s-report-larry-david-on-the-future-of-curb-your-enthusiasm-and-the-seinfeld-finale.

2. Rick Marin, "The Great and Wonderful Wizard of Odds," *New York Times*, July 16, 2000, https://www.nytimes.com/2000/07/16/style/the-great-and-wonderful-wizard-of-odds.html.

3. Maxton Walker, "Deep Down, I'm Really Shallow," *Guardian*, February 23, 2003. This interview includes some factual errors, such as saying David was hired for "the TV show *Saturday Night*" in 1980. He wrote for *Saturday Night Live* in 1984–1985. I'll forgive the Brits, though, as neither *Saturday Night Live* nor *Seinfeld* was much of a hit across the pond.

4. Roger Ebert, "Sour Grapes," RogerEbert.com, April 17, 1998, https://www.rogerebert.com/reviews/sour-grapes-1998.

5. For a more detailed discussion of many of the themes of this section, see Paul Arras, *The Lonely Nineties: Visions of Community in Contemporary US Television* (Cham, Switzerland: Palgrave Macmillan, 2018).

6. Matt Lauer, "'Friends' Creators Share Show's Beginnings," MSNBC.com, May 5, 2004, www.nbcnews.com/id/4899445/ns/dateline_nbc-newsmakers/t/friends-creators-share-shows-beginnings.

7. "The Last Show," *The Mary Tyler Moore Show*, season 7, episode 24 (CBS, March 19, 1977).

8. Michael Richards actually appeared as Cosmo Kramer in a season 1 episode of *Mad About You*. However, it must have been a different Kramer since *Mad About You* exists as a sitcom in the *Seinfeld* universe.

9. Denise Martin, "FX Takes Walk on 'Sunny' Side: Cabler, Known for Gritty Dramas, Tries Its Hand at Comedy Series with Tyro Creator," *Variety*, August 1, 2005, https://variety.com/2005/tv/news/fx-takes-walk-on-sunny-side-1117926741/.

10. Emily Nussbaum, "Bar None," *New Yorker*, November 11, 2013, 84, https://www.newyorker.com/magazine/2013/11/11/bar-none.

11. Ibid., 84–85.

12. Jonathan Storm, "DeVito a Fine Fit for 'Sunny' Business," *Philadelphia Inquirer*, June 29, 2006, E01.

13. Carina Chocano, "Julia Louis-Dreyfus Takes the White House," *New York Times*, April 12, 2012, https://www.nytimes.com/2012/04/15/magazine/julia-louis-dreyfus-takes-the-white-house.html.

14. Mandalit del Barco, "If It's Awkward, 'My Instinct Is to Make Fun of It,' Says Armando Iannucci," *Morning Edition*, National Public Radio, March 8, 2018, https://www.npr.org/transcripts/591143172.

15. Melena Ryzik, Cara Buckley, and Jodi Kantor, "Louis C.K. Is Accused by 5 Women of Sexual Misconduct," *New York Times*, November 9, 2017, https://www.nytimes.com/2017/11/09/arts/television/louis-ck-sexual-misconduct.html; "Louis C.K. Responds to Accusations: 'These Stores Are

True,'" *New York Times*, November 10, 2017, https://www.nytimes.com/2017/11/10/arts/television/louis-ck-statement.html.

16. Notaro's career is interwoven with C.K.'s as, among other connections, the latter helped produce and promote her breakout 2012 album, *Live*.

17. Emma Stafansky, "Aziz Ansari Accused of Sexual Misconduct," *Vanity Fair*, January 14, 2018, https://www.vanityfair.com/hollywood/2018/01/aziz-ansari-accused-of-sexual-misconduct.

18. Halle Kiefer, "Aziz Ansari Issues Statement after Sexual-Misconduct Accusation: 'I Took Her Words to Heart,'" Vulture, January 14, 2018, https://www.vulture.com/2018/01/aziz-ansari-issues-statement-on-sexual-misconduct-accusation.html.

## 11. CRITIQUES AND MISSTEPS

1. Jordan Hoffman, "*Seinfeld* at 25: Carol Leifer Reveals the Origins of the Marble Rye and the Elaine Stories We Never Saw," *Vanity Fair*, July 2, 2014, https://www.vanityfair.com/hollywood/2014/07/seinfeld-25th-anniversary-marble-rye.

2. Stacy Lavilla, "'Seinfeld' Edits Out Anti-Asian Joke: 'Chinaman's Nightcap' Schtick Won't Run in Reruns," *Asianweek*, July 15, 1998.

3. Jessica Chasmar, "'Seinfeld' Creators Axed 'Elaine Gets a Gun' Episode," *Washington Times*, July 14, 2014.

4. "Inside Look: 'The Outing,'" *Seinfeld: The Complete Series, Vol. 3: Season 4* (Culver City, CA: Sony Pictures Home Entertainment, 2005), DVD, disc 3.

5. See, for example, Ron Becker, "Gay-Themed Television and the Slumpy Class: The Affordable, Multicultural Politics of the Gay Nineties," *Television & New Media* 7, no. 2 (May 2006): 184–215.

## 12. *SEINFELD* TODAY

1. Esther Zuckeman, "Behind the New Modern Seinfeld Twitter Account, Which Is Not about Nothing," *The Wire*, December 10, 2012, https://www.theatlantic.com/entertainment/archive/2012/12/modern-seinfeld-today-twitter/320660. Funny enough, many of their 500+ tweets were rather topical, making the feed more tied to its historic context than the typical episode of *Seinfeld*.

2. Maureen Dowd, "Yada Yada Yuppies," *New York Times*, May 14, 1997, https://www.nytimes.com/1997/05/14/opinion/yada-yada-yuppies.html.

3. Maxwell Tani, "Maureen Dowd: The Only Thing I Wish I Could Take Back Is a Negative Column I Wrote about Seinfeld," *Business Insider*, September 14, 2016, https://www.businessinsider.com/maureen-dowd-seinfeld-amanda-hess-monica-lewinsky-2016-9.

4. Christopher Lasch, *Culture of Narcissism: American Life in an Age of Diminishing Expectations* (New York: W. W. Norton, 1979).

5. Joshua Green, "This Man Is the Most Dangerous Political Operative in America," *Bloomberg Businessweek*, October 8, 2015, https://www.bloomberg.com/politics/graphics/2015-steve-bannon.

6. Marlow Stern, "Rob Reiner on Steve Bannon Getting Rich off 'Seinfeld': 'It Makes Me Sick,'" *Daily Beast*, November 17, 2016, https://www.thedailybeast.com/rob-reiner-on-steve-bannon-getting-rich-off-seinfeld-it-makes-me-sick.

7. Rory Carroll, "Seinfeld Writer Says 'It's Pretty Galling' That Steve Bannon Still Earns Royalties," *Guardian*, December 9, 2016, https://www.theguardian.com/us-news/2016/dec/09/steve-bannon-seinfeld-royalties-peter-mehlman-trump.

8. Joel Achenbach, "Seinfeld Leaves His Mark on History," *Washington Post*, November 19, 2004, https://www.washingtonpost.com/archive/lifestyle/2004/11/19/seinfeld-leaves-his-mark-on-history/bdefda11-b2f3-4568-853f-64433712def4.

9. Asawin Suebsaeng, "'Seinfeld' Writer Takes on Conservative Outrage over Holiday Festivus Pole Protests," *Mother Jones*, December 12, 2013, https://www.motherjones.com/politics/2013/12/festivus-pole-protest-christmas-seinfeld-dan-okeefe-fox-news.

10. Quoted in Steve Johnson, "'Seinfeld' Finale: Yada, Yada, Yada," *Chicago Tribune*, May 15, 1998, https://www.chicagotribune.com/news/ct-xpm-1998-05-15-9805150196-story.html.

11. Judith Trevino et al., "Effect of Biting before Dipping (Double-Dipping) Chips on the Bacterial Population of the Dipping Solution," *Journal of Food Safety* 29, no. 1 (February 2009): 37–48.

# BIBLIOGRAPHY

Achenbach, Joel. "Seinfeld Leaves His Mark on History." *Washington Post*, November 19, 2004. https://www.washingtonpost.com/archive/lifestyle/2004/11/19/seinfeld-leaves-his-mark-on-history/bdefda11-b2f3-4568-853f-64433712def4.

Alexander, Amy. "Not Everyone Will Miss 'Seinfeld': Some Resent Paucity of Black Faces." *Boston Globe*, January 30, 1998, C1.

Alexander, Jason. "Oh Dear God, Leave Heidi Alone." @IJasonAlexander, June 4, 2015. https://twitter.com/IJasonAlexander/status/606414256427442176.

Arras, Paul. *The Lonely Nineties: Visions of Community in Contemporary US Television.* Cham, Switzerland: Palgrave Macmillan, 2018.

Associated Press. "NBC Apologizes for 'Seinfeld' Episode on the Puerto Rican Day Parade." *New York Times*, May 9, 1998. https://www.nytimes.com/1998/05/09/nyregion/nbc-apologizes-for-seinfeld-episode-on-the-puerto-rican-day-parade.html.

Bark, Ed. "Nothing Doing—As Elaine Would Say, 'Seinfeld' Finale Just Wasn't Sponge-worthy." *Dallas Morning News*, May 15, 1998, 1G.

Battaglio, Stephen. "The Biz: The Research Memo That Almost Killed *Seinfeld*." *TV Guide*, June 30, 2014. https://www.tvguide.com/news/seinfeld-research-memo-1083639.

Bauder, David. "'Seinfeld' Finale." Associated Press, May 15, 1998.

Becker, Ron. "Gay-Themed Television and the Slumpy Class: The Affordable, Multicultural Politics of the Gay Nineties." *Television & New Media* 7, no. 2 (May 2006): 184–215.

Bianculli, David. "'Seinfeld' Delivers Finale." *New York Daily News*, May 15, 1998.

Braxton, Greg. "For Many Black Viewers, 'Seinfeld's' End Is Nonevent." *Los Angeles Times*, May 12, 1998, F9.

Calhoun, John. "Seinfeld." *Theater Crafts International* 26, no. 7 (August 1992): 44–47.

Carlozo, Louis. "Alexander Revisits 'Seinfeld' Finale." *Chicago Tribune*, November 6, 2007. https://www.chicagotribune.com/news/ct-xpm-2007-11-06-0711020445-story.html.

Carroll, Rory. "Seinfeld Writer Says 'It's Pretty Galling' That Steve Bannon Still Earns Royalties." *Guardian*, December 9, 2016. https://www.theguardian.com/us-news/2016/dec/09/steve-bannon-seinfeld-royalties-peter-mehlman-trump.

Carter, Bill. "Seinfeld Says It's All Over, and It's No Joke for NBC." *New York Times*, December 26, 1997. https://www.nytimes.com/1997/12/26/us/seinfeld-says-it-s-all-over-and-it-s-no-joke-for-nbc.html.

Chasmar, Jessica. "'Seinfeld' Creators Axed 'Elaine Gets a Gun' Episode." *Washington Times*, July 14, 2014.

Chocano, Carina. "Julia Louis-Dreyfus Takes the White House." *New York Times*, April 12, 2012. https://www.nytimes.com/2012/04/15/magazine/julia-louis-dreyfus-takes-the-white-house.html.

Cronin, Brian. "TV Legends Revealed: Why Did 'Seinfeld' Replace Its Original Female Lead?" CBR.com, August 3, 2016. https://www.cbr.com/tv-legends-revealed-why-did-seinfeld-replace-its-original-female-lead.

Darowski, Joseph J., and Kate Darowski. Frasier: A Cultural History. Lanham, MD: Rowman & Littlefield, 2017.

Davis, Francis. "Recognition Humor." Atlantic, December 1992. https://www.theatlantic.com/past/docs/issues/92dec/seinfeld.htm.

Del Barco, Mandalit. "If It's Awkward, 'My Instinct Is to Make Fun of It' Says Armando Iannucci." Morning Edition, National Public Radio, March 8, 2018. https://www.npr.org/transcripts/591143172.

Dowd, Maureen. "Yada Yada Yuppies." New York Times, May 14, 1997. https://www.nytimes.com/1997/05/14/opinion/yada-yada-yuppies.html.

Dudek, Duane. "Seinfeld Is Moving Up in NBC's Stable of Top-Seeded Comics." Milwaukee Journal Sentinel, June 12, 1991, D6.

Dunlea, Reed. "The Wolff of 116th Street: How Seinfeld's Theme Song Was Created." Noisey: Music by Vice, March 17, 2015. https://www.vice.com/en_us/article/689n7a/how-seinfelds-theme-song-was-created.

Ebert, Roger. "Sour Grapes." RogerEbert.com, April 17, 1998. https://www.rogerebert.com/reviews/sour-grapes-1998.

Edgers, Geoff. "How Julia Louis-Dreyfus Quietly Became the Most Successful Sitcom Star Ever." Washington Post, October 17, 2018. https://www.washingtonpost.com/entertainment/tv/how-julia-louis-dreyfus-quietly-became-the-most-successful-sitcom-star-ever/2018/10/16/b434a03a-ce2e-11e8-a3e6-44daa3d35ede_story.html.

Elber, Lynn. "'Seinfeld' Creators Beg Audience to Keep Quiet." Associated Press, April 10, 1998.

Enrico, Dottie. "'Seinfeld' Finale Advertisers Put on Game Faces." USA Today, April 29, 1998.

Esterly, Glenn. "Sweating It Out with Newman: Here's What Seinfeld, Jurassic Park and Basic Instinct Have in Common." St. Louis Post-Dispatch, November 30, 1995.

Evans, Bradford. "The Lost Roles of Seinfeld." Vulture, April 14, 2011. https://www.vulture.com/2011/04/the-lost-roles-of-seinfeld.html.

Fee, Gayle, and Laura Raposa. "Ssssshhhhh! Secret's out on 'Seinfeld' Finale." Boston Herald, May 13, 1998.

"Forever Seinfeld." People, Special Seinfeld Farewell Issue, May 14, 1998. https://people.com/archive/cover-story-forever-seinfeld.

Fox, Jesse David. "Talking to the Seinfeld Writer behind 'Yada Yada Yada' and 'Double-Dipping.'" Vulture, July 2, 2014. https://www.vulture.com/2014/07/classic-seinfeld-episodes-writer-peter-mehlman-yada-yada-shrinkage-double-dipping.html.

Freeman, John. "Subtle 'Seinfeld' Succeeds by Refusing to Try Too Hard." San Diego Union-Tribune, March 24, 1992.

Gajewski, Ryan. "Jason Alexander: 'Seinfeld' Killed Off Susan Because Actress Was 'F—ing Impossible' to Work With." Hollywood Reporter, June 4, 2015. https://www.hollywoodreporter.com/live-feed/jason-alexander-seinfeld-killed-susan-800031.

Getlen, Larry. "The Backstage Drama That Nearly Brought Down 'Seinfeld.'" New York Post, July 10, 2016. https://nypost.com/2016/07/10/the-backstage-bickering-that-almost-brought-down-seinfeld.

Gilbert, Matthew. "Endgame: Dreaming of a 'Seinfeld' Finale." Boston Globe, March 1, 1998.

Goldberg, Lee. Unsold Television Pilots: 1955–1989. Calabasas, CA: Adventures in Television, 2015.

Goldman, William. Adventures in the Screen Trade: A Personal View of Hollywood and Screenwriting. New York: Warner Books, 1983.

Goldstein, Ian. "Steve Buscemi: Seinfeld Audition Never Happened." Entertainment Weekly, August 8, 2015. https://ew.com/article/2015/08/08/steve-buscemi-seinfeld-audition-never-happened.

Graham, Jefferson. "Seinfeld's Oddball Alter Ego: Series Co-Creator Larry David Adds His Own Twists." *USA Today*, February 4, 1993, 3D.

Green, Joshua. "This Man Is the Most Dangerous Political Operative in America," *Bloomberg Businessweek*, October 8, 2015. https://www.bloomberg.com/politics/graphics/2015-steve-bannon.

Green, Tom. "Comic Seinfeld Stands Up for His Personal 'Chronicles.'" *USA Today*, July 3, 1989, 3D.

Hickey, Jennifer. "Knowing Who Watches What." *Insight on the News* 14, no. 21 (June 8, 1998): 12–13.

Hobson, Jeremy. "One Former 'Seinfeld' Writer Reflects on the Show's Impact, 20 Years after Its Finale." *Here & Now*, WBUR, May 14, 2018. https://www.wbur.org/hereandnow/2018/05/14/seinfeld-finale-20-years-later.

Hoffman, Jordan. "*Seinfeld* at 25: Carol Leifer Reveals the Origins of the Marble Rye and the Elaine Stories We Never Saw." *Vanity Fair*, July 2, 2014. https://www.vanityfair.com/hollywood/2014/07/seinfeld-25th-anniversary-marble-rye.

"How Larry David Earned Your Enthusiasm." *Rolling Stone*, July 20, 2011. https://www.rollingstone.com/movies/movie-lists/how-larry-david-earned-your-enthusiasm-17626/saturday-night-live-1984-1985-20225.

Huff, Richard. "Competing Networks Plot Countermoves for 'Seinfeld' Finale." *Dallas Morning News*, April 5, 1998.

Inskeep, Steve. "Interview: Michael Richards Discusses 'Seinfeld.'" *Morning Edition*, National Public Radio, November 23, 2004.

Itzkoff, David. "Julia Louis-Dreyfus on Clinton, Trump and an Election-Year 'Veep.'" *New York Times*, April 14, 2016. https://www.nytimes.com/2016/04/17/arts/television/julia-louis-dreyfus-on-clinton-trump-and-anelection-year-veep.html.

James, Caryn. "'Seinfeld' Goes Out in Self-Referential Style." *New York Times*, May 15, 1998. https://www.nytimes.com/1998/05/15/arts/television-review-seinfeld-goes-out-in-self-referential-style.html.

Johnson, Ross. "Getting a Piece of a DVD Windfall: Sales Are Soaring and Hollywood Is Split over Dividing Profits." *New York Times*, December 13, 2004. https://www.nytimes.com/2004/12/13/business/media/getting-a-piece-of-a-dvd-windfall.html.

Johnson, Steve. "'Seinfeld' Finale: Yada, Yada, Yada." *Chicago Tribune*, May 15, 1998. https://www.chicagotribune.com/news/ct-xpm-1998-05-15-9805150196-story.html.

Kalman, Matthew. "Pact Brings Peace to the Seinfeld Cast." *Globe and Mail*, February 27, 2004. https://www.theglobeandmail.com/arts/pact-brings-peace-to-the-seinfeld-cast/article4087758.

Kaplan, James. "Angry Middle-Aged Man." *New Yorker*, January 19, 2004. https://www.newyorker.com/magazine/2004/01/19/angry-middle-aged-man.

Kiefer, Halle. "Aziz Ansari Issues Statement after Sexual-Misconduct Accusation: 'I Took Her Words to Heart.'" *Vulture*, January 14, 2018. https://www.vulture.com/2018/01/aziz-ansari-issues-statement-on-sexual-misconduct-accusation.html.

King, Susan. "Alexander's Big-Time Band of Characters." *Los Angeles Times*, March 27, 1994. https://www.latimes.com/archives/la-xpm-1994-03-27-tv-38811-story.html.

Kogan, Rick. "Short and Funny 'Seinfeld Chronicles' Stands Out as Standup Sitcom." *Chicago Tribune*, July 5, 1989. https://www.chicagotribune.com/news/ct-xpm-1989-07-05-8902140989-story.html.

Koltnow, Barry. "It's OK to Call Him George." *Orange County Register*, October 9, 2000, F01.

Kreps, Daniel, James Montgomery, David Fear, Kory Grow, and Gus Wenner. "And They're Spectacular! 10 Actors on Their Memorable 'Seinfeld' Roles." *Rolling Stone*, July 8, 2014. https://www.rollingstone.com/tv/tv-lists/and-theyre-spectacular-10-actors-on-their-memorable-seinfeld-roles-17322/teri-hatcher-sidra-115186.

Kronke, David. "Kramer Gets Serious: Michael Richards of 'Seinfeld' Reveals Another Side in 'Unstrung Heroes.'" *Los Angeles Times*, September 20, 1995. https://www.latimes.com/archives/la-xpm-1995-09-20-ca-47891-story.html.

Lasch, Christopher. *Culture of Narcissism: American Life in an Age of Diminishing Expectations*. New York: W. W. Norton, 1979.

Lauer, Matt. "'Friends' Creators Share Show's Beginnings." MSNBC.com, May 5, 2004. www.nbcnews.com/id/4899445/ns/dateline_nbc-newsmakers/t/friends-creators-share-shows-beginnings.

Lavilla, Stacy. "'Seinfeld' Edits Out Anti-Asian Joke: 'Chinaman's Nightcap' Schtick Won't Run in Reruns." *Asianweek*, July 15, 1998.

Levy, Ariel. "Julia Louis-Dreyfus Acts Out." *New Yorker*, December 17, 2018. https://www.newyorker.com/magazine/2018/12/17/julia-louis-dreyfus-acts-out.

Littlefield, Kinney. "Sein-off, Alas, Was Nothing Much." *Orange County Register*, May 15, 1998, F01.

Littlefield, Warren, and T. R. Pearson. *Top of the Rock: The Rise and Fall of Must See TV*. New York: Doubleday, 2012.

"Louis C.K. Responds to Accusations: 'These Stores Are True.'" *New York Times*, November 10, 2017. https://www.nytimes.com/2017/11/10/arts/television/louis-ck-statement.html.

Lyman, Rick. "Touching Moments with Leifer? Get Real!" *New York Times*, September 7, 1997. https://www.nytimes.com/1997/09/07/tv/touching-moments-with-leifer-get-real.html.

Major, Jack. "TV Highlights: What's Funny These Days? Try 'Seinfeld.'" *Providence Journal*, May 23, 1991, E5.

Marin, Rick. "The Great and Wonderful Wizard of Odds." *New York Times*, July 16, 2000. https://www.nytimes.com/2000/07/16/style/the-great-and-wonderful-wizard-of-odds.html.

Martin, Denise. "FX Takes Walk on 'Sunny' Side: Cabler, Known for Gritty Dramas, Tries Its Hand at Comedy Series with Tyro Creator." *Variety*, August 1, 2005. https://variety.com/2005/tv/news/fx-takes-walk-on-sunny-side-1117926741.

"Michael Richards." *People*, May 14, 1998. https://people.com/archive/michael-richards.

Mitchell, Pamela. "Peterman Mum on 'Seinfeld' Finale." *Hartford Courant*, April 13, 1998. https://www.courant.com/news/connecticut/hc-xpm-1998-04-13-9804110044-story.html.

Moore, Frazier. "No Laughs for You! 'Seinfeld' Finale Turned Out to Be a Real Stinker." Associated Press, May 15, 1998. Printed in *Sheboygan Press* (WI), May 16, 1998, 19.

Noonan, David. "The Power of Self-Loathing." *New York Times Magazine*, April 12, 1998. https://www.nytimes.com/1998/04/12/magazine/the-power-of-self-loathing.html.

Nussbaum, Emily. "Bar None." *New Yorker*, November 11, 2013, 84–85. https://www.newyorker.com/magazine/2013/11/11/bar-none.

Oldenburg, Ray. *The Great Good Place: Cafés, Coffee Shops, Community Centers, Beauty Parlors, General Stores, Bars, Hangouts, and How They Get You through the Day*, 2nd ed. New York: Marlowe, 1997.

Pennington, Gail. "'Seinfeld' Finale Draws Mixed Reviews, OK Ratings." *St. Louis Post-Dispatch*, May 16, 1998.

Remnick, David. "Interview with Jerry Seinfeld." New Yorker Festival, October 6, 2017. https://www.newyorker.com/culture/new-yorker-live/videos-from-the-2017-new-yorker-festival.

Rennison, Billy. "Seinfeld Comes Home, Performs at Alma Mater Queens College." *Queens Courier*, October 23, 2012. https://qns.com/story/2012/10/23/seinfeld-comes-home-performs-at-alma-mater-queens-college.

Richmond, Ray. "Seinfeld Special Brightens Up Boring Summer Fare." *Orange County Register*, July 5, 1989, L10.

Rose, Charlie. "Who Is Larry David?" *60 Minutes*, CBS, March 1, 2015.

Rose, Lacey. "Julia Louis-Dreyfus Reveals Awkward Fan Letter from Hillary and Her Panic on That 'Last F—able Day.'" *Hollywood Reporter*, April 20, 2016. https://www.hollywoodreporter.com/features/julia-louis-dreyfus-reveals-awkward-885385.

Rosenberg, Howard. "Past Comes Back to Haunt 'Seinfeld.'" *Los Angeles Times*, May 15, 1998. https://www.latimes.com/archives/la-xpm-1998-may-15-mn-49999-story.html.

Ryzik, Melena, Cara Buckley, and Jodi Kantor. "Louis C.K. Is Accused by 5 Women of Sexual Misconduct." *New York Times*, November 9, 2017. https://www.nytimes.com/2017/11/09/arts/television/louis-ck-sexual-misconduct.html.

"Salaries Reported in Deal for Cast of 'Seinfeld.'" *New York Times*, May 12, 1997. https://www.nytimes.com/1997/05/12/us/salaries-reported-in-deal-for-cast-of-seinfeld.html.

Saunders, Dusty. "Plot Thickens over 'Seinfeld' Finale." *Rocky Mountain News*, March 30, 1998.

Schembri, Jim. "Seinfeld's Legacy." *Sydney Morning Herald*, November 9, 1998, 14.

Schruers, Fred. "Jerry Seinfeld: King of Prime-Time Comedy." *Rolling Stone*, September 22, 1994. https://www.rollingstone.com/tv/tv-news/jerry-seinfeld-king-of-prime-time-comedy-47034.

Schwarzbaum, Lisa. "'Seinfeld' Is Back, Baby! The Show Gains an 8th Season, but Loses Larry David." *Entertainment Weekly*, February 2, 1996. https://ew.com/article/1996/02/02/seinfeld-back-baby.

*Seinfeld: The Complete Series*. Seasons 1–9. DVD. Culver City, CA: Sony Pictures Home Entertainment, 2004–2007.

Shales, Tom. "Guilty Pleasures: 'Seinfeld' Goes up the River." *Washington Post*, May 15, 1998. https://www.washingtonpost.com/archive/lifestyle/1998/05/15/guilty-pleasures-seinfeld-goes-up-the-river/ea8fa5d7-93ec-47ed-9543-6274a5d785df.

———. "So Long, 'Seinfeld.' Let Me Show You to the Door." *Washington Post*, April 16, 1998. https://www.washingtonpost.com/archive/lifestyle/1998/04/16/so-long-seinfeld-let-me-show-you-to-the-door/ced8dc1a-a8af-42ad-8dd9-75965ab15b22.

Siegemund-Broka, Austin. "Larry David's Best Advice on Dealing with Network Execs: 'Just Say No.'" *Hollywood Reporter*, September 29, 2014. https://www.hollywoodreporter.com/news/larry-davids-best-advice-dealing-736325.

Simmons, Bill. "Larry David on the Future of 'Curb Your Enthusiasm' and the 'Seinfeld' Finale." *B.S. Report*, ESPN, December 16, 2014. http://grantland.com/hollywood-prospectus/b-s-report-larry-david-on-the-future-of-curb-your-enthusiasm-and-the-seinfeld-finale.

Smith, Chris. "Jerry Seinfeld: Making Something out of Nothing." *New York*, 30th Anniversary Issue, April 6, 1998. http://nymag.com/nymetro/news/people/features/2430.

Stafansky, Emma. "Aziz Ansari Accused of Sexual Misconduct." *Vanity Fair*, January 14, 2018. https://www.vanityfair.com/hollywood/2018/01/aziz-ansari-accused-of-sexual-misconduct.

Stanhope, Kate. "Former NBC Execs Look Back on the Births of 'ER,' 'Seinfeld,' and 'Will & Grace.'" *Hollywood Reporter*, February 7, 2017. https://www.hollywoodreporter.com/live-feed/nbc-execs-look-back-er-seinfeld-will-grace-973094.

Stern, Marlow. "Rob Reiner on Steve Bannon Getting Rich off 'Seinfeld': 'It Makes Me Sick.'" *Daily Beast*, November 17, 2016. https://www.thedailybeast.com/rob-reiner-on-steve-bannon-getting-rich-off-seinfeld-it-makes-me-sick.

Storm, Jonathan. "DeVito a Fine Fit for 'Sunny' Business." *Philadelphia Inquirer*, June 29, 2006, E01.

Suebsaeng, Asawin. "'Seinfeld' Writer Takes on Conservative Outrage Over Holiday Festivus Pole Protests." *Mother Jones*, December 12, 2013. https://www.motherjones.com/politics/2013/12/festivus-pole-protest-christmas-seinfeld-dan-okeefe-fox-news.

Tani, Maxwell. "Maureen Dowd: The Only Thing I Wish I Could Take Back Is a Negative Column I Wrote about Seinfeld." *Business Insider*, September 14, 2016. https://www.businessinsider.com/maureen-dowd-seinfeld-amanda-hess-monica-lewinsky-2016-9.

Thompson, Robert J. *Television's Second Golden Age: From "Hill Street Blues" to "ER."* New York: Continuum, 1996.

"A Timeline of HIV and AIDS." HIV.gov, U.S. Department of Health and Human Services, n.d. https://www.hiv.gov/hiv-basics/overview/history/hiv-and-aids-timeline.

Trevino, Judith, Brad Ballieu, Rachel Yost, Samantha Danna, and Genevieve Harris. "Effect of Biting before Dipping (Double-Dipping) Chips on the Bacterial Population of the Dipping Solution." *Journal of Food Safety* 29, no. 1 (February 2009): 37–48.

Tucker, Ken. "White House Showcase, Jerry Seinfeld Sitcom." *Philadelphia Inquirer*, July 5, 1989, E1.

Vilkomerson, Sara. "When Woody Met Larry." *Independent*, May 8, 2009. https://www.independent.co.uk/arts-entertainment/films/features/when-woody-met-larry-1680901.html.

Walker, Maxton. "Deep Down, I'm Really Shallow." *Guardian*, February 23, 2003.

Waters, Harry E. "Can Tinker Save NBC?" *Newsweek*, no. 99, June 14, 1982, 97.

Zehme, Bill. "Jerry & George & Kramer & Elaine: Exposing the Secrets of Seinfeld's Success." *Rolling Stone*, July 8, 1993. https://www.rollingstone.com/music/music-news/jerry-george-kramer-elaine-162060.

Zuckeman, Esther. "Behind the New Modern Seinfeld Twitter Account, Which Is Not about Nothing." *The Wire*, December 10, 2012. https://www.theatlantic.com/entertainment/archive/2012/12/modern-seinfeld-today-twitter/320660.

Zurawik, David. "Not His Finest Hour." *Baltimore Sun*, May 15, 1998. https://www.baltimoresun.com/news/bs-xpm-1998-05-15-1998135029-story.html.

# INDEX

# ABOUT THE AUTHOR

**Paul Arras** has a PhD in history from Syracuse University where he studied the history of television and American culture. He is an assistant professor in the Department of Communication and Media Studies at SUNY Cortland. He has written about television before, in *The Lonely Nineties: Visions of Community in Contemporary US Television* (2018).